Unsolved Mysteries
of American History

Unsolved Mysteries of American History

An Eye-Opening Journey through 500 Years of Discoveries, Disappearances, and Baffling Events

PAUL ARON

John Wiley & Sons, Inc.

New York ★ Chichester ★ Weinheim ★ Brisbane ★ Singapore ★ Toronto

Copyright © 1997 by Paul Aron.

Published by John Wiley & Sons, Inc.

This publication is designed to provide accurate and authoritative information in regard to the subject matter covered. It is sold with the understanding that the publisher is not engaged in rendering legal, accounting, or other professional services. If legal advice or other expert assistance is required, the services of a competent professional person should be sought.

Library of Congress Cataloging-in-Publication Data
Aron, Paul.
    Unsolved mysteries of American history: an eye-opening journey
  through 500 years of discoveries, disappearances, and baffling
  events / Paul Aron.
      p. cm.
    Includes index.
    ISBN 0-471-15369-9 (cloth : alk. paper)
    1. United States—History—Miscellanea. 2. America—History—
  Miscellanea.   I. Title.
  E179.A75 1997
  973—dc21   97-7319

Printed in the United States of America
10 9 8 7 6 5 4 3 2 1

Contents

Acknowledgments

For much useful advice, thanks to Stephen Aron, John Kingston, Robert Thompson, and my agent, John Thornton.

Judith McCarthy has been the ideal editor: her judgments have always been incisive but never been discouraging. Others at Wiley who have been helpful are Chris Jackson, Elaine O'Neal, and John Simko.

Finally, I am grateful to my wife, Paula Blank, for her perceptive readings of the manuscript and its author.

Introduction

Ellery Queen's 1934 novel *The Chinese Orange Mystery* presents us with a murder scene that's completely backwards. The rug and table are upside down, the grandfather clock and bookcases face the wall, a set of Hebrew books (Hebrew being a language written from right to left, *i.e.,* backwards) is missing.

It turns out the murderer has turned around everything in the room just to conceal the one thing which would normally be backwards: the dead man's collar. (The dead man was a priest, and priests always wear their collars backwards.) At this point, the rest of the puzzle pieces easily fit together and the mystery is solved.

"The detective," wrote Queen, "is a prophet looking backwards."

So is the historian. Like a detective, he or she must look backwards, trying to figure out what happened and why. And, like the detective in Queen's story, the historian must examine evidence which is often not what it seems.

Take, for example, the mystery of whether Leif Ericsson and his band of Norsemen (and Norsewomen, too, if one is to believe the ancient Icelandic sagas) discovered America, about five hundred years before Columbus. By the early nineteenth century, Leif's advocates had scoured the east coast of North America; no stone was left unturned in the search for evidence of Leif's settlement. And a remarkable number of those stones turned out to have Norse inscriptions on them. In towns from Newfoundland to Florida, the claim that "Leif Ericsson was here" was as common as the claim that "George Washington slept here." Alas, both claims were equally improbable; on closer examination most of these reputed Norse relics turned out to be crude hoaxes.

Then, in 1964, near a small fishing village in northern Newfoundland, the Norwegian archaeologist, Helge Ingstad, uncovered an ancient Norse spindle-whorl. Here, at last, was genuine proof of Leif's settlement. This was better than finding a Viking sword, for it proved that the sagas were right not only about Norsemen coming to

America but about Norsewomen, too. (It was the women who would have used the spindle-whorl to spin wool.)

Case closed?

By no means. According to the sagas, Leif had named the country he found Vinland (or Wineland), after the wild grapes he found there. *But:* botanists assure us that grapes can't grow any further north than Massachusetts—and a glance at any map shows Newfoundland atop Massachusetts. So how could Vinland have been in Newfoundland?

To make sense of something so backwards—or, in this case, so upside-down—required a detective of Ellery Queen's ingenuity. Was Ingstad up to the task? To find out, see chapter 2.

And that, as they say, is just the beginning. Did Pocahontas really rescue John Smith? Was Daniel Boone a traitor? Was Sally Hemings the mistress of Thomas Jefferson? Was Amelia Earhart a spy? Were the Rosenbergs guilty? Who killed JFK? How much did Reagan know about the Iran-contra affair? These are mysteries that have intrigued, sometimes baffled, but never deterred our most resourceful historians. These are mysteries with all the twists and turns, all the intellectual challenges, all the espionage and murder that you could hope for from Ambler or Chandler, Parker or Paretsky.

After all, these are the greatest mysteries of our history.

Unsolved Mysteries of American History

Chapter 1

When Did the First People Arrive in America?

Soon after Columbus landed in America, Europeans began speculating about the people of this New World. To Columbus himself there was no mystery: since he assumed he'd reached some island off the shore of India (as all of Asia was then sometimes known), he had few doubts about who these people were (or what to call them). But once it became clear that the Indians were not, in fact, Indians, theories about who they were and where they came from abounded.

One theory which was especially popular in Spain was that the Indians were survivors of the lost continent of Atlantis. Atlantis, according to stories dating back as far as Plato's dialogues, once stretched from Spain to America but had sunk in a great flood. The first to tie the people of Atlantis to those of America was Francisco López de Gómara; in 1552 he explained that the Indians had been stranded in America when Atlantis sunk. As evidence, Gómara pointed out that the Mexican Indians used the word "atl" for water.

Another persistent theory was that the Indians were descendants of the lost tribes of Israel, whose exile to Assyria had been chronicled in the Old Testament and who hadn't been heard from since. A Dutch theologian named Joannes Fredricus Luminus seems to have been the first to make the connection between Jews and American Indians, arguing in 1567 that both had big noses and strange burial customs.

The first to move beyond such myths toward a serious study of American Indians were Spanish friars, among them the Jesuit missionary José de Acosta. In 1589 Acosta hypothesized that the Indians had reached the New World via an overland route from Asia. Here was a man ahead of his time; by the twentieth century, most scholars agreed he was right on the mark.

This consensus began to emerge in the mid-nineteenth century after Charles Darwin theorized that human beings first evolved in Africa, then spread around the rest of the world. Fossil evidence seemed to bear Darwin out: Africa and Europe could boast of numerous archaeological sites indicating the presence of humans tens of thousands of years ago; America had none (or at least none that weren't strongly disputed). Advances in geology strengthened the case for an overland route by demonstrating that a land bridge once existed between Siberia and Alaska, where today the waters of the Bering Strait are found.

So it seemed the mystery had been solved. Native Americans were not *truly* native; they had come from Asia. But an equally intriguing mystery remained: *when* had they arrived?

Until the 1960s and 1970s this mystery also seemed nearly solved. The consensus was that people crossed into America about 12,000 years ago.

This was near the end of the last Ice Age, when so much of the earth's water was locked up in glaciers that the Bering land bridge, also known as Beringia, was left exposed. Beringia had, to be sure, an inhospitable climate—worse even than that of Alaska and Siberia today. But the climate had warmed up enough for humans to survive in the area. Fossils found there indicate that woolly mammoths, steppe bison, wild horses, and caribou all lived in the region, and their human hunters might very well have followed them onto and across the land bridge. So the 12,000-year estimate made sense: any earlier, and it would have been too cold for people to survive so far north; any later, and the water from the melting glaciers would have submerged the land bridge and blocked the passage across.

This geological logic was buttressed by archaeological evidence. In 1908 a black cowboy named George McJunkin was riding near the small town of Folsom, New Mexico, searching for a lost cow. Instead, he came across some bones with a stone spearpoint beside them. The bones were much too large to belong to a cow; intrigued, McJunkin

Stone spearpoints found between the ribs of Ice Age mammoths prove people were living in America 10,000 to 12,000 years ago. If human hunters arrived in America about that time, that might also explain—according to some paleoecologists—why such Ice Age animals as mammoths (like this one, from an Arizona State Museum diorama reconstruction) quickly became extinct. By permission of the Arizona State Museum.

took them back to the ranch house. There they stayed until 1925, when they landed on the desk of Jesse Figgins of the Colorado Museum of Natural History. Figgins easily identified the bones as those of a long-extinct form of bison that had roamed the plains at the end of the Ice Age. But it was the stone spearpoints McJunkin had found beside the bones that had the more far-reaching implications. If these spearpoints were manmade weapons used to kill the bison, that meant humans had been hunting (and living) in America during the Ice Age.

More indications of Ice Age hunters followed soon after. In 1932 two amateur collectors exploring near Clovis, New Mexico, found the bones of some animals with stone spearheads between the ribs. In this case, the animals turned out to be woolly mammoths, also extinct since the Ice Age. And with the spearpoints right between the ribs, there could be little doubt that people were in America during the Ice Age.

In the 1950s a University of Chicago scientist named Willard Libby developed "radiocarbon dating," which allowed scientists to determine the age of the Folsom and Clovis finds more precisely; they turned out to date back between 10,000 and 11,500 years ago—thus fitting in very neatly with the puzzle being pieced together.

So, too, did evidence that came right from the prehistoric Indians' mouths—or rather, teeth. After examining more than 200,000 prehistoric teeth from the remains of about 9,000 prehistoric Indians, anthropologist Christy Turner determined that all Native American teeth shared certain genetic traits with northeast Asian teeth. These traits were unique—no other people had them besides the North American Indians and the northeast Asians. From this, Turner concluded that the Indians' ancestors must have come from northeast Asia. What's more, by examining the differences between northeast Asian and American Indian teeth and by comparing them to general dental evolution patterns, Turner calculated that the two populations must have separated in the vicinity of—you guessed it—12,000 years ago.

If people first entered America about 12,000 years ago, that explained another mystery as well: the rapid extinction of mammoths, mastodons, saber-toothed cats, native camels, giant beavers, and other large animals that roamed North America until about 10,000 years ago. When the bones of these animals were found at sites dated 12,000 years or older, there were no human artifacts nearby. When human artifacts less than 10,000 years old were found at similar sites, none of these animals' bones were around. Only in finds dating back between 12,000 and 10,000 years ago, such as those at Clovis and Folsom, did human artifacts (for example, spearheads) and these bones appear together. From this, paleoecologist Paul Martin formulated his hypothesis of "Pleistocene overkill" in 1967. Martin was convinced that human hunters crossed the Bering land bridge about 12,000 years ago and then moved south through an ice-free corridor just east of the Canadian Rockies. Here they found mammals so completely unadapted to human predators that they quickly hunted them to extinction.

Not all scientists accepted Martin's arguments. Some countered that climatic changes, or at least some combination of human hunting and climate, could better account for the extinctions. But there was no denying that the extinctions were yet another indication that people had crossed the Bering land bridge about 12,000 years ago. The mystery of when the first Americans arrived was, it seemed, solved.

In the 1970s and 1980s this consensus fell apart as not one, but many, archaeologists claimed to uncover evidence of a human presence in America earlier—in some cases, *much* earlier—than 12,000 years ago.

Between 1973 and 1977 James Adovasio excavated Meadowcroft Rockshelter in southwest Pennsylvania. There he found remnants of baskets and small stone blades at levels that radiocarbon dating indicated were occupied almost 20,000 years ago.

In 1976 in a Chilean peat bog called Monte Verde, Tom Dillehay unearthed the wooden foundations of huts occupied 13,000 years ago. At even deeper levels he found three hearths and some tools made from pebbles that radiocarbon dating showed to be about 34,000 years old.

Also in 1976 the husband-and-wife archaeologist team of Alan Bryan and Ruth Gruhn found the skeleton of a mastodon with a stone point inside it, at a site called Taima-taima in Venezuela. Radiocarbon dating placed the kill 13,000 years ago.

And in 1978 Niede Guidon dated some prehistoric art from a Brazilian rock shelter called Pedra Furada back to about 32,000 years ago, making it among the oldest art in the world.

How could these people have traversed a continent still covered with glaciers? And how did they get to America in the first place—before there was a land bridge across the Bering?

Proponents of a pre-12,000-year-old human presence in America have suggested a couple of possibilities. Some have suggested that people crossed into America during an earlier period when the land bridge was exposed but when conditions had warmed somewhat. And even during the heart of the Ice Age there may have been an ice-free corridor along which people might have headed south.

Another hypothesis, this one championed by the Canadian archaeologist Knut Fladmark, was that people traveled across the Bering Sea and down the west coast of the Americas by boat. The boats would have been very primitive, but perhaps the Pacific coast of North America might have sustained enough life for people to make it far enough south, after which they could have headed inland. After all,

Fladmark pointed out, people reached Australia about 40,000 years ago—also from Asia—and there was never a land bridge between those continents.

Proponents of the traditional 12,000-year date have sharply attacked all of these findings and theories. One traditionalist, Brian Fagan, mockingly referred to the ice-free corridor as a "prehistoric superhighway" beckoning the Paleo-Indians south from Beringia into warmer climes. Even at the warmest points during the Ice Age, Fagan argued, this corridor could barely support animal or human life, and people had little incentive to venture into it.

As for Fladmark's boat theory, traditionalists responded that, though the distance between Asia and America across the Bering Strait was about the same as between Asia and Australia, the trip to Australia was across fairly placid, tropical seas. In contrast, the Bering Strait—even during the warmer times of the Ice Age—was full of dangerous ice floes, hardly an appealing trip for people who, from all other evidence, survived by hunting and not fishing.

How, then, have traditionalists explained the pre-12,000-year-old finds? Many have claimed that the findings were simply wrong. In some cases the artifacts supporting earlier dates may have been natural and not man-made: trees may have fallen in ways that could be mistaken for human dwellings, natural deposits may appear to be hearths, pebbles eroded by streams may seem to be tools. In other cases the dating process may have been corrupted; radiocarbon dating depends on finding organic material (which can be carbon-dated) at the same level as human artifacts (which can't be carbon-dated), and then assuming that the latter are the same age as the former—but all sorts of geological disturbances could result in older organic matter ending up in the same layer as more recent human artifacts.

The majority of archaeologists today still stand by the 12,000-year date. Besides questioning the validity of the claims for sites like Monte Verde and Pedra Furada, these archaeologists point to the relatively small number of such sites. In Europe and Asia, on the other hand, there are thousands of well-documented sites that have yielded numerous and indisputably human artifacts dating back more than 30,000 years. If people lived here more than 12,000 years ago, most archaeologists insist, there ought to be more record of it. Or, as some traditional archaeologists have put it, the absence of evidence is evidence of absence.

But—to a much greater extent than was the case just a few years ago—archaeologists are willing to entertain the possibility that at least a few people might have arrived here earlier than 12,000 years ago. And even the most conservative archaeologists can't preclude the possibility that someday someone will find definitive proof that people were in America long before the Ice Age ended.

☆ To investigate further:

Fladmark, Knut. "Getting One's Berings." *Natural History,* November 1986. This and the following articles from *Natural History* were part of a series on the first Americans written by specialists and reporting on their original research but in nontechnical terms. Fladmark's article considers the likelihood of Ice Age Americans migrating by boat.

Adovasio, J. M. and Ronald Carlisle. "Pennsylvania Pioneers." *Natural History,* December 1986. A report on the Meadowcroft Rock Shelter excavations.

Turner, Christy. "Telltale Teeth." *Natural History,* January 1987. Dental evidence of Indians' Asian ancestry.

Ruhlen, Merritt. "Voices from the Past." *Natural History,* March 1987. What Indian languages reveal about the migrations to and in the Americas.

Dillehay, Tom. "By the Banks of the Chinchihuapi." *Natural History,* April 1987. A report on the Monte Verde excavations.

Grayson, Donald. "Death by Natural Causes." *Natural History,* May 1987. Considers whether human hunters or climate caused the extinction of North America's Ice Age animals.

Bryan, Alan. "Points of Order." *Natural History,* June 1987. A report on excavations in Venezuela and Colombia by a leading proponent of Americans' greater antiquity.

Guidon, Niede. "Cliff Notes." *Natural History,* August 1987. A report on the Pedra Furada excavations.

Martin, Paul. "Clovisia the Beautiful!" *Natural History,* October 1987. A summary of the conservative case against New World peopling prior to 12,000 years ago.

Fagan, Brian. *The Great Journey: The Peopling of Ancient America.* New York: Thames and Hudson, 1987. A scholarly but nontechnical overview of the subject by an archaeologist who is conservative in his assessment of the site data but open to the possibility of pre-Clovis finds. (This essay is much indebted to Fagan's work.)

Dillehay, Tom and David Meltzer. *The First Americans: Search and Research.* Boca Raton, FL: CRC Press, 1991. A collection of essays that go beyond discussions of particular sites to discuss general issues relating to the peopling of the Americas, and which compare the migrations to America with those of other places and other times. Technical but readable.

Dixon, E. James. *Quest for the Origins of the First Americans.* Albuquerque: University of New Mexico Press, 1993. A highly speculative but fascinating analysis by a proponent of early settlement.

Chapter 2

Did Leif Ericsson
Discover America?

I f one is to believe the ancient Icelandic sagas, the first European to discover America was not Christopher Columbus, nor was it Leif Ericsson. It was none other than Biarni Heriulfson.

Biarni was a trader who regularly crossed the part of the Atlantic between Norway and his home in Iceland. In the summer of 985 he left Norway to spend the winter with his father. He arrived to find his father had departed for Greenland—a land recently discovered by Eric the Red. Biarni set off after him. But on his way to Greenland he got lost and came upon some new land. This new land was America—at least according to those who believed the sagas to be historical documents and not just literary epics.

The discovery didn't excite Biarni. "To me this land looks good for nothing," he told his crew, and then he headed back to Greenland. There he was reunited with his father, thus securing his place in history as the world's most devoted son and least venturesome explorer.

Others, however, found Biarni's stories intriguing. These new lands sounded appealing, especially compared to Greenland; in spite of Eric the Red's efforts to attract other settlers by giving the land an attractive name, Greenland was anything but green. Among those stirred by Biarni's stories was Eric's son, Leif Ericsson. He bought Biarni's ship, assembled a crew, and set sail for the land that he would call Vinland. He lived there for a year before returning to Greenland.

Other Norse expeditions soon followed, including one led by Leif's brother, Thorvald. Thorvald spent the winter of 1004–1005 at Leif's settlement but, the sagas say, was killed by "Skrellings." (Presumably these were Indians or Eskimos.) The surviving members of his party then returned to Greenland. Yet another brother of Leif, Thorstein, and a sister, Freydis, then tried to colonize Vinland, but again, the Skrellings drove the intruders away. Only Freydis showed any Viking spirit: after failing to rally the fleeing men, she slapped a sword across her bared breasts and screamed so loud that the Skrellings retreated. But the men had had enough: This land may have been more hospitable than Greenland; its inhabitants, on the other hand, were not. For another five hundred years, the Indians had America to themselves.

Or so the story went. To most historians, however, it was just that—a story. Granted, there were some scholars who argued it was true, but these were mostly Scandinavians whose conclusions were tainted by chauvinism. For the sagas to be accepted as history, there had to be proof.

The search for that proof began in earnest in 1837 when the Royal Danish Society of Antiquaries published the original saga texts. The book's editor, Carl Rafn, also included in the book the results of his correspondence with Americans about various ruined towers and inscribed stones found along the east coast of North America and reputed to be of Norse origin.

Alas, Rafn's enthusiasm overwhelmed his judgment. He included almost anything anyone claimed might be Norse, even though he himself had never even been to America, let alone examined the evidence. On closer examination most of these finds turned out to be crude hoaxes. In towns from Newfoundland to Florida, the claim that "Leif Ericsson was here" became as common and as improbable as the claim that "George Washington slept here."

Among the evidence discovered was the Newport Tower. In one sense the tower couldn't really be discovered: it stood about 25 feet high on top of a hill in Newport, Rhode Island, so you didn't need an archaeologist to find it. The tower certainly *looked* medieval; with thick floors and round arches, it would have seemed at home in eleventh-century France or Belgium—or Norway. The case for the Tower's Norse origins was strengthened when its measurements turned out to be readily divisible by old Norse measures. But something just didn't make sense: if the Tower dated back to medieval times, how could Rhode Island's first English settlers have failed to notice it when they arrived? Not one of their writings makes any mention of it. In fact the earliest mention of the tower is in the 1677 will of Benedict Arnold (not the traitor—this Benedict Arnold was the governor of Rhode Island). Arnold referred to it as "my stone built wind mill," and later investigations confirmed it was built, probably by Arnold, around 1675.

The next major find was the Kensington Stone, uncovered in the roots of a 500-year-old tree on Olof Ohman's farm in Minnesota. In an alphabet that was used in medieval Scandinavia, the stone told of "8 Swedes and 22 Norwegians on an exploration journey from Vinland westward." It was dated 1362.

But the word *opdagelsefard* (exploration journey) didn't occur in any Scandinavian language until hundreds of years after 1362. The stone had to be forgery. As one Icelandic linguist put it: "If a telephone book for the year 1957 were to be found under the roots of a 500-year-old tree, one would admire the skill with which it had been placed there; but one should not find it necessary to accept the antiquity of the volume in question."

By this point most of Leif's boosters were despairing of ever proving their case. One archaeologist—granted, a *Norwegian* archaeologist—refused to give up. During the 1950s Helge Ingstad traveled thousands of miles up and down the North American coast in search of Vinland. If the sailing times recorded in the sagas were accurate, he reasoned, then the land Leif called Vinland ought to be northern Newfoundland. The sagas' descriptions of these lands also fit.

In 1960, close to the small village of L'Anse aux Meadows near Epaves Bay in northern Newfoundland, Ingstad noted some indistinct overgrown elevations in the ground. They appeared to be sites of houses—very old ones. Their shapes were similar to ancient Norse buildings uncovered in Iceland and Greenland. Could these houses have been built by Leif Ericsson and his crew? Ingstad began excavating.

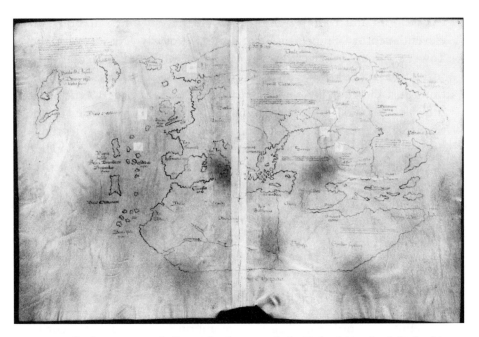

Supposedly drawn 50 years before Columbus set sail, the Vinland Map *(with Vinland in the upper left corner) would—if it's authentic—be proof that the Norse reached America first. By permission of Yale University Press.*

In 1964 he found exactly what he'd hoped for. In the southern-most room of the largest house site, one of Ingstad's colleagues found a small ring of stone which was clearly a Norse spindle-whorl. It was exactly the kind of spindle-whorl that Norse women had used in Swe-den, Norway, Iceland, and Greenland, and it was unlike anything the Indians and Eskimos of Newfoundland would have used. This was as dramatic a find as a Viking sword would have been; in fact it was even better since it proved that the sagas were right—not just about Norse-men reaching America, but about a settlement with Norsewomen (who would have been the ones to use the spindle-whorl) and sheep (whose wool the women would have spun).

There was no question that Ingstad had found a pre-Columbian Norse settlement. But a big problem remained. This was the name Vinland, sometimes translated as Wineland. Leif had named the coun-try after the wild grapes found there. Yet botanists assert that the northern limit for wild grapes along the east coast is somewhere in Massachussetts. Which means: *there are no wild grapes in Newfoundland.*

And one cannot simply ignore the name, since *The Greenlanders' Saga* describes in detail how it was given. Leif, the saga tells us, was very worried when one of his company, a German named Tyrkir, disappeared. When Tyrkir finally returned, the following exchange took place:

> "Why are you so late . . ." Leif asked him, "and parted this way from your companions?"
>
> By way of a start Tyrkir held forth a long while in German, rolling his eyes all ways, and pulling faces. They had no notion what he was talking about. Then after a while he spoke in Norse. "I went no great way further than you, yet I have a real novelty to report. I have found vines and grapes."
>
> "Is that the truth. . . ?" Leif asked.
>
> "Of course it's the truth," he replied. "I was born where wine and grapes are no rarity."

Given how sure Tyrkir was that Vinland was a land of wild grapes, how could it be in Newfoundland?

Historians have ventured a number of guesses.

Farley Mowat, a botanist and climatologist as well as a historian, suggested that even though grapes don't grow in Newfoundland today, they may have grown there between 1000 and 1200. We do know that the vineyards of western Europe at that time extended farther north than they do today.

Ingstad himself offered a number of explanations: that Vinland might be translated as Meadowland rather than Vineland or Wineland or Grapeland; that Tyrkir, for all his apparent certainty, may have mistaken wild berries for grapes; that the saga-writers, in an effort to make Vinland more appealing, may have exaggerated its fertility. (After all, Eric the Red had no qualms about giving Greenland its very misleading name.)

Most historians were convinced for one reason or another. And even if L'Anse aux Meadows isn't Vinland and is simply a different Norse settlement, it's still incontrovertible evidence that the Norse did discover and settle North America five hundred years before Columbus.

☆ To investigate further:

Jones, Gwyn. *The Norse Atlantic Saga*. New York: Oxford University Press, 1986. The most widely respected translation of the sagas, along with a history of the Norse voyages. The translation from *The Greenlanders' Saga* is Jones's.

Haugen, Einar. *Voyages to Vinland*, New York: Knopf, 1942. The history is dated, and the translations have been superseded in scholarly circles by Jones's, but Haugen's account and translations are still the most dramatic.

Holand, Hjalmar. *Explorations in America Before Columbus*. New York: Twayne Publishers, 1956. The case for the authenticity of the Newport Tower and the Kensington Stone; generally discredited but still fun.

Wahlgren, Erik. *The Kensington Stone*. Madison: University of Wisconsin, 1958. The case against the authenticity of the stone; definitive but dry.

Mowat, Farley. *Westviking*. Boston: Atlantic Monthly Press, 1965. A fascinating combination of climatology, anthropology, zoology, seamanship, and various other disciplines. Mowat claims he's located Vinland in Newfoundland, though not at L'anse aux Meadows. He also argues—contrary to generally accepted opinion—that Columbus knew of and was influenced by the Norse discoveries.

Skelton, Raleigh, et al. *The Vinland Map and the Tartar Relation*. New Haven: Yale University Press, 1965. The book features a map from 1440 which included Vinland. If authentic, the map would be the only pre-Columbian document, besides the sagas, to include Vinland. But whether it's "the most exciting cartographic discovery of the century" or a twentieth-century fraud remains a source of heated scholarly debate.

Ingstad, Helge. *Land Under the Polar Star*. New York: St. Martin's Press, 1966. Ingstad's account of his expedition to Greenland, during which he came to the conclusion that he should search for Vinland in Newfoundland.

———. *Westward to Vinland*. New York: St. Martin's Press, 1969. Ingstad's account of his discoveries at L'Anse aux Meadows. Scholarly but exciting.

Pohl, Frederick. *The Viking Settlements of North America*. New York: Clarkson Potter, 1972. Uses the sailing directions and topographical descriptions in the saga to locate Vinland in New England, contrary to most current thinking.

Morison, Samuel. *The European Discovery of America*. New York: Oxford University Press, 1971. The section on the Norse voyages is a concise yet comprehensive history and historiography. While you're at it, read the rest of the book—there's no better historian of the sea than Morison.

Chapter 3

Why Did the Anasazi Abandon Their Cities?

The first white men to explore Chaco Canyon, in northwestern New Mexico, arrived in 1849, led by Army Lieutenant James Simpson. What Simpson found there convinced him that the Aztec empire of Mexico must once have extended this far north. Only such an advanced civilization, he concluded, could have constructed the massive and beautiful buildings whose ruins he now surveyed. The largest of them—Pueblo Bonito—stood five stories tall and had several hundred rooms. It was larger than any apartment building in North America (and it remained so until 1882, when it was surpassed by one in New York City).

Simpson was wrong: in the twentieth century, archaeologists dated the Chaco Canyon buildings to the end of the tenth century, well before the rise of the Aztecs. From numerous other sites in the area, archaeologists were able to chronicle the rise of the civilization that culminated in these buildings. This was, they determined, a homegrown civilization, one which had been built by a people called the Anasazi by the Indians Simpson encountered.

But who could blame Simpson for looking outside of Chaco Canyon for its architects? The ruins at Chaco Canyon bore little resemblance to the buildings of the Hopi or Zuni or any other Indians then living in the area. At least Simpson, in attributing the Chaco Canyon buildings to the Aztecs, was willing to give the credit to Native

Americans, albeit the wrong ones; others would later argue that the buildings must have been a Roman outpost.

In the eleventh century all roads did not lead to Rome; many led—quite literally—to Chaco Canyon. Straight, broad avenues connected Pueblo Bonito to nine "Great Houses" and to some 75 other settlements in and around Chaco Canyon. Archaeologists have mapped more than four hundred miles of roads, many of them 30 feet wide, radiating out from the canyon center. The Anasazi must have used these roads to carry the timber that made up the vast roofs and support systems of their buildings. Judging from the tremendous quantities of turquoise found in the area, the roads were also used to transport the gems from distant mines to Chaco Canyon. After being made into small tiles, the turquoise was then sent as far away as California and Mexico.

The Anasazi were remarkably wealthy: along with exotic gems, archaeologists have found huge quantities of discarded pots—at one Chaco building, a single trash heap contained 150,000 broken pots. This must also have been a remarkably egalitarian society, for there were no palaces or special buildings mixed in among the huge apartment buildings. Supporting all this was a sophisticated irrigation system that used dams and dikes, contoured terraces, and reservoirs to make the most of the sandy soil and limited rainfall.

About one hundred years after they built the Great Houses of Chaco Canyon, the Anasazi moved north into southwest Colorado, creating an architecture that was, if possible, even more stunning. Here they built their homes right inside the caves that sculpt the steep cliffs of the area's canyons. Protected by the caves, many of these cliff dwellings (including the huge Cliff Palace at Mesa Verde) are still largely intact.

But the civilization that built these houses was not nearly so durable. By 1200 Chaco Canyon's houses were empty; by 1300 Mesa Verde's cliff dwellings were, too. Why did the Anasazi abandon their great cities, in many cases only a hundred or so years after they built them? And where did they go? This is a mystery that has intrigued historians—not to mention archaeologists, anthropologists, demographers, biologists, and visitors to the American Southwest—ever since James Simpson and his men first stumbled upon Chaco Canyon.

☆ ☆ ☆

To the historian and archaeologist Harold Gladwin, writing in 1957, the solution was obvious: the Anasazi were under attack. This would

Built 900 years ago, the Cliff Palace in Mesa Verde, Colorado, has proven a lot more durable than the civilization that built it. By permission of the Arizona State Museum.

explain why people who had been widely scattered came together in the huge apartment buildings of Chaco Canyon. The large pueblos offered more protection than smaller, scattered villages—hence the building spree in Chaco Canyon at the end of the tenth century. It would also explain why they had abandoned the Chaco Canyon buildings so soon after they'd built them. When the Chaco Canyon towns failed to hold off their attackers, the Anasazi retreated to the cliff dwellings of Mesa Verde, built during the eleventh and twelfth centuries. The cliff dwellings were, to put it mildly, inconvenient—but at least that made them inaccessible to enemies as well.

So, protected by deep canyons and sheer escarpments and warned of the dangers by refugees from Chaco Canyon, the Anasazi held out for another hundred years. But eventually their attackers wore them down, and by the end of the thirteenth century the cliff dwellings of Mesa Verde had gone the way of the pueblos of Chaco Canyon.

Who were the people who drove away the Anasazi? Gladwin believed they were the people who later became known as the Navajo and Apache. Sweeping down from western Canada, they were the last people to reach the Southwest before the Spanish invasion. Navajo tradition seems to confirm this theory: the word "Anasazi" comes from the Navajo word for "ancient enemies." Other historians have proposed it was the Southern Paiute or Ute, not the Navajo or Apache. (Ute legends, too, tell how they conquered people as they moved south.) Whoever their enemies were, the Anasazi outnumbered them, but the raiders' hit-and-run attacks against their settlements and fields eventually took their toll.

But there was one major problem with these "military" solutions to the mystery: there is no archaeological evidence that the Apache or Navajo or Ute or Paiute entered the area until long after the pueblos and cliff dwellings had been abandoned. Granted, the Apache and Navajo were traditional enemies of the Pueblo people of the Southwest, but some historians argued that this tradition originated in the seventeenth century after the Indians acquired horses from Europeans (giving them a tremendous tactical advantage). Finally, if the Anasazi went down in battle, why didn't archaeologists find any mass graves or other signs of war? Anyone looking at the ruins of Pueblo Bonito or Cliff House today can see they were deserted—not burned or sacked.

☆ ☆ ☆

And so we turn to an alternative solution to the mystery: the great drought.

This theory depends on advances in the science of dendrochronology, which uses the growth rings of trees to supply precise information about past climates. Each year a tree produces a growth ring; the wider the ring, the more rain there was that year. It was A. E. Douglass, on a National Geographic expedition to the Southwest in 1929, who developed new techniques of tree-ring dating, then charted the tree rings in living trees and overlapped and matched them with those found in wooden beams from increasingly older archaeological sites. Douglass found there was a severe drought in the area between 1276 and 1299—exactly the time the Anasazi cities were finally and fully abandoned.

But Gladwin's followers struck back: there had been previous droughts in the area, they pointed out, and the cities hadn't been abandoned. And there were nearby areas with more rainfall—but there was no evidence that the Anasazi had moved there.

So the environmental explanations became more complex, taking into account not just rainfall amounts but the times of the year the rain fell, water table levels, land-clearing practices, the changing mix of subsistence strategies.

Other explanations emerged as well.

Could there have been a massive epidemic? Unlikely: there was no sign of large burial areas.

Could there have been a disruption of the turquoise trade? Perhaps Lieutenant Simpson wasn't so wrong after all; if the Anasazi were dependent, not on the Aztecs, but on some earlier Mexican civilization, then might not the Anasazi demise be tied to problems down south? Also unlikely. Most archaeologists are skeptical of this explanation for the same reason they originally rejected Simpson's theory: the only pre-Aztec Mexican civilization that might have extended so far north was that of Teotihuacán, and that had declined long before the rise of the Anasazi. Although there was trade between the Anasazi and Mexico, there is no evidence that the Anasazi civilization depended on it.

Could there have been a civil war among the Anasazi? Perhaps. But there were still no signs of massive burials or sacked cities. And why wouldn't the victors have stayed on?

Could there have been some sort of religious upheaval? Some archaeologists have argued that the Anasazi may have been drawn south by the emerging Kachina religion. But others question whether the archaeological record of Kachina icons and artifacts puts the religion in the area early enough to have attracted the Anasazi. Besides, why would the religion have required the Anasazi to leave their cities?

And so the debate goes on.

☆ ☆ ☆

There are some signs, though, that it may someday be resolved. Most of the archaeologists, anthropologists, and historians working on the mystery today agree that there will never be a single solution, whether military, environmental, or social. Rather, they believe a variety of factors came into play. Perhaps, for example, drought or crop failures set off internal fighting, or undermined people's religious faith. Perhaps a combination of many factors chipped away at a complex system until it could barely maintain itself, and then some final force—a massive drought, an outside attack—was just the last straw.

Almost all scholars agree on one point: the Anasazi did not simply vanish into the sands. Whatever the reason for abandoning their cities, the Anasazi went somewhere. Some probably settled along the Rio Grande, some at the foot of Black Mesa. Some may even have stayed on in Mesa Verde or Chaco Canyon, but in a less structured society that built nothing new to reveal its presence to archaeologists. After all, before Chaco Canyon and Mesa Verde were built, the Anasazi had survived for hundreds of years in smaller, more nomadic groups. That type of life may have seemed as natural and appealing to them as their more complex, urban society seems to us.

Part of the problem, historian Kendrick Frazier points out, is the use of the term "Anasazi." It sounds like a particular tribe of Indians, just like the Navajo or Hopi, and since there are no Anasazi today we think of its people as having disappeared. But they didn't disappear. The Anasazi merged with the tribes who became the modern Pueblo Indians and—though the passage of eight hundred years may make it difficult for us to recognize them—the descendants of the Anasazi are living today in Arizona and New Mexico. To think otherwise is to repeat the mistake James Simpson made almost one hundred and fifty years ago.

☆ To investigate further:

Douglass, A. E. "The Secret of the Southwest Solved by the Talkative Tree Rings," *National Geographic*, December 1929. How Douglass advanced the science of dendrochronology and discovered the great drought.

Gladwin, Harold. *A History of the Ancient Southwest*. Portland, ME: Bond Wheelwright Co., 1950. One of the first comprehensive histories, and still the most dramatic, to make the case that the Anasazi were attacked by outside tribes.

Colton, Harold. *Black Sand*. Albuquerque: University of New Mexico Press, 1962. The case for an epidemic.

Pike, Donald and David Muench, *Anasazi*. New York: Crown, 1974. Striking photos of Anasazi ruins.

Euler, R. C., T. N. V. Karlstrom, J. S. Dean, R. C. Hevley, "The Colorado Plateaus: Cultural Dynamics and Paleoenvironment." *Science,* September 1979. A multidisciplinary approach arguing that though the causal relationships were not as direct as previously supposed, environmental factors led to the abandonments. Technical but compelling.

Cordell, Linda S. *Prehistory of the Southwest.* San Diego: Academic Press, 1984. An anthropology textbook with a useful synthesis of research.

Frazier, Kendrick. *People of Chaco.* New York: Norton, 1986. A history of Chaco archaeology that succeeds in capturing the mystique as well as the mystery of the Anasazi.

Ambler, J. Richard and Mark Sutton, "The Anasazi Abandonment of the San Juan Drainage and the Numic Expansion." *North American Archaeologist* 10, no. 1 (1989). One of the most recent revivals of the case that outside attackers (in this case the southern Ute and Paiute) drove away the Anasazi.

Rafferty, Kevin. "The Anasazi Abandonment and the Numic Expansion." *North American Archaeologist* 10, no. 4 (1989). Makes the case that the disruption of ties with the Toltec empire in Mexico precipitated the Anasazi collapse.

Gumerman, George, ed. *Themes in Southwest Prehistory.* Santa Fe: School of American Research Press, 1994. A multidisciplinary collection including a provocative essay on the need to focus on "push" as well as "pull" factors, i.e., what drew the Anasazi to new locations as well as what drove them away from old ones.

Chapter 4

Where Did Columbus Land?

Leif Ericsson beat him here and perhaps others did as well. But it was Christopher Columbus's discovery of America that mattered most; once Columbus set foot on American soil, the New World and the Old were forever linked. Columbus's landfall was arguably the most momentous occasion in western history. Yet more than five hundred years later, historians are still arguing about where it took place.

☆ ☆ ☆

To most historians the solution to the mystery was to be found in the *Diario,* a summary of Columbus's own shipboard log of the journey. Unfortunately the original version of the *Diario* has been lost; when Columbus returned to Spain, he presented it to Queen Isabella, and it hasn't been seen since. Fortunately two copies of the log were made. One ended up in the hands of a Dominican friar named Bartolomé de Las Casas who included it in his *Historia de las indias;* that same copy (or the other one) was also at some point in the hands of Columbus's son Fernando who used it as a source for his biography of his father.

With the *Diario* in hand, historians have attempted three ways of solving what's become known as the "landfall problem." First, they've tried to track Columbus's westbound journey, starting from the Canary Islands off the coast of Africa and following the log's directions to

Columbus's first encounters with Native Americans most certainly did not include naval battles or cannibal barbecues (as portrayed in this 1621 illustration by the Venetian artist Honorario Philopono). By permission of the Houghton Library, Harvard University.

see where he ended up. Second, they've tried going backward, taking as their starting point the north coast of Cuba (which is the first place Columbus visited whose identity is certain) and reconstructing his track between there and his first landing. And third, they've tried to match the log's descriptions of the islands Columbus visited with the current topography of the various possible landing places.

Using all three methods, historians have come up with about a dozen serious candidates for the honor of being the site of the first landfall. Foremost among them is the island of San Salvador, a small island in the northern Bahamas. San Salvador was first cited as the landfall by the Spanish historian Juan Bautista Muñoz in 1793. And San Salvador was also the name Columbus gave to the island of his landfall—but that's irrelevant to the case for this particular island because it was known as Watlings Island until 1926. At that time the island's British colonial government, trying to preempt other claimants, gave it the name San Salvador.

What mattered much more than the local government's endorsement was that of Samuel Eliot Morison in 1942. That was the year Morison published what is still considered the standard biography of Columbus. In it he stated in no uncertain terms that only San Salvador/Watlings fit Columbus's course and description as set down in the log. Morison's prestige as both historian and navigator—he was a rear admiral in the navy and he scoffed at "dryadusts" who studied Columbus's voyages from their armchairs—all but ended the discussion for 40 years.

Gradually, however, other claimants chipped away at Morison's and San Salvador's position. In 1986 *National Geographic,* after spending one million dollars on a new study, lent its considerable prestige to the case for Samana Cay, a Bahamian island about 65 miles southeast of San Salvador. Samana Cay, too, had had many previous advocates, among them Gustavus Fox, who had been Lincoln's assistant secretary of the navy. (Morison and Fox were just two of the many admirals to be found on Columbus's track.) The *Geographic* study argued that Morison had failed to take into account the effects of currents and leeway (a ship's slow skid downwind), and it enlisted the aid of a computer to resail the routes electronically.

In 1991 other researchers, arguing that neither Morison nor the *Geographic* study had taken into account the effects of magnetic variation (don't ask!), located the first landfall further southeast, on the island of Grand Turk. Grand Turk, too, had had many early advocates, the first being Martin Fernández de Navarette in 1825.

As the landfall's quincentennial approached, the debate intensified, with proponents of one island or another seizing upon different passages in the *Diario* to demonstrate why no other island besides their choice fit the bill. San Salvador, which remained the orthodox position, came under the most attack, but strong cases were made for and against all the leading candidates. The only thing everyone agreed on was that Columbus's landfall took place somewhere in the Bahamas.

Why couldn't all these sophisticated historians and mariners come to some sort of consensus? What was so difficult about comparing Columbus's words with the locations and characteristics of Bahamian islands?

For one thing, it's not so clear what Columbus's words were. Only 20 percent of the *Diario* is in his words; the rest consists of summaries and paraphrases by Las Casas. We can't even be sure that what Las Casas used hadn't been altered before it got to him.

Furthermore, even when you take the words that we're fairly sure are Columbus's own, you run into problems. To take just one example, the *Diario* says the landfall island has *una laguna en medio muy grande*—a very large lagoon in the center. Advocates of Watlings have been especially vehement in pointing out that only Watlings, of all the leading candidates, has a large body of water in the middle of the island. Advocates of Grand Turk and Samana Cay have argued that their islands may have dried up in the past five hundred years, that ground water is seasonal in the Bahamas, and that we can't know for sure how much water there was on any given island then. But undeniably these are efforts to make the best of a description that favors Watlings.

What neither supporters nor detractors of Watlings take into account is that we have no idea what Columbus meant by a "large lagoon." Large compared to what? Landfall advocates compare the size of their various islands' waters but Columbus couldn't compare them; this was the first New World island he'd seen. What's more, the rest of the phrase—*en medio*, or in the middle—has been taken to mean in the middle of the island as it would be viewed from above, that is, a lake in the middle of the island. But what if you take "in the middle" to mean halfway up the shoreline? Then "laguna" might not mean lake, but "lagoon," as we use the word today. Suddenly Watlings, which has a lake but no lagoon, has lost its most compelling piece of evidence.

The point here is not to make a case *against* Watlings, or *for* any other island. Rather, it is to show, as the historian David Henige did most thoroughly in his 1991 book, that all these cases are based on a primary source that may be unreliable and is certainly vague. One revisionist historian has even speculated that Columbus was intentionally vague. Kirkpatrick Sale, a writer who admittedly doesn't like Columbus (he blames him for just about every instance of exploitation of land and people that has taken place in America since 1492), suggests that Columbus's descriptions were vague because he wanted to keep the location secret. If gold and glory were to be found on the landfall island or any other, Columbus wanted it for himself. As evidence, Sale points to a September 1493 letter from Ferdinand and Isabella to Columbus, in which the sovereigns demand more details about "the degrees within which the islands and land you discovered fall and the degrees of the path you traveled." There's no record of Columbus ever answering that letter.

But one needn't attribute Columbus's vagueness to greed to ad-mit the *Diario* isn't as useful a source as we'd like it to be. Perhaps it was that Columbus was (understandably) preoccupied. Perhaps he just didn't care about this island; had he returned to it during any of his three subsequent voyages to the New World, this mystery might be easily solved. Alas, the first time Columbus stepped on the landfall is-land was also the last time he did so.

☆ ☆ ☆

So, we can't help asking: if this island didn't matter to Columbus, why should it matter to us?

One answer is that it shouldn't. Neither our understanding of American or European history, nor our understanding of Columbus's character, have changed the slightest bit as the result of conclusions on behalf of one island or the other. Except for a minor blip in a few is-lands' tourist trade, not much is at stake.

Many historians have, therefore, put the landfall question behind them, moving on to other questions. Perhaps the most hotly contested issue in recent Columbus scholarship has been not where the landfall island is, but where Columbus *thought* it was. Morison maintained that Columbus died believing that he'd found a new route to the Far East, and that the islands he visited were somewhere off the coast of Asia. This remains the majority view. Nonetheless, an increasing number of historians have been convinced that Columbus knew he'd discovered a truly New World, and some have even argued that this was always his goal.

And yet, even as other questions about Columbus have taken precedence, the landfall mystery has continued to intrigue historians, mariners, and others. With its tantalizing mixture of just enough evi-dence to get us close but not quite enough to get us there, it has again and again proven an irresistible challenge. Columbus's San Salvador, the native's Guanahani: this was, after all, the place where two worlds first collided.

☆ To investigate further:

Fuson, Robert. *The Log of Christopher Columbus.* Rockport, ME: International Marine Publishing Co., 1987. Like most translations of the log, this one has an agenda: it was prepared in conjunction with the *National Geographic* case for Samana Cay. Still, it's a lively version.

Morison, Samuel Eliot. *Admiral of the Ocean Sea*. New York: Little, Brown, 1942. Still the definitive biography, with the case for Watlings/San Salvador.

De Vorsey, Louis, Jr. and John Parker, editors. *In The Wake of Columbus*. Detroit: Wayne State University Press, 1985. A wide-ranging collection of scholarly essays, with a concise historiography by Parker.

Judge, Joseph and James Stanfield. "The Island Landfall." *National Geographic*, November 1986. The case for Samana Cay.

Marvel, Josiah and Robert Power. "In Quest of Where America Began." *American History Illustrated*, Jan/Feb 1991. The case for Grand Turk.

Sale, Kirkpatrick. *The Conquest of Paradise*. New York: Knopf, 1990. Even if you don't buy Sale's argument that Columbus embodies everything wrong with America, from enslaving blacks and Indians to destroying the environment, you'll still find him lively and provocative.

Henige, David. *In Search of Columbus*. Tucson: The University of Arizona Press, 1991. A critique of the flaws of the *Diario* as a primary source, and of the way it's been misinterpreted and manipulated.

Wilford, John Noble. *The Mysterious History of Columbus*. New York: Knopf, 1991. A readable review of the ways historians from Columbus's time on have mythologized, debunked, and otherwise interpreted the man and his journeys.

Chapter 5

How Did Cortés Conquer the Aztecs?

ernán Cortés and his band of four hundred or so Spanish adventurers first sighted Tenochtitlán, the capital of the Aztec empire, in November 1519. With its busy canals, bustling markets, and beautiful buildings, Tenochtitlán might have reminded some of the Spaniards of Venice. For most of them, though, this was a far larger city than any they'd seen; Tenochtitlán's population of about 250,000 was larger than that of any city in Europe. The city was built on an island in the middle of a large lake near present-day Mexico City. Broad causeways stretched many miles across the lake, connecting the island to the mainland and to an Aztec empire that ruled over nearly four hundred cities and more than 125,000 square miles.

Two years after the Spaniards first set foot in Mexico, Tenochtitlán was in ruins and the remains of the empire were presided over by Cortés. How Cortés defeated the Aztecs is one of the greatest mysteries of history. For unlike the other Native American groups encountered by Europeans, the Aztecs were a highly organized, highly militarized people. Montezuma II, the Aztec emperor, commanded an army of more than 200,000 warriors, many seasoned in the far-reaching campaigns that had gained the Aztecs their empire. How was it possible for a few hundred Spaniards—acting on their own, with no support or supplies from the Crown, and operating in territory that no European had even seen before—to conquer the Aztec empire?

Most of our knowledge of the conquest comes to us from the conquistadores themselves. Cortés described the events in a series of letters to the Spanish king, Charles I. So did a number of others, most notably the foot soldier Bernal Díaz del Castillo, who participated in the conquest and wrote his recollections twenty years later, and Francisco López de Gómara, who wasn't a witness to the events but who later became private secretary and chaplain to Cortés.

Cortés set off for Mexico in March 1519 under the auspices of the Spanish governor of Cuba, Diego Velázquez. Velázquez ordered him to explore the Mexican coast and trade with any Indians he found there. Cortés, however, had bigger things in mind. Upon reaching Mexico's east coast, he announced (through an interpreter he'd picked up along the way) that he'd been sent by Charles I of Spain, the greatest king on earth, to speak to their leader. This was Montezuma, he learned. Cortés added that he'd also like some gold because, "I and my companions suffer from a disease of the heart which can be cured only with gold." Montezuma's messengers carried this message to Tenochtitlán and then returned with lavish gifts—including gold. But the emperor regretted he would not be able to meet with Cortés, they said.

If Montezuma thought gold would get rid of Cortés, he was tragically mistaken. The gold only whetted Cortés's appetite. He and his motley crew set off for Tenochtitlán, discovering to their delight that many of the cities en route deeply resented the tribute they were forced to pay the Aztecs. Far from resisting the Spanish advance, these people were happy to join forces with Cortés. Most significant of these allies were the Tlaxcalans, fierce enemies of the Aztecs whom the latter had never subdued.

And so it was that on November 8, 1519, Cortés, now accompanied by about five thousand Indian allies, reached the causeway leading to Tenochtitlán. Again, Montezuma chose a policy of appeasement; he welcomed Cortés and his army into his city, put them up in a luxurious palace, and served them sumptuous feasts. Still, after a few days, Cortés became uneasy. Though Montezuma continued to play the generous

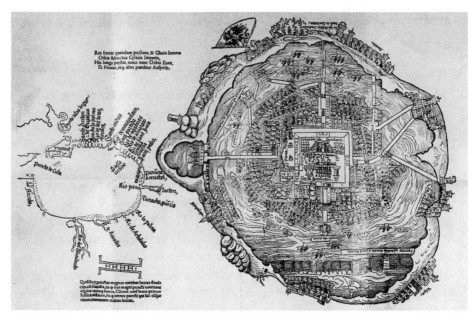

A map of Tenochtitlán and the Gulf of Mexico, made for Cortés in 1524. Although the European-style houses are certainly not authentic, the map does show Aztec temples, causeways across Lake Texococo, and other features of the city prior to its conquest. Courtesy of the British Museum.

host, Cortés could sense the growing hostility of other Aztecs. Whatever its emperor's policies, this was, after all, a nation of warriors.

Cortés then came up with one of the most audacious plans in the history of war: he would take the emperor hostage in his own city. In the midst of one of the emperor's social calls, Cortés and his men did just that. For the next six months, with Montezuma as their prisoner, the Spaniards had the run of the city. But trouble was brewing on two fronts. The more hawkish Aztecs, uniting under the emperor's brother Cuitláhuac, seemed increasingly willing to attack the Spaniards, even if it meant risking Montezuma's life. Then, to make matters worse, a Spanish fleet sent by the Cuban governor Velázquez arrived on the Mexican coast. Velázquez was not at all happy that Cortés had turned his little trading mission into a major expedition; if there were riches to be had in Mexico, the governor felt, they were for *him* to discover, not Cortés.

So Cortés headed back to the coast, taking about 120 soldiers with him. He left just a hundred or so at Tenochtitlán under the command of Pedro de Alvarado. Once he reached the coast, Cortés put to work the same admirable powers of persuasion that had won over so many Indians. And again he succeeded: after some minor skirmishes with Velázquez's soldiers, Cortés convinced most of them to join him. So he headed back to Tenochtitlán with his new recruits.

Alas, in leaving Alvarado in charge in Tenochtitlán, Cortés had erred as greatly as Velázquez had when he chose Cortés. Alvarado had none of Cortés's subtlety, and in the midst of an Aztec religious festival he'd attacked and massacred the celebrants. The Aztecs, led by Cuitláhuac, counterattacked, and full-scale fighting had broken out. When Cortés reached Tenochtitlán, he discovered that his carefully cultivated Indian allies had fled, leaving the Spaniards trapped in the palace. Again, Cortés tried to use Montezuma to quell the Aztecs: he sent the emperor up to the palace roof to speak on behalf of the Spaniards. But by now the Aztecs would have none of this, and Montezuma was killed by stones thrown by his own people.

Cortés then decided his best chance was to sneak out at night and, on June 30, 1520, the Spaniards stuffed their pockets with Aztec treasure and headed for the causeways. But the Aztecs discovered them and attacked, killing more than half of the Spaniards. Many drowned in the waters around Tenochtitlán, weighed down by the gold in their pockets. "Those who died," Gómara wrote, "died rich."

Cortés regrouped at Tlaxcala, his most loyal ally. He set to work building boats, which would cut off all access to Tenochtitlán. In late April 1521, the Spaniards set siege to the city, then began a bloody, house-by-house advance. Three months later, they again ruled Tenochtitlán—or what remained of the once great capital.

This was the Spanish version of the conquest. The Spanish won because they were braver, more tenacious, more resourceful and, when necessary, ruthless in the service of their king and God; the Aztecs, and Montezuma in particular, were indecisive and cowardly. Still, a mystery remained. Why would Montezuma, whose past included many battlefield victories, suddenly lose all heart when faced by the Spaniards? Cortés's letters to the king of Spain contain his answer. When Montezuma first welcomed the Spaniards into Tenochtitlán, the emperor spoke to Cortés, and Cortés's letter quotes him as follows:

> For a long time we have known from the writings of our ancestors that neither I, nor any of those who dwell in this land, are natives of it, but foreigners who come from very distant parts; and likewise we know that a chieftain, of whom they were all vassals, brought our people to this region. And he returned to his native land . . . and we have always held that those who descended from him would come and conquer this land and take us as their vassals. So, because of the place from which you claim to come, namely, from where the sun rises, and the things you tell us of the great lord or king who sent you here, we believe and are certain that he is our natural lord. . . . So be assured that we shall obey you and hold you as our lord in place of that great sovereign of whom you speak.

Montezuma, Cortés explained, had first mistaken Cortés for the Aztec god, Quetzalcoatl, who, according to Aztec legend, would someday return to rule his people. Later, as in the above speech, Montezuma realized Cortés was not a god but still thought he was the god's emissary. Either way, Montezuma's superstitious nature prevailed over his military judgment, and Cortés took full advantage of it.

It was not just the conquistadores themselves who explained the conquest thus. Most historians followed suit, admiring Cortés for his courage and strategy, and ridiculing Montezuma's superstition-induced paralysis. Even those historians who have denounced Cortés as a greedy imperialist, the destroyer of Indian culture, could only pity Montezuma.

And yet, to many historians today, the above portraits of Cortés and Montezuma don't ring true. Cortés's letters to King Charles I ought not to be considered an accurate historical narrative, they argue. Rather, Cortés had a very specific purpose in mind: to convince Charles that Cortés, and not Velázquez, ought to be granted the right to explore (and conquer) Mexico. To make his case, Cortés was capable of grossly distorting history: for example, according to some historians, the speech about Quetzalcoatl that Cortés put into Montezuma's mouth is entirely apocryphal. Quetzalcoatl was indeed an Aztec god, but he was worshipped in Cholula, not Tenochtitlán. Cortés may have heard the legend on his way to Tenochtitlán and used it in his letter to show Charles how well he—as opposed to Velázquez—had mastered and manipulated the Aztecs on the king's behalf.

Alternative explanations for Montezuma's behavior have come from recent studies of the Indian accounts of the conquest. To be sure, these accounts are also problematic; they're fragmentary and, since the Aztec language was not a written one, they've come down to us in versions recorded by Spaniards soon after the conquest. Still, the Aztecs' own accounts, along with other studies of Aztec culture, do present another side of the story. The Montezuma who emerges from these studies is reluctant to fight, but not because he's superstitious or cowardly. This Montezuma shies away from battle with the Spaniards for many reasons: he's not sure whether to trust the Spaniards' talk of peaceful intentions, but he's very aware that they've arrived toward the end of the harvest season, and that many of his warriors are busy in the fields. At the very least, he may have been biding his time, hoping his emissaries could break up the alliances between the Spaniards and other Indian groups.

Historians have spent a great deal of energy debating what was going on in Montezuma's head. At this point we must admit that we can't know for sure why he let the Spaniards enter Tenochtitlán. In one sense, however, this debate is irrelevant to explaining the conquest: whatever Montezuma's motives, whatever the efficacy of his appeasement strategy, a better understanding of these issues could only help explain the *first* phase of the conquest—up until the death of Montezuma. After Montezuma's death, the Aztecs were ruled by the openly anti-Spanish Cuitláhuac. There was no longer any question that this was war, and that the Aztec empire was at stake. Yet even at this point, with the massive Aztec forces mobilized by a brave and competent chieftain, it took the Spaniards only a bit more than a year to regroup and return to besiege and overrun Tenochtitlán. To explain this second phase of the conquest, historians have had to shift their focus away from the debate about the relative merits of Cortés and Montezuma to other factors.

One obvious factor was the superiority of Spanish weapons. Against the Aztec arrows, the Spanish had cannons; while the Aztecs were on foot, the Spanish had horses. Yet the importance of this factor is easily overstated. The Aztecs were quick to figure out how to neutralize Spanish war technology. They would fall back to positions such as towns or ravines where the Spanish horses couldn't maneuver. And cannons were not so powerful an advantage as they might sound—the Spaniards only had a few of them and their supply of gunpowder was limited and at times too wet to be of much use. Besides, a few horses and cannons couldn't make up for the vast numerical advantage the Aztecs held.

Another factor was disease. A member of the crew sent by Velázquez had smallpox, and the disease swept across Mexico, whose people had never been exposed to the disease and who therefore had no resistance to it. By 1558, the population of Mexico had been reduced from a preconquest figure of about ten million* to a mere two or three million, and disease was undeniably a major factor in this. But smallpox struck down as many of Cortés's Indian allies as it did Aztecs, and it did not spread fast enough to account for the conquest on its own.

Yet another factor was the Aztec tradition of trying to capture, rather than kill, their enemies on the battlefield. This was hardly a compassionate tradition—many of those captured were later sacrificed to the gods and *eaten* by their captors, a practice that struck terror into the hearts of the most courageous Spaniards. But it did mean that in their efforts to capture rather than kill their enemies, the Aztecs often let them get away. And given the limited number of Spaniards, this undeniably aided Cortés's campaign.

All these factors played a role in the conquest. So, too, did Cortés's courage and strategy. Without a doubt, however, Cortés's greatest contribution to the Spaniards' success was his ability to enlist the support of Indian allies. More than anything else, this evened out the numbers on the opposing sides. Cortés admitted this; so did the Indian accounts of the conquest. Reliable numbers are hard to come by, but the Tlaxcalans alone added thousands of warriors to the Spanish ranks.

The empire that the Spaniards conquered was indeed a huge and powerful one. The Aztecs received tribute from far-flung cities and, in the absence of a major competing power, there was little these cities could do about it. But they deeply resented the Aztecs, and when the Spaniards arrived on the scene they offered a rallying point around

---

*The preconquest population of Mexico is itself a major source of debate. Estimates range from thirty million to four million, with those denouncing the conquest as immoral tending to favor the higher numbers (to make the Spaniards look guiltier) and those defending the conquest and the Spaniards coming up with lower numbers. Whatever the preconquest numbers, however, it is clear that by the late 1540s, when statistics were for the first time systematically gathered, the population had been considerably reduced.

which these disaffected cities could unite. For all of Cortés's efforts to portray himself as the only figure the king could trust to handle the Indians, it was not Cortés alone who brought down the Aztec empire; it was the Tlaxcalans and their allies, as much as the Spaniards, who were the *conquistadores*.

☆ To investigate further:

Pagden, Anthony, translator and editor. *Hernan Cortés: Letters from Mexico*. New Haven: Yale University Press, 1986. This translation of Cortés's letters includes a fascinating introduction in which J. H. Elliott convincingly demonstrates how Cortés's accounts of the conquest were slanted by his efforts to gain the king's support.

del Castillo, Bernal Díaz (translated by A. P. Maudslay). *The Discovery and Conquest of Mexico*. New York: Farrar, Straus and Cudahy, 1956. A Spanish soldier's account of the conquest, written in 1555.

de Gómara, Francisco López (translated by Lesley Byrd Simpson). *Cortés*. Berkeley: University of California Press, 1964. Cortés's secretary and chaplain's account of the conquest, written with Cortés's cooperation.

de Fuentes, Patricia, editor and translator. *The Conquistadors*. Norman: University of Oklahoma Press, 1993. A handy volume of excerpts from all the major first-person Spanish accounts of the conquest (except Díaz's).

de Sahagún, Bernardino (translated by Howard Cline). *Conquest of New Spain*. Salt Lake City: University of Utah Press, 1989. Sahagún, a Franciscan friar, wrote this history in 1585 based on his interviews with Indians who'd survived the conquest. Though the Aztecs' recollections may have been colored both by Sahagun's mediation and by their own feelings toward the conquest, this is nonetheless the most valuable source of knowledge on the Aztec world.

Leon-Portilla, Miguel, editor. *The Broken Spears*. Boston: Beacon Press, 1962. An English translation (from the Spanish, which was itself a translation from the Aztec language, Nahuatl) of surviving Aztec descriptions of the conquest.

Prescott, William Hickling. *The Conquest of Mexico*. New York: Harper & Brothers, 1843; reissued by Modern Library (New York) 1936. Though dated by Prescott's nineteenth-century prejudices in favor of Cortés and against Indians, this remains a classic work of narrative history.

Todorov, Tzvetan. *The Conquest of America*. New York: HarperCollins, 1984. Todorov, a French critic, attributes the conquest to the superiority of the Spaniards, not as fighters or strategists, but as communicators.

Hassig, Ross. *Aztec Warfare*. Norman: University of Oklahoma Press, 1988. An ethnohistorian's view of the rise and fall of the Aztec empire, this makes clear the extent to which the empire's downfall was brought about by cleavages that preceded Cortés's arrival.

Clendinnen, Inga. "Fierce and Unnatural Cruelty." *Representations*, Winter 1991. A highly provocative essay emphasizing how both the Spaniards and the Aztecs misunderstood each other and misrepresented the conquest.

Thomas, Hugh. *Conquest*. New York: Simon & Schuster, 1993. While Thomas is not quite as masterful a writer as Prescott, this comprehensive narrative is as close as the twentieth century has come to Prescott's history, and the wide range of twentieth-century scholarship incorporated in Thomas's work certainly supplants Prescott's.

Chapter 6

What Happened to the Lost Colony of Roanoke?

90 men. 17 women. 9 children.

These were the colonists who landed on Roanoake Island off the coast of what is now North Carolina in July 1587—20 years before John Smith reached Virginia and 35 years before the Pilgrims reached Massachussetts. Among them was Eleanor Dare, the daughter of the colony's governor, John White. She was about to give birth, and that child—the appropriately named Virginia Dare—would be the first European child born in the New World, assuming no anonymous Norse child had preceded her.

White stayed in America for the birth of his granddaughter, then set sail for England to arrange additional supplies for the colony. When he returned three years later, the colonists had vanished; the only clues to their whereabouts were the letters CROATAN, carved on a post, and CRO on a nearby tree.

Had the colonists quickly carved these messages while under attack from Indians? White thought not: he'd instructed them to carve a cross if they were in trouble. Did the colonists mean they'd gone to join the friendly Indians on nearby Croatoan Island? That, too, perplexed White: he'd discussed with the colonists the possibility of heading north towards the Chesapeake Bay, but Croatan Island was south of Roanoke Island.

Bad weather prevented White from looking further and forced him to return to England, but by no means did that end the search. To the Jamestown settlers later on, the fate of the Roanoke colonists was no mere history exercise; they believed, quite reasonably, that it might be the key to understanding how they themselves could survive in the New World, and John Smith led a number of expeditions in search of his predecessors. More recently, historians and archaeologists have continued the search. And though no white person ever again saw the "lost colonists," those on their trail have turned up some tantalizing clues and proposed some engaging scenarios.

The fate of the Lost Colony is very much bound up with the fate of Sir Walter Raleigh. This was the same Walter Raleigh who, legend has it, spread his best cloak over a puddle before the queen. Perhaps, perhaps not. In any case, whatever he did to charm the queen was worth hundreds of cloaks—for Raleigh became such a favorite that in 1584 Elizabeth granted him an exclusive patent to colonize America.

Within a month he arranged a reconnaissance voyage to North America. It returned later in the year with enthusiastic reports of abundant Carolina resources and friendly Carolina Indians. Raleigh did not delay: in April 1585 he sent off one hundred colonists in seven ships. They arrived at Roanoke Island later in the year, built a fort, and appointed Ralph Lane as Governor.

This, then, was the first Roanoke colony, and the first British colony in America. It was founded two years before the Lost Colony, and whose fate, in contrast, is well-known.

It was a remarkably ill-conceived colony. Lane was a soldier, as were most of the colonists. What they had in mind for Roanoke was a base for attacking Spanish ships en route from South America. Their plan was to get rich on Spanish treasure; building houses and toiling in the American soil was not for them. They quickly came to depend on friendly Indians for food, and they almost as quickly alienated the Indians. (Lane's idea of diplomacy was to kidnap the favorite son of the powerful chief Menatonon and hold him hostage until the chief gave Lane information about other tribes' defenses.) By the spring of 1586 the colonists were out of supplies and allies and in desperate straits.

Fortunately help appeared on the horizon in the form of a fleet of ships commanded by Sir Francis Drake. But Drake was as much a privateer as the Roanoke colonists. He had come in order to use the colony as a base for his attacks on the Spanish; he could offer the colonists guns but no butter. And when a storm sunk four of his ships he could barely offer them passage home. In fact, to make room for the Roanoke colonists, Drake had to leave behind some African slaves and Indians he had liberated from the Spanish. These slaves and Indians were never heard from again; they were as "lost" as the more celebrated "lost colonists" of John White.

A few weeks after Drake, Lane, and the rest of the colony set sail for England, a relief party sent by Raleigh arrived. (On the way they'd been delayed by an irresistible urge to attack some Spanish ships.) When they found the colony deserted, they turned around, leaving behind a holding party of 15 men. None of them were ever heard from again, either.

Now we get to the "real" lost colony, a colony which ironically was much better prepared to survive in the New World than Lane and company. However greedy a privateer Raleigh was, he was a man who could understand what had gone wrong and act to correct it. For his next colony, instead of the authoritarian Ralph Lane, he chose as governor the artist John White. (White was a superb artist; his drawings of Indian life are still among the best sources for anthropologists and historians.) Instead of soldiers, Raleigh chose colonists whose interest was in building a colony, and he granted them land as incentive to work and stay. Women and children came along, with more planning to follow. And instead of the sandy soil of Roanoke, this new group was to settle in the Chesapeake Bay, not far from where Jamestown would eventually take root. In short, the colony Raleigh sent to America in 1587 was, much more even than Jamestown, the prototype for later successful colonies.

So what went wrong?

To begin with, the ships somehow ended up at Roanoke again, instead of on the Chesapeake. Then the ships' pilot, a Portuguese named Simon Fernandes, announced it was too late in the year to take the colonists any further. According to White's letters (one of the primary sources for exploring the mystery of the Lost Colony), greed was the motive of Fernandes; like so many associated with the Roanoke ventures he was a privateer. He dumped the colonists at

If John White made an ineffectual governor of Roanoke, he was nonetheless a superb artist; witness his drawings of Indian life, such as these engraved in 1590 by Theodor De Bry. Library of Congress.

Roanoke so he could run off and attack some Spanish ships. More generous interpreters have argued that Fernandes might have been trying to do the colonists a favor. The pilot had had some previous experience in Chesapeake Bay while in Spanish service, and he may have told the colonists (quite accurately) how warlike the Indians in the area were, and how they had wiped out a Jesuit mission there in 1570.

Whatever reasons Fernandes had for staying at Roanoke, White acquiesced. Perhaps he felt Fernandes had the upper hand and there was nothing he could do about it. Perhaps, though he wouldn't admit it, he was happy to be back on familiar ground—despite the inadequacy of the site and the bad relations Lane had generated with the Indians. Perhaps—and this is the most likely explanation—White was an admirable artist but an ineffectual leader.

In any case, Fernandes stuck around for a month, departing in August 1587 and taking White with him. Here's another mystery: why would the colony's governor leave the colony, not to mention his newborn granddaughter? According to White, the colonists insisted that only *he* could be counted on to make sure that they were not forgotten by their backers. More likely, they were fed up with his vacillating leadership and decided he'd be more use to them back in England.

Again White let them down; it was not until three years later that he returned and by then, as we've seen, it was too late. For this, however, it's not really fair to blame White. He worked tirelessly on behalf of the colonists but his timing couldn't have been worse. For one thing, Raleigh's interest was waning: he had put a lot of money into the venture and didn't feel he could keep doing so, especially since the Earl of Essex had replaced him as the queen's favorite. More ominously, the Spanish had grown tired of British privateering and had decided to cut it off at its base. With the Spanish Armada on its way, Elizabeth was taking no chances. In April 1588 she ordered all ships capable of war service—including those White was putting together to go back to Roanoke—to stay put. Even after the Armada was defeated, Elizabeth feared a new attack and was reluctant to let ships go. And so it was not until 1590 that White finally returned to find—or rather, not find—his colony.

What happened to the colonists?

White himself was sanguine. He knew they had planned to move eventually anyway. He found no cross anywhere, and he clearly remembered instructing them "that if they should happen to be distressed in any of those places, that they should carve over the letters or name, a Crosse." White couldn't explain why they would have changed plans and gone south instead of north, nor did he explain how they were supposed to carve a cross at Roanoke if they ran into problems elsewhere. Still, everything seemed pretty much in order at the fort and there definitely was no cross there. White was relieved.

Meanwhile, back in England, Raleigh's position was deteriorating. He'd secretly married, and when Elizabeth found out she did not take it well, imprisoning both groom and bride in the Tower of London. When he was finally released, he found himself exiled from the court. In 1595 Raleigh finally made it to America—but now it was the South American coast that attracted him. Roanoke seemed far away and unimportant. Some historians have argued that Raleigh intentionally abandoned the search to protect his patent, which required him to have a settlement. As long as he could claim the colonists were alive somewhere in the area his patent was safe; further searches might risk proving they were dead. In 1602 Raleigh did send a party to search further but it turned up nothing new.

It was not until after Jamestown was settled in 1607, therefore, that the search continued in earnest. That same year George Percy of Jamestown described seeing an Indian with "a head of haire of a perfect yellow and a reasonable white skinne, which is a Miracle amongst all Savages." And John Smith, in *A true relation of such occurrences and accidents of noate as hath hapned in Virginia,* told of meeting an Indian chief who told him "of certaine men cloathed at a place called Ocanahonan, cloathed like me." William Strachey's 1612 *Historie of Travell Into Virginia Britania* describes how Indians told him of "howses built with stone walls, and one story above another, so taught . . . by the English."

Strachey also told of the slaughter of the lost colonists by Powhatan, the father of Pocahontas. Strachey's story went as follows: The colonists did head north, as White planned, eventually finding their way to the Chesapeake Bay. There they lived in peace for about 20 years with the Chesapeake Indians. Then, just about the time the first Jamestown colonists were arriving, Powhatan went to war with the Chesapeakes, slaughtering both the Indians and the settlers.

This was the story the Jamestown settlers settled on. It explained both the persistent rumors of lost colonists in the area and the failure to actually find them.

Other solutions to the mystery have been proposed in the centuries since then. Some suggested the lost colonists were lost at sea, trying to get back to England. But that's unlikely—they didn't have a large enough boat to cross the Atlantic. Others have suggested they were killed by Spaniards. Also unlikely—since Spanish documents show they were still looking for the English colony as late as 1600. Still others claim today's Croatan Indians are the direct descendants of the lost colonists, pointing to some linguistic similarities between the Indians' language and English. But these can more easily be explained by hundreds of years of contacts with European immigrants.

So Strachey's story, which the Jamestown settlers believed, may very well be the truth. One modern historian, David Beers Quinn, has added a new twist. Most of the colonists, he believes, moved north, thus accounting for the rumors and reports that reached Jamestown. At least a few stayed behind for a while longer, however, perhaps to wait for White or to hold the fort, and these were the colonists who ultimately headed south to Croatan, thus accounting for the signs on the tree.

Archaeologists continue to search for clues and they may someday be able to tell us more about what happened to Raleigh's lost colonists, or Drake's lost freedmen. As for Raleigh himself, though he may have given up on his Roanoke colony, he never gave up on America. He found himself even more out of favor with Elizabeth's successor, James I, than he'd been with Elizabeth, and he spent twelve years in the Tower. He was released in 1616, tried to win back his wealth and power with another expedition to South America, failed, and was executed.

And the much maligned John White? A John White, "late of parts beyond the seas," was declared dead in Ireland in 1606. But his was such a common name historians can't be sure this was the former governor. The fate of John White, like that of his daughter and granddaughter, remains something of a mystery.

☆ To investigate further:

Harriot, Thomas. *A briefe and true report of the new found land of Virginia.* Frankfort, 1590, reprinted by Dover, NY, 1972. One of the greatest mathematicians of the Renaissance, Harriot accompanied the 1585 expedition and produced this report, which includes White's drawings.

Hakluyt, Richard. *The Third and Last Volume of the Voyages, Navigations, Traffiques and Discoveries of the English Nation.* London: George Bishop, Ralph Newberie, and Robert Barber, 1600; reissued by Viking (New York) 1965. What we know about the lost colony and about all the British expeditions to America is largely thanks to Hakluyt, who collected the narratives, letters, and reminiscences of Raleigh, White, Lane, and others.

Quinn, David Beers. *England and the Discovery of America, 1481–1620.* New York: Knopf, 1974. No one has devoted more time and pages to the mystery of the lost colony, or to the British explorations and settlements in general. Sometimes Quinn goes way out on a limb, as when he suggests that the British discovered America before Columbus, or (some say) when he explains what happened to the lost colonists. But Quinn always lets you see the evidence on which his theories are based and, given the evidence we have so far, his theory about the lost colony is more plausible than anyone else's.

Stick, David. *Roanoke Island.* Chapel Hill: University of North Carolina Press, 1983. One of a number of very readable histories to appear around the settlement's 400th anniversary.

Kupperman, Karen. *Roanoke: The Abandoned Colony.* Totowa, NJ: Rowman & Alanheld, 1984. An attempt to present Quinn's ideas in a less academic, more popular style; as such, it's successful, but it's well worth the effort to read Quinn's own work.

Hume, Ivor Noel. *The Virginia Adventure.* New York: Knopf, 1994. The latest reports from the area's leading archaeologist; informative and entertaining.

Chapter 7

Did Pocahontas Save John Smith?

In December 1607, just a few months after the first permanent British colony in America was established at Jamestown, Captain John Smith led a trading party up the Chickahominy River. He was captured by Indians and taken before the great chief, Powhatan, who ruled over much of Tidewater Virginia. In *The Generall Historie of Virginia, New-England, and the Summer Isles,* Smith himself told what happened next:

> A long consultation was held, but the conclusion was, two great stones were brought before Powhatan: then as many as could layd hands on him, dragged him to them, and thereon laid his head, and being ready with their clubs to beate out his braines, Pocahontas the Kings dearest daughter, when no intreaty could prevaile, got his head in her armes, and laid her owne upon his to save him from death: whereat the Emperour was contented he should live to make him hatchets and her bells.

Is Smith's story true? Did the Indian princess throw herself between Smith and the tomahawks heading toward his "braines"?

Among the first and most adamant to call Smith a liar was Henry Adams in the mid-nineteenth century. He pointed out that Smith's ear-

From The True Travels, Adventures and Observations of Captaine John Smith. *In this 1629 book, Smith himself described how Powhatan "commanded him to be slaine" but then "Pocahontas saved his life." Library of Congress.*

lier histories of Virginia made no mention of Pocahontas saving him; it was not until the 1624 *Generall Historie* that Smith published the story. By then, Adams argued, those who could have refuted it—such as Pocahontas herself—were dead. With no other English-speaking witnesses besides Pocahontas, it came down to Smith's word.

The rest of the *Generall Historie* didn't do much to increase the value of that word. Smith told some remarkable—some would say incredible—tales. Seemingly least credible of all was that Pocahontas was just one of four foreign ladies who, unable to resist Smith's charms, came to his rescue. Before coming to Virginia, Smith had joined the Austrian armies fighting against the Turks in Hungary. He was captured by the Turks and made a slave in Constantinople. There his luck improved: his mistress, "the beauteous Lady Tragabigzanda," took a liking to him, treated him well, and then sent him to her brother in Tartary, from where he escaped. He ultimately reached a Russian garrison where "the good Lady Callamata . . . largely supplied all his wants." And when Smith escaped some pirates, it was "the good Lady Madam Canoyes" who "bountifully assisted me."

All this from the *Generall Historie*—all this about a very short, bearded, battle-scarred man whose portraits are distinctly underwhelming. No wonder that some of Smith's contemporaries called him a braggart and a liar, and many historians agreed.

But then, in 1953, the tide of opinion turned. That year Bradford Smith's biography of Smith appeared, with an appendix on the captain's Hungarian adventures written by Laura Striker Polanyi. Polanyi carefully checked Smith's narrative of the wars against the Turks; to almost everyone's surprise, everything that could be checked turned out to be accurate.

The case for Smith was further strengthened by ethnohistorians. Their work showed that Smith's descriptions of Indian life and culture were realistic. In fact, his works are considered an important primary source for those studying Indian history and culture. Geographers, too, came to admire the accuracy of Smith's maps of Chesapeake Bay and New England.

Smith's defenders took the offense, accusing Henry Adams and his followers of denigrating the man because he was a southerner. After all, Adams was the great-grandson of John Adams and the grandson of John Quincy Adams. Both Adamses were New Englanders to the core and were bitter political enemies of John Randolph, a Virginian—and a descendant of none other than Pocahontas. (Yet another noncoincidence: the first to answer Henry Adams in print was William Hirt Henry, grandson of Virginia's Patrick Henry.)

With Smith's reputation on the upswing, it was time to put aside sectionalist politics and Balkan adventures, and look anew at his relationship to Pocahontas.

The strongest case against the Pocahontas rescue story remained that Smith never published it until his 1624 *Generall Historie.* That he left it out of his 1612 work, *A Map of Virginia,* was fairly easy to explain: that dealt mostly with geography and ethnology and not with Smith's own explorations and adventures.

But why was the story nowhere to be found in Smith's 1608 work, *A True Relation of Such Occurrences and Accidents of Noate as Hath Hapned in Virginia?*

Smith's apologists have offered a number of suggestions. Perhaps, they've argued, it was for the sake of public relations. *A True Relation* was written to encourage investment and settlement in Virginia, and stories of hostile Indians didn't help that cause. Some speculated that the Pocahontas story might have been cut by an over-zealous editor. But, Smith's detractors were quick to point out, *A True Relation* contained plenty of stories about Indians attacking Jamestown settlers—with endings much bloodier and unhappier than that of the Pocahontas story.

So the pro-Smith, pro-truth-of-the-story faction presented a variety of other arguments. In 1608, they said, Smith respected Powhatan; in 1609 he learned of Powhatan's role in killing the Roanoke colonists and his later works therefore portrayed the chief as much more bloodthirsty. Smith's supporters even used his reputation as a braggart to defend him, arguing that he might have left out the Pocahontas story simply because he was embarrassed that he needed an Indian princess—and an eleven-year-old at that—to save him. They also noted that the *Generall Historie* was a longer book with lots of details and stories that weren't in the earlier works. Perhaps Smith left out the Pocahontas story from his earlier works for no particular reason at all; his was a life full of hairbreadth escapes from death and, until Pocahontas later became a celebrity in England, Smith's encounter with her might not have seemed of much importance to him. He had no way of knowing that a few words in the *Generall Historie* were to become the basis of

America's version of Romeo and Juliet, or of what Henry Adams called "the most romantic episode in the whole history of his country."

Finally, Smith's supporters pointed out that Smith *had* included the Pocahontas story in at least one work prior to the *Generall Historie*. This was his letter to Queen Anne, dated June 1616. Pocahontas had by then married the Englishman, John Rolfe, and moved to England. With plans underway for her to meet the royal family, Smith took it upon himself to do the introductions. His letter to the queen tells a story much like that in the *Generall Historie*: "... at the minute of my execution, she hazarded the beating out of her owne braines to save mine, and not onely that, but so prevailed with her father, that I was safely conducted to James towne ..."

The letter was dated 1616, when Pocahontas was still alive and presumably could have denied the story. But it did not appear in print until 1624, as part of the *Generall Historie*. By then, Pocahontas had died. So, again, we have only John Smith's word to go by.

☆ ☆ ☆

Perhaps the best way to determine the truth of Smith's story is to ask, simply: does it make sense?

Some of the legend that's surrounded it makes no sense at all and can be summarily dismissed. For one thing, it is absolutely certain there was never a love affair between John Smith and Pocahontas. In 1607 Pocahontas was eleven years old; John Smith was 27. She may have had a crush on him but it was no more than that. It was John Rolfe, not John Smith, whom she married in 1614. If there was any sort of special relationship between Smith and Pocahontas—and, according to the *Generall Historie*, she did come to his aid and the colony's a number of other times—it was not a romantic one. Nor did Smith ever claim otherwise.

As for the claims Smith *did* make: do they make sense?

No.

Smith said he was spared "to make him hatchets, and her bells." Powhatan had no shortage of hatchets or bells; he knew very well that Smith was a leader of the English and worth a lot more than a few hatchets or bells. Nor is there any reason to believe a powerful warrior and chief would be swayed because of his daughter's plea.

But this does not mean Smith was a liar. More likely, the incident did take place much as Smith described but he misunderstood what was going on. According to Smith's account, Indians prepared to "beate out his braines" by feeding him extravagantly and parading him before the various tribes; right before they were to kill him one Indian woman brought him water to wash his hands and another brought feathers to dry them. All this sounds like a carefully orchestrated ceremony. In all likelihood, the "rescue" of Smith by Pocahontas was also part of the ceremony.

Many historians have suggested that the rescue was part of a traditional ritual of death and rebirth that accompanied adoption into an Indian tribe. Recently, the archaeologist and historian Ivor Noel Hume argued that it was not a traditional ritual but a conscious effort on Powhatan's part to try to turn Smith into an ally. To have executed Smith, Hume wrote, would have been to bring down on Powhatan the wrath of the English, and Smith had made clear there were plenty more Englishmen across the water. Better to stage a ceremony that might leave Smith both intimidated and grateful.

Smith, of course, understood none of this. He was indeed intimidated by Powhatan and grateful to Pocahontas. And who can blame him?

☆ To investigate further:

Barbour, Philip L., editor. *The Complete Works of Captain John Smith.* Williamsburg, VA: Institute of Early American History and Culture, 1986. Decide for yourself whether you believe him.

Kupperman, Karen Ordahl. *Captain John Smith.* Williamsburg, VA: Institute of Early American History and Culture, 1988. Selected writings for those who don't quite need all of the above.

Smith, Bradford. *Captain John Smith.* Philadelphia: Lippincott, 1953. Includes Striker's groundbreaking work on the Hungarian episodes and, until Barbour's, the best defense and biography of Smith.

Barbour, Philip L. *The Three Worlds of Captain John Smith.* Boston: Houghton Mifflin, 1964. Still the most widely respected biography, this argues that the Pocahontas episode was true (though Barbour later expressed some doubt about it).

———. *Pocahontas and Her World.* Boston: Houghton Mifflin, 1970. Adds little to the above.

Vaughan, Alden T. *American Genesis.* New York: Little, Brown, 1975. A short—and on the subject of the Pocahontas story, inconclusive—biography of Smith.

Gerson, Noel B. *The Glorious Scoundrel.* New York: Dodd, Mead, 1978. Argues that Smith not only made up the story but that he never even met Pocahontas until she came to England.

Lemay, J. A. Leo. *The American Dream of Captain John Smith.* Charlottesville: University Press of Virginia, 1991. Part of a backlash against the "politically correct" scholarship that has placed Smith at the front of a long line of Europeans who have exploited Native Americans, this polemic portrays Smith as a friend and admirer not just of Pocahontas but of all Indians. However, it doesn't add much substance to Barbour's work and even Smith, braggart that he was, might have been embarrassed by so much praise.

————. *Did Pocahontas Save John Smith?* Athens: University of Georgia Press, 1992. A history of the controversy, which concludes the answer is yes.

Hume, Ivor Noel. *The Virginia Adventure.* New York: Knopf, 1994. The latest report from the area's leading archaeologist.

Chapter 8

What Caused
the Salem Witch-Hunt?

In February 1692 in the town of Salem, Massachussetts, two children in the house of the Reverend Samuel Parris—nine-year-old Betty Parris and her eleven-year-old cousin Abigail Williams—began acting very strangely. They ran around the house, flapping their arms, screaming "Whish, Whish, Whish." They pulled burning logs out of the fireplace and threw them around the room. It was as if, another local minister observed, they "were bitten and pinched by invisible agents; their arms, necks, and backs turned this way and that way, and returned back again, so as it was impossible for them to do of themselves, and beyond the power of any Epileptick Fits, or natural Disease to effect." Local doctors were at a loss to explain what was going on. Finally, Dr. William Griggs suggested the girls were bewitched.

The authorities sprang into action, demanding that the children tell them who was tormenting them. The girls first named Tituba, the Parris family's West Indian slave. Then they added the names of two other local women, Sarah Good and Sarah Osborne. Tituba admitted she'd read palms and told fortunes and perhaps dabbled in some voodoo, but she denied harming the girls; that was the doing of Good and Osborne, she said. Good, in turn, said Osborne was the witch.

So far this was no big deal. There had been other accusations of witchcraft in other New England towns, usually resulting in a lot of gossip and perhaps an occasional arrest or even a conviction. But in Salem this was just the beginning. More and more of Salem's teenage and preteen girls began having fits; more and more of Salem's adults were accused of witchcraft. Even the four-year-old daughter of Sarah Good was accused and sent to prison with her mother, where she remained in heavy irons for nine months. By summer the town's jail was filled with more than a hundred accused witches; by the end of the year, 19 people had been hanged—more than in all the previous New England witch trials. Another victim was pressed to death under heavy stones because he refused to testify before the magistrates.

It was clear things had gone too far. Influential ministers and magistrates, many of whom had been quick to see the devil's work in the girls' behavior, now realized this had gotten out of hand (a realization aided no doubt by the fact that some of them and their wives were being accused). The trials came to a halt, as did the witch-hunt. But the question did not go away: What drove the people of Salem to behavior so extreme that, ever since, Salem has been a metaphor for persecution and intolerance?

To the rationalists of the eighteenth and nineteenth centuries, the question barely merited analysis. Since there was obviously no such thing as a witch, the girls were simply liars. Those who supported the girls acted out of fear of being themselves accused; those who confessed to being witches and who named other witches did so only to save themselves from the gallows.

In the twentieth century, Freudian interpretations came to the fore. The girls' fits were a classic case of hysteria, the result of repressed adolescent and preadolescent sexuality. It is easy enough to believe the girls were repressed—the Puritans, after all, could be puritanical.

Freudian interpretations reigned until the early 1970s, when social historians began to probe the social and economic background of the witch-hunts. The 1690s, they stressed, were years of extreme instability in Massachussetts. Indian wars had been devastating; so had epidemic illnesses. The King had revoked the charter under which the colony was governed, leaving the entire structure of the government unsettled. And the traditionally agrarian culture of the area was increasingly threatened by the influence of a more cosmopolitan merchant class.

What possessed the girls of Salem? Explanations for the witch-hunt have included ergot poisoning, sexual repression, social tensions, family feuds, corrupt judges—and the devil. From Augustus Mason's 1883 book, The Romance and Tragedy of Pioneer Life. *Library of Congress.*

With their world seemingly coming apart, it was not so surprising that New Englanders, steeped as they were in Puritan theology, would blame Satan. Some people took all the fire-and-brimstone talk with a grain of salt, but others undoubtedly believed in witches. In any case, the particular people they accused fit the bill. Tituba was a black slave, an obvious pariah. Sarah Good was a beggar whose pleas had gotten on everyone's nerves. Sarah Osborne was more financially secure than Sarah Good, but she had been involved in some nasty disputes over land with her own sons and was widely suspected of having lived with her husband before they were married—no small transgression in Puritan society. To make matters worse, she hadn't been to church for more than a year. Many of the others accused early on were also conveniently vulnerable scapegoats.

But if all this illuminated the social strains and social divisions that led New Englanders to cry witch, it did little to explain why the witch-hunt materialized in Salem and not elsewhere in New England. To solve that mystery, two social historians, Paul Boyer and Stephen Nissenbaum, took a close look at Salem. What they found was that Salem was actually more like two towns. Near the coast stood Salem Town, a flourishing commercial center dominated by merchants and tradesmen; a little further inland lay Salem Village, a traditional and increasingly impoverished agricultural hamlet. To a remarkable extent, the accusers and their supporters lived in the interior and the accused and their defenders lived near or in town; the former tended to be poorer and more devout; the latter tended to be richer and more secular.

Nowhere else in New England did these two ways of life confront each other so directly and so unavoidably. Had Salem Village been situated somewhat further inland, its inhabitants might not have felt so threatened by Salem Town, nor would they have known its residents well enough to accuse them of anything, let alone witchcraft. Had this been the case, the name Salem might today conjure up nothing more than a pleasant coastal village. But with Salem's particular situation, daily contact meant a continual build up of the Villagers' resentment of their rich and godless neighbors. Worse, some of the Villagers, Boyer and Nissenbaum found, had a particular grudge against their neighbors. In fact, underlying the Salem witch-hunt was a family feud that made the Capulets and the Montagues seem the closest of friends.

On the one side were the Putnams, on the other were the Porters. Both lived in the Village, but the Porters lived on the town side, and the Putnams further inland. Trouble started brewing in 1686, when Thomas Putnam Sr. died, bequeathing the best part of his estate to his second wife, Mary Veren Putnam, and his only son by that wife, Joseph. Like the biblical Joseph, Joseph Putnam was deeply resented by his older half brothers. Thomas Putnam Jr., the eldest, was especially bitter as he watched Joseph become one of the richest men in town with money and land that Thomas felt was rightfully his. His bitterness only deepened in 1690, when Joseph Putnam married Elizabeth Porter, a member of the only town family that rivalled the Putnams' wealth and prestige. To the Putnams, the Porters personified the evils of Salem Town.

No wonder, then, that the Putnams and Porters could be found on opposite sides of almost every issue dividing the town. The Putnams and their wives belonged to the church of Samuel Parris (father and uncle, you'll recall, to the two girls who started the whole witch-hunt).

The Porters, on the other hand, led a drive to replace Parris with a new minister. And throughout the witch trials, the Putnam name appeared again and again among the accusers. Eight Putnams were involved in the prosecution of 46 accused witches, and Ann Putnam, the 12-year-old daughter of Thomas Putnam Jr., was by far the most active of all the afflicted girls. Meanwhile, the Porters' friends and family were prominent among the accused.

Three years after the witch trials were over, the feud was still going strong. In 1695 Mary Veren Putnam died, leaving everything that was hers (and that had once belonged to Joseph Putnam Sr.) to Joseph. The Putnams challenged the will, claiming it had actually been written by Israel Porter, Joseph's father-in-law. Furthermore, the Putnams claimed, Mary Veren Putnam had not been of sound mind when she signed the will. And what doctor did they call to testify this was so? None other than William Griggs, the doctor who had first suggested the children in the Parris household had been bewitched.

The Putnam/Porter feud brings to mind not just Bible stories but also fairy tales. Think of Thomas Putnam Jr. and his brothers as Hansel and Gretel, exploited by their father's evil second wife, who abandons them to the forest and its witch. How did Hansel and Gretel survive? The Putnams knew the answer: *they killed the witch.*

Alas, for the Putnams, it was all in vain. Throughout his life, Thomas Putnam Jr. had to sell off what little land his father did leave him in order to pay his increasing debts. When he died in 1699, there was little left for his three sons, all of whom moved away from the area, or his five daughters, three of whom remained spinsters. Joseph Putnam, in contrast, remained rich, and his sons and daughters prospered in Salem. (The only son who moved away from Salem was Israel Putnam, who became a highly successful soldier, known best for his bravery at Bunker Hill, where he uttered the famous line: "Don't shoot until you see the whites of their eyes.")

☆ ☆ ☆

Whether the Putnams consciously sought revenge, or whether they actually believed the accused were witches, is unclear. But the Boyer/Nissenbaum analysis convinced most historians that the social tensions between the two families and communities were at the root of the witch trials. A few historians, however, disagreed.

As Bernard Rosenthal saw it, the trials could only be understood through a study of the surviving trial records. What he found there convinced him that the trials were part of a scam perpetrated by the county sheriff, George Corwin. Rosenthal backed up the charge by demonstrating that Corwin profited from the illegal seizure of the property of the wealthier defendants. More damning still, Corwin's uncle and father-in-law were both among the judges who sent the witches off to jail or to be hanged. Although no evidence exists that they conspired with Corwin, they must certainly have known what was going on, as did the other judges.

Rosenthal's close reading of the records revealed other motives were also at work. For example, the influential minister Cotton Mather backed the court proceedings because he felt that one of the defendants, the dissenting minister George Burroughs, was a dangerous threat to the religious hegemony. Mather, in spite of his fire-and-brimstone image, had mixed feelings about the trials in general, but he was willing to legitimize the other hangings to get rid of Burroughs.

Rosenthal strongly criticized social historians for focusing too much on the background and losing sight of the foreground; namely, the individual motives of people like Corwin and Mather. In this, he was not being entirely fair to Boyer and Nissenbaum; after all, although they certainly paid a lot of attention to socioeconomic factors, they also wrote about the very personal motives of the Putnams and the Porters.

Nor was the Boyer/Nissenbaum theory quite so at odds with Rosenthal's evidence as his criticism of it implied. The Salem witch-hunts were caused by both the underlying patterns in the community (which the social historians brilliantly illuminated) and the more immediate motives of the participants (as revealed by Rosenthal). Not all of the participants were driven by the same motive, and some were undoubtedly driven by more than one. Corwin might have been driven by greed, Mather by theology, Putnam by jealousy and resentment, the girls by boredom or frustration. So many different problems converged in 1692 Salem that it didn't take much to cause an explosion. All that was needed was a spark—which appeared in the form of a West Indian slave who dabbled in voodoo.

☆ To investigate further:

Boyer, Paul and Stephen Nissenbaum, editors. *Salem-Village Witchcraft*. Boston: Northeastern University Press, 1972. A documentary record, including transcripts of the preliminary trial proceedings and much of the testimony. (The actual trial records have not survived.)

Upham, Charles. *Salem Witchcraft*. Boston: Wiggin and Lunt, 1867. This standard "rationalist" approach to the witchcraft was reprinted in 1959 by F. Unger Publishing Co. (New York).

Starkey, Marion. *The Devil in Massachussetts*. New York: Knopf, 1950. Though it preceded much of the modern scholarship, this remains the most dramatic narrative history of the crisis.

Hansen, Chadwick. *Witchcraft at Salem*. New York: George Braziller, 1969. In a society where most people believed in witchcraft and where many practiced black magic, spells might actually work—if only through the power of suggestion. So, at least according to this iconoclastic work, some of the accused might actually have been guilty of witchcraft.

Boyer, Paul and Stephen Nissenbaum. *Salem Possessed*. Cambridge: Harvard University Press, 1974. How social tensions between Salem Town and Salem Village led to the witch-hunt.

Caporael, Linnda. "Ergotism: The Satan Loosed in Salem?" *Science*, April 1976. A biologist's proposal that the girls' fits and visions were symptoms of convulsive ergotism, a disease contracted from contaminated grain.

Spanos, Nicholas and Jack Gottlieb. "Ergotism and the Salem Village Witch Trials." *Science*, December 1976. Disputes Caporael's diagnosis by arguing that the fits and visions seemed to start and stop on cue, thus implying a social rather than physiological cause.

Demos, John. *Entertaining Satan*. New York: Oxford University Press, 1982. Though not exclusively about Salem, this is the most thorough and sophisticated study of New England witchcraft; Demos approaches the subject from the perspectives of biography, psychology, and sociology as well as history.

Karlsen, Carol F. *The Devil in the Shape of a Woman*. New York: Norton, 1987. A feminist investigation, which contends that many of the accused were singled out because they owned or were in line to inherit property that would otherwise go to men.

Gragg, Larry. *The Salem Witch Crisis*. Westport, CT: Praeger, 1992. A straightforward history of the crisis with an excellent chapter on how prison conditions led many to confess.

Rosenthal, Bernard. *Salem Story*. New York: Cambridge University Press, 1993. The case that systematic fraud caused the witch-hunt; also includes fascinating discussions of how the Salem story has been used in American literature and culture.

Chapter 9

Was Daniel Boone a Traitor?

Boonesborough, Kentucky. September 1778. To the east and north: the British army. To the west: equally hostile Shawnee Indians. Yet what entranced the people of Boonesborough was a drama of another sort. This was the court-martial, by authority of the Kentucky militia, of the man after whom the town had been named—Daniel Boone.

Boone, his fellow officers charged, had left the fort in February 1778 with 27 men, heading for some nearby salt springs. That was in itself perfectly reasonable. The Shawnee had burned the town's crops and kept the men pinned inside the fort, unable even to hunt. What little meat the townspeople had would spoil without salt to preserve it.

But then Boone had left his party, only to return leading a Shawnee war party and demanding that the salt-makers surrender. Worse, the salt-makers had then witnessed Boone conspiring with the Shawnee and their British allies, and agreeing to surrender Boonesborough to them. And when the Shawnee did attack Boonesborough later that year, Boone had persuaded the town's leaders to meet with the Indians outside the fort so that the Shawnee could ambush them.

And so it was that Daniel Boone, the man whose exploits on the frontier had already made him a legend, came to be charged with treason.

☆ ☆ ☆

Remarkably, Boone denied none of these acts. But the story he told put quite a different spin on them. This is how it went.

While scouting for the salt-makers, Boone was spotted by four Indians. He tried to flee but—for all his skills as a frontiersman—he was 45 years old and not as fast as he used to be. They caught him.

The Indians took Boone to their camp, where he found 120 warriors painted for war. The Shawnee chief, Blackfish, told Boone they had already seen the camp of the salt-making party and they planned to kill them and then attack Boonesborough.

Realizing that neither the salt-makers nor Boonesborough could withstand such an attack, Boone hatched a plan (or so he said—remember, this is all Boone's version of the story). He told Blackfish that he'd get the salt-makers to surrender, if Blackfish would promise to treat them well. And he convinced the chief that he couldn't take Boonesborough now, but that it would be weaker in a few months. Wait until then, Boone said, and he would turn the fort over to the Shawnee.

All this, Boone claimed, he did to buy time to build up the fort's defenses.

Blackfish agreed to the deal. So Boone convinced the salt-makers to surrender, and the prisoners and their captors headed north. Along the way Boone ingratiated himself further with Blackfish—so much so that by the time they reached the Shawnee village of Chillicothe, the chief had decided to adopt Boone as his own son. He named him Sheltowee. (The ceremony was no fun for Boone—it involved having his hair plucked out and his skin scrubbed to purge him of his whiteness.)

The Shawnee then took Boone and the other captives to the fort of their British allies in Detroit. There Boone again agreed to surrender Boonesborough, this time convincing the British commander, Lieutenant Governor Henry Hamilton, that both he and his fellow settlers were loyal to the crown.

Having gained the trust of both the Shawnee and the British, and knowing they were readying their attack, Boone escaped and returned to Boonesborough. In September the Indians emerged in the meadow before the fort. A voice called for Sheltowee; it was Blackfish calling his

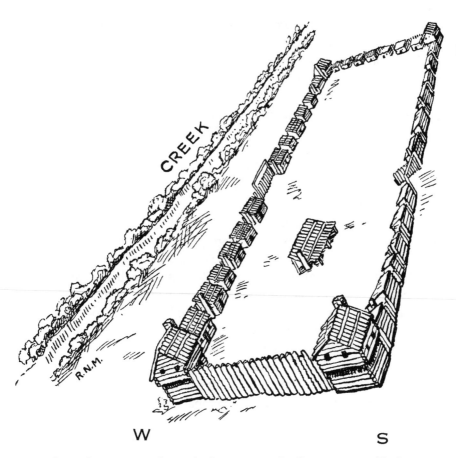

Boonesborough, as seen in this early drawing, was hardly an impregnable fortress—which might have accounted for some of Boone's questionable defensive strategies. Library of Congress.

son. The chief reminded Boone of the promises he'd made; Boone replied, truthfully, that he was no longer in command of the fort. Blackfish agreed to negotiate, if Boone and his fellow chiefs would do so in front of the fort.

Clearly this would be risky; Blackfish may have had a great deal of faith in his adopted son, but Boone's escape must surely have tested that. Everyone in the fort knew the offer to negotiate might be a trap. But the more they could prolong negotiations, the better chance they had to prepare the fort's defenses. So Boone convinced a delegation from the fort to meet with Blackfish.

In the midst of negotiations the Shawnee attempted to take members of the delegation prisoner, fighting broke out, and the siege of Boonesborough began. But siege warfare was not the Shawnee style; after ten days they withdrew. Boonesborough was saved, and Boone was its hero.

Or was he? Should we believe Boone's story?

☆ ☆ ☆

His judges did. The verdict of the court-martial was not guilty. Further vindication came right after the court-martial, when Boone was promoted to major.

Given Boone's importance as a symbol of the winning of the West, it's not surprising that most early biographers also bought his story. His earliest biographer, John Filson, wrote *The Adventures of Col. Daniel Boone* in 1784, just six years after the siege of Boonesborough. Boone cooperated in the writing; in fact, the book was written in the first person, and if it wasn't so obvious that the language was too high-falutin to be Boone's, this might even be called his autobiography. Certainly it did much to establish the legend of Boone as frontier hero. And it's therefore hardly surprising that, though it recounts Boone's version of the captivity and siege, it doesn't even mention the court-martial which followed. Filson and Boone probably considered it too embarrassing.

Others followed in Filson's footsteps. Boone's first twentieth-century biographer, Reuben Thwaites, was a bit more objective than Filson, going so far as to concede that Boone's "services in defense of the West . . . were not comparable to those of George Rogers Clark or Benjamin Logan." But on the question of Boone's loyalty, there could be no doubt. To Thwaites, writing in 1902, it was obvious that Boone just pretended to like the Indian life. How could anyone want to eat food "prepared in so slovenly a manner as to disgust even so hardy a man of the forest as our hero"? And there were "many other discomforts intensely irritating to most white men," Thwaites added.

Thirty-seven years later, historians still could not entertain any doubt on the matter. Boone's 1939 biographer, John Bakeless, attributed the court-martial to jealousy and gossip.

☆ ☆ ☆

Today, however, Boone's actions and motives are more suspect. We know, for example, that Boone's wife, Rebecca, came from a leading

Tory family and that Boone had accepted a captain's commission from the British-appointed governor in 1774. (This commission came in very handy, when the captured Boone met Hamilton in Detroit.)

John Mack Faragher, author of the definitive modern biography of Boone, concluded that Boone "aligned himself with neither ideological camp, a neutrality that became increasingly difficult to maintain as the conflict sharpened and grew bitter." While chauvinistic historians might have wished otherwise, this ambivalence was common throughout the country, especially in the western territories. For Boone and for many others in and around Boonesborough, loyalty to your immediate community was far stronger than loyalty to either America or Britain.

Just as the line between patriot and Tory has blurred, so too has the line between pioneer and Indian. Part of the Boone legend—at least the part that didn't become confused with Davy Crockett's—always included his ability to adopt Indian ways. And Boone was not alone in this. Appalling though it seemed to more genteel whites back East and to historians like Thwaites, pioneers and Indians had a great deal in common: they hunted the same game, they lived off the same land, they traded and made treaties together. Boone himself, in spite of his reputation as an Indian fighter, only killed one Indian in his entire life.

Blackfish and Boone could discuss turning over the fort because both could genuinely envision its inhabitants becoming Indians. Boone was just one of hundreds of European and American captives to be adopted into Indian tribes. Many refused to return to the white world, even when they were part of prisoner exchanges.

Does all this mean Boone was a traitor? By no means. Just because lines have been blurred does not mean that Boone crossed over them. Just because he could easily pass as a Tory or an Indian does not mean he betrayed either America or Boonesborough. We may never know for sure whether Boone's actions were all tricks, or treason, or something in-between.

What we do know is that the age of Boone was already passing. It had been an age when pioneers and Indians, in spite of all their clashes, had much in common, when Boone and Blackfish might at least consider making a deal. But soon the British who supplied the Shawnee with arms would be gone, as would the buffalo and other game that kept them alive. With the end of the Revolution, settlers flooded into Kentucky, changing forever the face of the countryside.

Blackfish's plan to convert all of Boonesborough to Indian ways went way beyond the scope of previous adoptions; it was a desperate effort to save a lost way of life. Ironically, it was also Boone's way of life that was lost. Though his judges exonerated him, Boone no longer had a place in Boonesborough. A year after his trial he left forever the town which bore his name.

☆ To investigate further:

Filson, John. *The Discovery, Settlement And Present State of Kentucke: . . . To which is added, An Appendix, Containing, The Adventures of Col. Daniel Boon.* Ann Arbor, MI: University Microfilms, 1966. Originally published in 1784, the primary source for much of the Boone legend.

Thwaites, Reuben G. *Daniel Boone.* New York: Appleton and Co., 1902. Dated, but lots of good stories.

Bakeless, John. *Daniel Boone.* New York: Morrow, 1939. Also dated, but fun.

Eckert, Allan W. *The Court-Martial of Daniel Boone.* New York: Bantam, 1973. A fictional account of the trial; the dialogue is invented but the rest of the story *could* be true.

Faragher, John Mack. *Daniel Boone.* New York: Henry Holt, 1992. The definitive modern biography.

Aron, Stephen. *How the West Was Lost: The Transformation of Kentucky from Daniel Boone to Henry Clay.* Baltimore: Johns Hopkins, 1996. A new revisionist approach from which are drawn this chapter's conclusions.

10

Why Did Benedict Arnold Turn Traitor?

For most of America's famous turncoats—Aaron Burr, Alger Hiss, the Rosenbergs—there is at least some question and in some cases much doubt as to whether they were guilty. In the case of Benedict Arnold, there is no doubt: his name has justly become a synonym for traitor. Nor is there any doubt as to the magnitude of his treachery. Arnold commanded the American forces at West Point and his plan was to turn over the fort there to the British. Had he done so, the British might easily have captured George Washington (who was in nearby Peekskill meeting with the Marquis de Lafayette). Even if Washington had escaped, the British would have controlled the Hudson River crossings. This would have enabled them to cut off supplies to Washington's army, which was already underfed and underarmed. The American Revolution, in short, might very well have failed.

Yet if it's clear what Arnold did (or tried to do), *why* he did it is much less clear. Arnold himself, in a proclamation published soon after he switched sides, said the war had been "a defensive one until the French joined in the combination." Then his eyes had been opened and he saw how dangerous were "the insidious offers of France . . . the enemy of the Protestant faith." But few then or later bought this explanation. Never before had Arnold indicated any qualms about the French. Besides, the language of Arnold's proclamation was

suspiciously similar to much else written by the Loyalist writer
William Smith; clearly this was little more than propaganda. To understand what really motivated Benedict Arnold, therefore, historians had
to look elsewhere, and the obvious place to start was Arnold's life prior
to his treason.

By far the most striking aspect of his life prior to turning traitor was
that Arnold had been a genuine hero of the Revolution. Along with
Ethan Allen, in May 1775, he had captured Fort Ticonderoga on the
northern New York frontier; with the fort came cannon and powder
crucial to the American war effort. In September 1775 he'd led 1,100
men on a wilderness expedition from Massachussetts to Quebec City.
There, though 40 percent of his men were lost to death or desertion,
he besieged a city manned by twice his number of troops until May
1776, when 10,000 British reinforcements forced the Americans to retreat. Next, during the summer of 1776, Arnold supervised the construction of a fleet on Lake Champlain; under his command, the
makeshift navy was largely destroyed but managed to hold out until
winter set in and forced the British to return to Canada. A year later,
when the British again swept down from Canada, Arnold led the crucial charge at the Battle of Saratoga that precipitated the British surrender there. Twice wounded, Arnold was honored and trusted by
George Washington for his bravery and leadership.

And yet with each victory came frustration and disappointment.
At Ticonderoga Arnold clashed with Ethan Allen; each had indepen-
dently conceived of the attack on the fort and each felt he should lead
the charge. Arnold had the official backing of Massachussetts; Allen
was backed by Connecticut and most of the troops. Their compromise—a joint command—was an uneasy one that was further marred
by Allen's subsequent charges that Arnold had overstepped
his orders and misappropriated funds. Arnold's invasion of Canada,
though heroic, failed to capture Quebec. His enemies were quick to label it a failure and to accuse him of confiscating provisions and materi-
als from Montreal merchants for his own profit. Even the battle of
Lake Champlain—which, in retrospect, is seen to have bought the
American army the time it needed to prepare for its defense of
Saratoga—was at the time seen only as a naval defeat. And Arnold's
decisive victory at Saratoga came in defiance of his commanding

Engraved by H.B.Hall.

MAJ. GEN. BENEDICT ARNOLD.

Major General Benedict Arnold of, for the moment, the Continental Army. Library of Congress.

officer, Horatio Gates, who disliked him and had ordered him to stay in his tent; in Gates's official report, Arnold's name was omitted.

Understandably, Arnold was bitter. He must have been further shocked and angered when Congress promoted five others to major general, each one of whom was far less experienced than Arnold. Instead of the renown he felt he deserved, he found himself defending himself against Ethan Allen's charges that he had misappropriated funds.

Since Arnold's injuries left him unfit for field duty, in 1778 Washington appointed him military governor of Philadelphia. Here again, Arnold soon found himself at odds with other revolutionary leaders. He closed the city's shops to inventory all captured goods, and was promptly accused of doing so to line his own pockets. Then he was accused of using army wagons to haul private goods to Philadelphia and granting an illegal pass for a ship, again for his own profit. Arnold was indignant. In May 1779 he wrote Washington that he had "little expected to meet the ungrateful returns I have received from my countrymen."

In December the charges against Arnold culminated in a court-martial, the results of which must have frustrated both Arnold and his accusers. The court found there was insufficient evidence to convict him on most of the counts but did find him guilty of two misdemeanors. It recommended that Washington reprimand him, which he did.

Was Arnold's indignation justified? Was he (up to this point) a patriot or a profiteer? Most historians have concluded he was both: the Revolution offered him a chance for fame and fortune and he wasn't about to turn away either. There is little doubt that he used his positions, especially as military governor of Philadelphia, to further his moneymaking schemes. But his contributions to the Revolutionary effort were undeniable, as was his courage under fire. Arnold must have felt unappreciated—and this must have been a factor in his decision to switch sides.

What, specifically, pushed him over the edge?

For 160 years, most historians assumed it was the court-martial, when Washington, once his great supporter, turned on Arnold. Then, in 1941, Carl Van Doren took a careful look at the recently rediscovered letters from the files of the British headquarters. To his surprise, he found that Arnold had been negotiating with the British *before* the court-martial. As early as May 1779 there are letters between the British commander in chief, Henry Clinton, and his adjutant general, John André, discussing Arnold's terms for turning traitor. The correspondence between André and Clinton, as well as between Arnold and André, also made very clear that Arnold was looking for money. Specifically, he wanted 20,000 pounds if his plan to turn over his new command at West Point succeeded, and 10,000 pounds if it failed. André countered with an offer of 6,000 pounds. This treason, it seemed, was a transaction motivated less by disillusionment than by sheer greed.

Arnold was especially eager for cash in May 1779 because he'd recently married. His new wife, the 19-year-old Peggy Shippen, had expensive habits; marriage meant new wardrobes for both of them, new furniture, and a continuing round of parties. Pointing as well to her Tory family and friends, many speculated that it was Shippen's influence that pushed Arnold over the brink. The British headquarters papers contain no hard evidence that Peggy Shippen influenced Arnold, but they did establish that she knew of the treason and had participated in its planning.

When the treason plot was discovered, however, with the capture of André, Arnold quickly ditched his wife. This was no time for chivalry. Arnold grabbed a boat and fled across the Hudson—leaving her behind. George Washington then paid her a visit. He found her hysterical and concluded she'd known nothing about her husband's treachery. Was her hysteria merely a show for Washington, this Lady Macbeth's latest act of deceit? Or was Peggy Shippen Arnold genuinely terrified because she feared her role in the treason would be discovered? No one can be sure.

As for Arnold himself, historians have continued to debate the particular mix of bitterness and greed that prompted him to turn traitor. These are not mutually exclusive motives—the British offered him both recognition and money. It's even possible that his love for Peggy was a factor in his decision. But there could no longer be any question that at the center of Arnold's treachery was his craving for money.

Characteristically, one of Arnold's first actions after putting on a British uniform was to present Clinton with a bill for 10,000 pounds. Two weeks after his coconspirator André was executed as a British spy,

Arnold again wrote Clinton insisting on the money. Clinton agreed to pay 6,000 pounds (André's final offer), plus 350 pounds for expenses. For some, especially someone as rich as Arnold, this might have been the end of the story. But not for Benedict Arnold: more than ten years later, with the Revolution over and both Arnold and Clinton living in England, Arnold was still writing Clinton, and still insisting on being paid.

☆ To investigate further:

Van Doren, Carl. *Secret History of the American Revolution*. New York: Viking, 1941. The first examination of the British headquarters papers, including an appendix with the text of letters from Arnold, André, Clinton, and others.

Flexner, James. *The Traitor and the Spy*. New York: Little, Brown, 1975. Originally published in 1953, this dual biography of Arnold and André portrays Peggy as a Lady Macbeth manipulating her husband into treachery.

Wallace, Willard. *Traitorous Hero*. New York: Harper & Brothers, 1954. A balanced biography of Arnold.

Boylan, Brian Richard. *Benedict Arnold*. New York: Norton, 1973. Of all of Arnold's biographers, Boylan is the kindest to his subject.

Randall, William Sterne. *Benedict Arnold*. New York: Morrow, 1990. An able retelling of Arnold's life, though there's nothing particularly new here.

Brandt, Clare. *The Man in the Mirror*. New York: Random House, 1994. A psychological portrait of Arnold that attributes most of his actions, including his treachery, to feelings of insecurity stemming from his father's alcoholism and bankruptcy; that this was a factor is certainly credible, but Brandt's argument that it was the primary factor in almost everything Arnold did is unconvincing.

Chapter 11

Was Sally Hemings the Mistress of Thomas Jefferson?

I t is well known that the man, *whom it delighteth the people to honor,* keeps, and for many years past has kept, as his concubine, one of his own slaves. Her name is SALLY. The name of her eldest son is TOM. His slaves are said to bear a striking although sable resemblance to the president himself.

So wrote James Callender in the September 2, 1802, issue of the Richmond *Recorder.* The charge that Jefferson had a slave mistress named Sally Hemings was picked up by other Federalist newspapers throughout the country; a Philadelphia magazine even commemorated it in verse, to be sung to the tune of "Yankee Doodle Dandy":

Of all the damsels on the green
On mountain or in valley
A lass so luscious ne'er was seen
As Monticellian Sally.

Stories of his slave mistress haunted Jefferson throughout the 1804 election campaign. Jefferson himself never commented on the charges publicly, though he denied them in a private letter to Robert Smith, his secretary of the navy. Other Republicans vehemently defended the president, however. They stressed that the stories were

MAD TOM in A RAGE

The Federalists accused Jefferson of more than having an affair with a slave; in this 1801 cartoon he and "Mad Tom" Paine are pictured trying to pull down the government. The Huntington Library.

politically motivated, and in this they were undeniably correct: not only was the *Recorder* a Federalist paper, but Callender had a personal grudge against Jefferson.

Callender had once been a leading propagandist for Jefferson's own Republican party. One of his earlier exposés had forced Alexander Hamilton to admit to an affair with a married woman; another of them had landed Callender in jail under the 1798 Alien and Sedition Acts. In 1801, when Jefferson became president, he pardoned Callender. But Callender felt his sufferings merited more than a pardon. He demanded that Jefferson appoint him postmaster at Richmond and that the president personally pay back the fines Callender had paid under the 1798 laws. When Jefferson refused, Callender threatened revenge; in switching to the Federalist side and writing the first of the Sally stories, he made good on that threat.

For Jefferson's defenders, then and since, Callender's blatantly malicious motives discredited his story. But to get to the truth, to determine whether or not Jefferson had a slave mistress, we must look beyond Callender's motives and examine the evidence.

Callender himself had little hard evidence to offer. He never visited Monticello, never talked directly to Sally Hemings or anyone else connected with the story. Nor, apparently, did any other writer of the period. But then, in 1873, an obscure Ohio newspaper, the *Pike County Republican,* published an interview with Madison Hemings, the son of Sally Hemings and—he claimed—Thomas Jefferson. Hemings, in fact, claimed that his mother had told him a great deal about her longtime relationship with Jefferson—namely that the two had first become lovers in Paris in 1787. Jefferson, a widower since 1782, was then minister to France; Sally Hemings was there as a servant to his daughter. Madison Hemings went on:

> During that time my mother became Mr. Jefferson's concubine, and when he was called home she was *enciente* [*sic*] by him. He desired to bring my mother back to Virginia with him but she demurred. She was just beginning to understand the French language well, and in France she was free, while if she returned to Virginia she would be re-enslaved. So she refused to return with him. To induce her to do so he promised her extraordinary privileges, and made a solemn

pledge that her children would be freed at the age of twenty-one years.

This promise Jefferson eventually kept. When Jefferson died, his slaves had to be sold to pay off creditors to whom he owed more than $100,000. But Jefferson made sure in his will that five of his slaves were to be freed; among these five were Madison Hemings and his brother Eston.

Madison Hemings's version of events was confirmed by another ex-slave memoir, that of Israel Jefferson. Israel Jefferson described how for fourteen years he'd cleaned and kept up Jefferson's bedroom and private chamber, and been on intimate terms with both Thomas Jefferson and Sally Hemings. Of Madison Hemings's claim to be the son of the president, Israel Jefferson said: "I can as conscientiously confirm his statement as any other fact which I believe from circumstances but do not positively know."

Israel Jefferson's memoir also confirmed another story that had been passed on for many years; namely, that Sally Hemings's mother, Betty Hemings, had been the mistress of Thomas Jefferson's father-in-law, John Wayles. This meant that Sally Hemings was the half sister of Thomas Jefferson's late wife, Martha Wayles Jefferson.

Strangely, many of Jefferson's defenders were quick to accept Israel Jefferson's testimony about the John Wayles-Betty Hemings liaison. Perhaps this was because the Wayles-Hemings affair provided an alternative explanation for why Thomas Jefferson treated the Hemings family so much better than other slaves, and why he eventually freed Madison and Eston Hemings. After all, if Jefferson knew they were related to his wife, then his special treatment of them might have had nothing to do with Sally Hemings in particular.

As for the rest of Madison Hemings's and Israel Jefferson's testimony, however, that they adamantly rejected. To discredit it, Jefferson's nineteenth-century biographer Henry Randall produced a letter from Jefferson's grandson, Thomas Jefferson Randolph, in which he revealed that Sally Hemings had indeed been the mistress of a white man—but it was Jefferson's nephew, Peter Carr, and not Jefferson himself who'd slept with her and fathered her children. One of Jefferson's granddaughters, Ellen Randolph Coolidge, came up with a similar story, this time placing the blame on Samuel Carr, Peter's brother, whom she described as "the most notorious good-natured Turk that ever was master of a black seraglio kept at other men's expence." If either Carr brother fathered Sally Hemings's children, that could account for the children's resemblance to Jefferson.

Further mitigating against the Madison Hemings-Israel Jefferson version of events was the fact that both memoirs were published in the *Pike Country Republican*. For a Republican newspaper in 1873, it was good politics to make the antebellum South—with which the Democrats could still be associated—look bad, and the *Republican* was almost as partisan a paper as Callender's *Recorder*. Also suspicious was the language in both the Madison Hemings and Israel Jefferson memoirs; it sounded a lot more like that of a newspaper editor than that of two ex-slaves, and Jefferson's defenders concluded that an editor might have worked on the content as well as the language. Furthermore, they argued, even if Madison Hemings had come up with the story himself, it was clearly in the interest of an impoverished ex-slave to turn out to be the son of Jefferson—and even if Sally Hemings had really told him Jefferson was his father, *she* might have made up the story for the same reason.

Of course, Jefferson's grandchildren had just as vested an interest in their version of events as his ex-slaves did in theirs. But most historians followed Randall's lead, or at least concluded the conflicting testimonies cancelled each other out. And in the absence of more hard evidence of the affair, most dismissed it as a nasty rumor.

This genteel consensus received its greatest test with the 1974 publication of Fawn Brodie's "intimate history" of Thomas Jefferson. The first major biographer to accept the Hemings story, Brodie presented a portrait in stark contrast to the traditional image of a monkish Jefferson, a man who, after his wife's death, devoted himself to philosophy and politics. Brodie's Jefferson remained a passionate lover. In France, before the arrival of Sally Hemings, Jefferson met an artist named Maria Cosway, to whom he wrote a remarkable love letter consisting mostly of a debate between "My Head and My Heart." Most biographers have interpreted the letter as a victory for Jefferson's head; Brodie, however, saw the heart as the winner. Brodie was convinced the Cosway-Jefferson relationship was both passionate and sexual.

But it was her portrait of the Hemings-Jefferson relationship that generated the most controversy. In addition to her efforts to rehabilitate the reputations and credibility of Callender and of Madison Hemings, Brodie presented a great deal of "psychological" evidence. For example, she noted that in his 1788 diary of a tour of Germany, Jefferson used the word "mulatto" eight times to describe the color of the soil; in Brodie's interpretation, it was Sally Hemings's mulatto color and not Germany's soil that was on Jefferson's mind. In a 1789 letter to Cosway, Jefferson described himself as "an animal of a warm climate, a mere Oran-ootan"; Brodie points out that in his *Notes on the State of Virginia*, Jefferson had indiscreetly written that "the Oran-ootan preferred the black woman over those of his own species."

In another letter to Cosway, Jefferson described a painting he'd just seen of Sarah delivering Hagar to Abraham. Jefferson called the painting "delicious" and added: "I would have agreed to have been Abraham though the consequence would have been that I should have been dead five or six thousand years." Brodie was quick to remind readers of the significance of the biblical story: Sarah, who was barren, gave Hagar (whom most artists depicted as dark-skinned) to Abraham so that she could bear him a child. To Brodie, Jefferson's lustful description could only be an unconscious admission of his love for Hemings.

Brodie's book was the best-selling nonfiction book of the year, and many general interest newspapers, including the *New York Times* and the *Washington Post* reviewed it favorably. The historical establishment, however, was unconvinced. Dumas Malone, whose multivolume Jefferson biography won a Pulitzer Prize, said the book ran "far beyond the evidence and carries psychological speculation to the point of absurdity; the resulting mishmash of fact and fiction, surmise and conjecture is not history as I understand the term." Merrill Peterson, author of the most widely respected one-volume biography of Jefferson, called Brodie "obsessive" and concluded there was "no need to charge off in defense of Jefferson's integrity when we have no solid grounds for doubting it."

Indeed, much of Brodie's psychological evidence does seem farfetched and some of it is just outright wrong; for example, according to the *Oxford English Dictionary*, the use of the word "mulatto" to describe the color of soil was common in eighteenth-century America. Even scholars with no vested interest in any particular image of Jefferson found Brodie's work long on speculation and short on hard evidence.

Still, the vehemence of the attacks on Brodie, and the even more vehement denials that someone of Jefferson's character could have slept with Hemings, were themselves revealing. Dumas, for example, wrote that "it is virtually inconceivable that this fastidious gentleman . . . could have carried on through a period of years a vulgar liaison." Clearly, Brodie had done more than repeat some old gossip; she'd touched a nerve.

What Brodie had done was to bring into the foreground of Thomas Jefferson's life the place of slavery and race, something most of his other biographers were loathe to do. By focusing on his purported relationship with Hemings, she'd reminded readers that, regardless of whether or not he'd slept with her, he'd *owned* her. Brodie herself did not believe the relationship was an abusive one; on the contrary, she was convinced Jefferson and Hemings shared a deep and lasting love. But Jefferson most certainly was not in love with the other two hundred slaves he owned—and his treatment of them and attitudes toward them were not so different from those of other wealthy Virginian slaveowners.

This is not to deny that Jefferson hated slavery; his writings make that clear. Nor is it to deny the extent to which Jefferson's ideals inspired later antislavery efforts. But Jefferson's actions definitely did not live up to his ideals. Unlike Washington, whose will freed all his slaves on his death, Jefferson freed only the two Hemings brothers and three others. Jefferson's 1783 draft of a new constitution for Virginia provided for the freedom of all children born of slaves after the year 1800, but that unsuccessful effort was his last on behalf of emancipation. After his return from France, wrote David Brion Davis, "the most remarkable thing about Jefferson's stand on slavery is his immense silence." On one of the few occasions he did speak out, during the Missouri crisis of 1820, he threw his considerable weight behind slavery's expansion.

It is in this context that Jefferson's relationship with Sally Hemings must be viewed. Probably he did not have an affair with her; Brodie's evidence is far from convincing. But he was supported by a slave system under which owners routinely did far worse things to slaves than Jefferson was ever accused of. And, when the chips were down, Jefferson supported the system that supported him.

☆ To investigate further:

Peterson, Merrill D. *The Jefferson Image in the American Mind.* New York: Oxford University Press, 1960. The evolution of Jefferson's image in the American imagination.

Jordan, Winthrop. *White Over Black.* Williamsburg, VA: Institute of Early American History and Culture, 1968. A study of American attitudes toward blacks up to 1812 that includes arguments against the affair.

Malone, Dumas. *Jefferson The President, First Term.* New York: Little, Brown, 1970. Volume 4 of the Pulitzer Prize-winning set.

Peterson, Merrill D. *Thomas Jefferson and The New Nation.* New York: Oxford University Press, 1970. The best one-volume biography.

Brodie, Fawn. *Thomas Jefferson, An Intimate History.* New York: Norton, 1974. Unconvincing—but undeniably provocative and entertaining.

Adair, Douglass. *Fame and the Founding Fathers.* Williamsburg, VA: Institute of Early American History and Culture, 1974. Adair's 1960 essay, "The Jefferson Scandals," is included here and remains one of the most convincing refutations of the affair.

Davis, David Brion. *The Problem of Slavery in the Age of Revolution, 1770–1823.* Ithaca, NY: Cornell University Press, 1975. A wide-ranging study of the complex and contradictory factors that influenced opinions on slavery, including a very unforgiving analysis of Jefferson's role.

Smith, Page. *Jefferson.* New York: American Heritage, 1976. A pictorial biography which follows Brodie's lead on the affair.

Miller, John Chester. *The Wolf by the Ears.* New York: The Free Press, 1977. "We have a wolf by the ears, and we can neither hold him nor safely let him go," wrote Jefferson in 1820. "Justice is in one scale, and self-preservation in the other." In Miller's book you can see how Jefferson chose the latter.

Chase-Riboud, Barbara. *Sally Hemings.* New York: Viking, 1978. A novel about Hemings and Jefferson that is sometimes moving but ultimately unconvincing as a portrait of either.

Dabney, Virginius. *The Jefferson Scandals: A Rebuttal.* New York: Dodd, Mead, 1981. The most thorough and also the most sanctimonious refutation of Brodie.

Randall, Willard Sterne. *Thomas Jefferson: A Life.* New York: Henry Holt, 1993. The latest biography; competent and readable though nothing dramatically new.

Chapter 12

Was Meriwether Lewis Murdered?

In September 1806 Meriwether Lewis—along with William Clark—received a hero's welcome as he entered St. Louis. Lewis and Clark had just returned from their epic journey across an unknown continent, a journey during which they had overcome Indians, grizzlies, mosquitoes, illness, and near starvation. At 33, Lewis was a national hero.

Just three years later he was dead, shot twice in a small cabin in the Tennessee wilderness. Who shot him has been one of the longest-lingering murder mysteries in American history.

☆ ☆ ☆

If there was an official inquest into Lewis's death, we don't know of it; the records of Maury County, Tennessee, where the shooting occurred, have been lost. But we do know that Thomas Jefferson took it upon himself to investigate the death personally.

Jefferson's interest was not surprising. Lewis had grown up on a plantation only eight or nine miles from Monticello, Jefferson's Virginia home. Jefferson had plucked Lewis from the army to serve as his private secretary, and the president had then chosen him to lead the expedition across the continent. After investigating his friend's death, Jefferson concluded it was suicide. The story he pieced together went as follows.

Meriwether Lewis, from the Analectic Magazine, *1816. Jefferson concluded his friend committed suicide; so did Lewis' partner in discovery, William Clark. But others were convinced it was murder. Library of Congress.*

After returning to St. Louis, Lewis was appointed governor of Upper Louisiana. Alas, it turned out this was a man who coped better in the actual wilderness than in the political jungle. Early in his term Lewis reversed some of the Indian policies of his chief assistant, Territorial Secretary Frederick Bates, and Bates worked from then on to undermine Lewis's authority and popularity. Once Jefferson left office, Lewis also managed to alienate his bosses in Washington, in particular Secretary of War William Eustis.

Matters came to a head when Lewis paid five hundred dollars more than Eustis had authorized to return an Indian chief to his tribe. The chief had come east with Lewis on the expedition's return trip, and Lewis felt responsible for getting him back home. Eustis, however, saw this as an example of Lewis's disregard for his higher authority. In addition, he was convinced there was a conflict of interest involved, since the company Lewis had contracted with to escort the chief home was a company in which Lewis's brother had invested.

To make matters worse, Lewis was deeply in debt. When Eustis refused to pay Lewis's expenses, Lewis was near bankruptcy. (He had to borrow some money from Clark—his partner in discovery—to get by.) In September 1809 the much-vexed Lewis set off for Washington to make his case to Eustis in person.

Along the way, Lewis stopped at Fort Pickering, near what is now Memphis. By this time, Lewis was more than vexed; according to the fort's commander, Captain Gilbert Russell, he was "in a state of derangement." Russell also reported that members of Lewis's crew had told him that Lewis had made two attempts at suicide, and that he'd taken it upon himself to keep Lewis in the fort's sick bay.

In about six days, according to Russell, Lewis's condition improved and he again set off for Washington, this time accompanied by Major James Neelly, the United States agent to the Chickasaw nation. For what happened next, during the last 23 days of Lewis's life, we are mostly dependent on Neelly's report. According to Neelly, Lewis's condition again deteriorated and he again "appeared deranged in mind." On October 9, two of their horses escaped and Lewis proceeded on to a small inn, while Neelly stayed behind to track down the horses.

From this point on Jefferson (and future historians) could no longer rely on Neelly's own eyewitness report. Instead, we can only depend on the story which Neelly had to reconstruct from the words of the innkeeper, Mrs. Grinder. According to the innkeeper, Lewis arrived there deranged. Not wanting to be around him, she gave him the house and slept in another one nearby, along with Lewis's and Neelly's servants. At about three in the morning she heard two pistol shots, went to Lewis's room, and found he'd shot himself in the head and a little below the chest. Lewis's last words, according to Grinder, were: "I have done the business my good Servant, give me some water."

This, then, was the story which Jefferson believed. As further evidence of Lewis's suicidal tendencies, Jefferson recalled that "Lewis had, from early life, been subject to hypochondriac affections," as had his father and other family members. Jefferson concluded that "during his Western expedition, the constant exertion which that required of all the faculties of body and mind, suspended these distressing occupations." But back in St. Louis these "affections" had returned, and "he was in a paroxysm of one of these" when he committed suicide.

Another who knew Lewis well also appeared unsurprised on being told he had committed suicide. William Clark reacted to the news by saying: "I fear O! I fear the weight of his mind has overcome him."

With the prestige of the presidency behind it, the verdict of suicide seemed settled.

☆ ☆ ☆

Yet, from the start, there were doubters.

Grinder's cabin lay on the Natchez Trace, a trail already well-known for the presence of bandits who wouldn't hesitate to rob and kill well-to-do travelers. About $120 that Lewis had with him when he left Fort Pickering was never found. Could not one of the Trace's notorious bandits have killed Lewis?

Nor was Grinder an entirely credible witness. Over the years she recounted the story to a number of different visitors, and these stories differed in many details. In some versions Grinder immediately aroused the servants, in others not; in some she was alone, in others her children were present; in some she gave Lewis the water he asked for, in others she refused; in some she described Lewis as crawling around and then heading over to the Trace, while in others he stayed in the cabin. In one version, Lewis's dying words became: "I am no coward; but I am so strong, so hard to die."

Some historians have suspected that Grinder couldn't keep her story straight because she was covering up her role in Lewis's murder—or perhaps the role of her husband. Others have been more sympathetic. After all, finding a world-famous explorer dead in your home would fluster most anyone, and Grinder was just a poor and uneducated innkeeper.

Neelly, too, has come under some suspicion, as have Lewis's and Neelly's servants. We know little about any of them, other than that Jefferson accepted their innocence (and in the case of Lewis's servant, Jefferson interviewed him at the White House).

Ultimately, with no eyewitnesses (unless Neelly or Grinder were lying), we can never know for sure whether Lewis was murdered or committed suicide. So, like Jefferson, historians have looked beyond the Grinders' cabin and into Lewis's psyche. And many, in contrast to Jefferson, concluded Lewis could *not* have killed himself.

How, they asked, could a man who had conquered the wilderness be so distraught by a few political and financial problems? In his 1947 dual biography of Lewis and Clark, John Bakeless wrote: "Though the government's financial methods drive men to distraction, they rarely drive them to suicide. If they did, the streets of Washinton would be littered with corpses." And in a 1965 biography of Lewis, Richard Dillon wrote: "If ever there is such a person as the anti-suicide type, it was Meriwether Lewis. By temperament, he was a fighter, not a quitter." For many of Lewis's biographers, especially his earlier ones, suicide just didn't make sense; it was the wrong ending to the epic tale they told.

Alas, Lewis was not bound by the need for an appropriately heroic ending to his life. Beset by debt and depression and perhaps disease, he may have seen no alternative to suicide. Perhaps he found it easier to escape Indians and grizzlies than his own despair. Perhaps, with his great adventure in the past, he saw nothing of promise in the future. Perhaps, even as he exhibited great courage during his expedition, he was courting death. Though Clark was certainly no coward, it was Lewis who unnecessarily climbed a dangerous cliff and nearly fell from it; it was Lewis who wandered off alone into country he knew was filled with grizzlies; it was Lewis who, with only two companions, went to meet the Shoshoni, who had never before seen white people, and then, with only three others, ventured into the land of the Blackfeet, whom he had been warned were hostile. Was he defying death—or embracing it? Did the same forces, however incompletely we understand them, drive him across the continent and then to his death?

We can't know for sure the answer to these questions; much about Lewis's death remains a mystery. But those who knew him best, Jefferson and Clark, concluded he committed suicide, and in the absence of more compelling evidence to the contrary, that seems the most likely solution.

☆ To investigate further:

Allen, Paul, editor. *History of the Expedition under the Command of Lewis and Clark*. Philadelphia: Bradford and Inskeep, 1814. This official account of the expedition, which Lewis was working on when he died, includes Jefferson's memoir and his conclusion that it was suicide.

Bakeless, John. *Lewis & Clark*. New York: Morrow, 1947. Includes a case for murder.

Phelps, Dawson A. "The Tragic Death of Meriwether Lewis." *William and Mary Quarterly*, July 1956. A good summary of the case for suicide.

Fisher, Vardis. *Suicide or Murder?* Denver: Alan Swallow, 1962. The most thorough of the cases for murder.

Dillon, Richard. *Meriwether Lewis*. New York: Coward-McCann, 1965. Includes a case for murder.

Kushner, Howard. "The Suicide of Meriwether Lewis." *William and Mary Quarterly*, July 1981. A psychoanalytic case for suicide which argues that both Lewis' excessive risk-taking and his suicide stemmed from his feelings that his father had abandoned him.

Lavender, David. *The Way to the Western Sea*. New York: Harper & Row, 1988. A thorough if uninspired retelling of the Lewis and Clark expedition, including Lavender's leanings toward the case for suicide.

Chandler, David Leon. *The Jefferson Conspiracies*. New York: Morrow, 1994. Argues that Lewis was murdered by agents of General James Wilkinson, and that Jefferson covered up evidence of the murder to keep secret his own intrigues with Wilkinson. Chandler's evidence is *extremely* circumstantial.

Ambrose, Stephen. *Undaunted Courage: Meriwether Lewis, Thomas Jefferson, and the Opening of the American West*. New York: Simon and Schuster, 1996. The most recent and most readable account of the expedition, with a strong case for suicide.

Chapter 13

Was Rachel Jackson a Bigamist?

From the moment the 1824 election ended in victory for John Quincy Adams, supporters of his opponent, Andrew Jackson, cried foul. Jackson had received a plurality of the popular and electoral votes, but he fell short of a majority, thus throwing the election into the House of Representatives. There, Henry Clay's support for Adams was decisive. When Adams then selected Clay as his secretary of state, Jacksonians charged both with a "corrupt bargain."

Four years later, the Jacksonians were out for revenge, and the election was one of the nastiest ever. Jackson's supporters denounced Adams as a gambler (the evidence was a billiard table Adams purchased for the White House) and as a pimp (the story—completely false but nonetheless widely circulated—was that while Adams was a diplomat in Russia he had supplied American virgins to the czar).

Adams's supporters responded in kind. They countered Jackson's reputation as a military hero by portraying him as a brute likely at any moment to explode in violence. That Jackson had fought eight duels and in one notorious tavern brawl didn't help his reputation, nor did his execution of six militiamen to quell a mutiny under his command during the 1813–1814 war against the Creek Indians. By far the most widely circulated charge against Jackson, however, was that he was an adulterer and that his wife, Rachel, was a bigamist.

KING ANDREW THE FIRST.

In the eyes of his opponents, Andrew Jackson was a monarchist, a mulatto, a murderer . . . and worst of all, married to a bigamist. The last charge may very well have been true. Library of Congress.

This charge presented a particularly difficult problem for Jackson; namely, that—at least technically—it was true.

☆ ☆ ☆

Jackson's supporters put together an 18-man committee to gather evidence and present his side of the story. Central to the Jacksonians' version of events was a narrative by John Overton, an eyewitness to much of what he reported.

Around 1787, Overton recalled, he became a boarder in the Kentucky house of the widow Robards; also living there were her son, Lewis Robards, and his wife, Rachel Robards—later to become Rachel Jackson. The Robardses' marriage was a disaster from the start. Lewis Robards was intensely antisocial and suspicious while Rachel, who loved to dance and ride horses and tell stories, was exactly the sort to bring out his jealous streak. At least once, Overton was called upon to intervene and bring about a reconciliation between the Robardses. All three—Lewis and Rachel Robards and John Overton—then moved to Tennessee, near Nashville, where they boarded with Rachel's mother, the widow Donelson.

Enter Andrew Jackson. Like Overton, he was a young frontier lawyer; like Overton, he became a boarder of the widow Donelson. On the Kentucky and Tennessee frontiers of 1789, this arrangement was not so unusual as it might sound: a widow would have been happy to have a couple of extra men around to fend off Indian attacks, and Overton and Jackson would have been happy to have someone to keep house for them. As boarders, Overton and Jackson shared a bed; this prompted one historian to comment, in light of how important Overton's account of what happened was to Jackson's 1828 campaign, that the saying that politics makes strange bedfellows ought in this case to have been reversed.

Inevitably, the tempestuous Jackson and the jealous Robards soon clashed. When Robards found Jackson talking with Rachel—a completely innocent meeting, Overton emphasized—Robards was incensed. Jackson attempted to reason with him but to no avail. The upshot was Robards stormed back to Kentucky, vowing never to live with Rachel again.

But sometime in the fall of 1790, he changed his mind—at least this was the rumor that reached Nashville at that time. On hearing that her husband intended to take her back to Kentucky—by force, if necessary—Rachel was understandably distraught. She decided to flee down the Mississippi River to Natchez, where she had friends who'd protect her.

Jackson was now "the most unhappy of men," according to Overton. Not because he'd done anything wrong, Overton emphasized, but for "having innocently and unintentionally been the cause of the loss of peace and happiness of Mrs. Robards." So Jackson decided to help out by joining the party going down the river. It was, after all, dangerous Indian country through which they'd pass.

In either the winter or spring of 1791, Overton continued, Rachel and Andrew set off for Natchez. By May, Jackson was back in Nashville, where he learned that the legislature had granted Robards a divorce. (Divorce was sufficiently rare that it required a legislative act.) Jackson then rushed back to Natchez, where in the summer of 1791 he married Rachel. They lived together there for a short time and in the fall of 1791 returned to Nashville together.

A happy ending, it seemed. But then, in December 1793—more than two years after they were married—the couple was horrified to learn that Robards hadn't gotten a divorce after all. The Virginia legislature had merely passed an act enabling Robards to take Rachel to court. That he had now done. Since Rachel and Andrew had been living together for more than two years, Robards had no problem convincing a jury that she was guilty of adultery. Worse, though the jury had no need to rule on this, if she had been married to Jackson during this period, she was also clearly guilty of bigamy.

But, Overton emphasized, this guilt was merely a technicality. When Rachel and Andrew married in 1791, both *thought* she was divorced. And when they learned that wasn't the case, they immediately got married again.

☆ ☆ ☆

This was the story the eighteen-man Nashville committee put forth in the midst of the 1828 presidential campaign. And though it was clearly a political document (Adams's supporters were quick to label the committee the "Whitewashing Committee"), it included a great deal of supporting evidence.

But there were also a lot of holes in the story. Jackson's most prominent nineteenth-century biographer, James Parton, basically accepted the committee's story but admitted that Jackson's conversations with Lewis Robards were probably "not characterized by that moderation of statement and demeanor which might be inferred from a hasty reading of Overton's narrative." Still, the basic story stood.

In 1940 Marquis James's biography of Jackson expressed somewhat more skepticism. How could Jackson, a lawyer, have rushed into a marriage without actually checking out the legislative act which supposedly made that marriage possible? And how could the two live together for more than two years, undisturbed by the slightest suspicion that there'd been no divorce? But, James concluded, "one must believe these things for they are true." Communications on the frontier were both slow and inaccurate; an error like that of the Jacksons was by no means inconceivable. Again, the story stood.

In the most recent major biography of Jackson, completed in 1984, Robert Remini was most skeptical of all. First, he wondered about Jackson's decision to accompany Rachel on her flight from Nashville to Natchez. Surely there was someone who could have accompanied her other than the man her husband had accused of being her lover. Couldn't one of Rachel's ten brothers or brothers-in-law have protected her on her journey? For that matter, why couldn't they have protected her in Nashville as easily as in Natchez? The story just didn't make sense. Remini concluded Jackson was already in love with Rachel at this point, and that he planned the trip with her in order to provoke Robards into granting her a divorce—a plan which succeeded. Not that this was an immoral plan—Rachel was trapped in a horrible marriage and this may have been the only way out she and Jackson could imagine. Still, this was a far cry from the completely innocent mistake Overton described.

Next Remini turned to the marriage ceremony itself—the first one, that is. Overton didn't actually witness the wedding; he merely said that "in the Summer of 1791, General Jackson returned to Natches, & as I understand, married Mrs. Robards." But Natchez was under Spanish rule in 1791, so only Catholic marriages were permitted. Both Andrew and Rachel were Protestant. A Protestant minister could have secretly (and illegally) married them, but no record of that first marriage has ever been found.

Yet there *is* a court record of the Jackson/Robards party's arrival in Natchez—and here the plot really thickens. According to the Spanish records, Jackson and Robards arrived in January 1790, not 1791 (as Overton claimed). If this is the case, then Rachel and Andrew Jackson were married, or living together, months before the divorce proceedings were initiated, let alone completed. And the charges made in 1827—for example, the *Cincinnati Gazette*'s claim that "Gen Jackson prevailed upon the wife of Lewis Roberts [*sic*] to desert her husband, and live with himself in the character of a wife"—were indeed true.

☆ ☆ ☆

So why the big fuss? Who cares if they lived together before they were married, or before she was divorced, or even before she *thought* she was divorced? It is a telling commentary on the difference between the frontier mores of the early 1790s and the national morals of the late 1820s that the Jacksons' eighteenth-century Nashville neighbors clearly didn't disapprove of the marriage; all evidence points to the high esteem in which the couple was held. Frontier life called for all sorts of improvisation, and the Jacksons were hardly unique in not standing on ceremony. Thirty years later, things had changed.

In any case, the accusations against the Jacksons mattered a great deal to Rachel Jackson. Though she was shielded from much of the campaign rhetoric, she came upon some pamphlets during a shopping trip right after the election. What she read staggered her, and many felt it contributed to the heart attack she soon suffered. She died just before she was to set off with her husband for the White House.

The accusations were also relevant for the impact they had on Jackson's presidency. When the wife of Vice President John Calhoun refused to call on the notoriously promiscuous wife of one of Jackson's cabinet members, the president—seeing the attacks on her as comparable to those on Rachel—rode to her defense. The incident became a major scandal, occupying a great deal of cabinet time and ultimately leading to a rift between Jackson and Calhoun that cleared the way for Martin Van Buren, rather than Calhoun, to succeed Jackson.

Finally, the vehemence and prevalence of the charges and countercharges during the 1828 campaign signaled a change in the nature of American politics. True, American politics had always been personal and often been nasty; witness the Federalists' charges that Jefferson had a slave mistress. But by 1828 the press and the parties were much better organized to disseminate negative stories about candidates.

Jackson was a central figure in this transformation. Though he was not personally involved in organizing his party's campaign, he came to symbolize many of the issues that galvanized both his supporters and opponents. To the former, he was the champion of the people, the common man standing against the commercial and banking interests that threatened to corrupt the nation; to the latter, he was a frontier brawler and military chieftain who would upset the orderly improvement of America's resources. What Jackson *actually* stood for was less clear and has been the basis of much historical debate. After his resounding victory in 1828, however, at least one thing was clear: running as the "common man" is an effective route to the White House.

☆ To investigate further:

Parton, James. *Life of Andrew Jackson* (3 volumes). Boston: Houghton Mifflin, 1859. Though many of its stories are apocryphal, there is much essential source material here for any study of Jackson.

James, Marquis. *The Life of Andrew Jackson* Indianapolis: Bobbs-Merrill, 1938. Dated but still entertaining.

Schlesinger, Arthur, Jr. *The Age of Jackson*. New York: Little, Brown, 1945. A classic work of history, this portrays Jackson as "the Man of the People" and his election and administration as a key stage in the growth of American democracy.

Hofstadter, Richard. *The American Political Tradition and the Men Who Made It.* New York: Knopf, 1951. Disputes Schlesinger's thesis by portraying Jackson, not as a champion of urban workers or small farmers, but as more concerned with the interests of entrepreneurs and other capitalists.

Curtis, James. *Andrew Jackson and the Search for Vindication.* New York: Little, Brown, 1976. A fascinating psychological portrait of Old Hickory.

Remini, Robert. *Andrew Jackson and the Course of American Empire.* New York: Harper & Row, 1977. With Remini's *Andrew Jackson and the Course of American Freedom* (1981) and *Andrew Jackson and the Course of American Democracy* (1984), this is the most recent major biography, and in many ways a return to Schlesinger's view of Jackson.

Watson, Harry. *Liberty and Power.* New York: Hill and Wang, 1990. A broad but concise survey of the period's politics, this portrays the Jacksonians as attempting to roll back the market revolution.

Cole, Donald. *The Presidency of Andrew Jackson.* Lawrence: University Press of Kansas, 1993. A nuanced portrait of a man more controlled by than in control of the political and economic forces of the age.

Chapter 14

How Did Davy Crockett Die?

To the millions of Americans who remember Fess Parker in ABC's 1954 *Davy Crockett, Indian Fighter* series or John Wayne in the 1960 movie *The Alamo*, the answer to this chapter's question is no mystery: Davy died fighting at the Alamo, along with all its other defenders. In the television version, he is last seen swinging his rifle like a club, with the bodies of the Mexicans he has slain at his feet; in the movie version he is if anything more heroic, blowing up the fort's powder magazine to make sure a score of Mexicans die with him.

So clear was this image in Americans' minds that when historian Dan Kilgore presented evidence in 1978 that Crockett surrendered at the Alamo and was executed after the battle, Kilgore was branded un-American. Yet Kilgore's evidence was not new, nor were Hollywood's versions the first fictionalized accounts of Crockett's life and death. Crockett himself was famous as a teller of tall tales, and historians attempting to uncover the truth about his death had first to peel away many layers of legends, lies, and half-truths.

☆ ☆ ☆

The mythic "Davy"—as opposed to the real person historians prefer to call "David"—was at least in part a creation of Crockett's own making. Crockett's autobiography, *A Narrative of the Life of David Crockett*, is more admired by literary critics than by historians. Still, it does present many of the facts of his life and reveals something, at least, of whether he was the type of man who'd fight to the end, or who'd prefer to live to fight another day.

Like Daniel Boone, the Crockett in *A Narrative of the Life* is a great hunter, a superman from the backwoods of Tennessee who killed 105 bears in a single season. So famed was he as a hunter that, so the story went, once a treed raccoon recognized him, it would yell, "Don't shoot, I'm a comin' down!"

Above all, however, the real Crockett was a politician. Using his comic drawl and his log-cabin background as proof that he would fight for the interests of the common man and of the westerner in particular, he was elected to the Tennessee House of Representatives in 1821 and 1823, and to the U.S. House in 1827, 1829, 1831, and 1833. At first he was an ardent supporter of that other "man of the people," Andrew Jackson. But Crockett broke with the president over his policies for disposing of western lands and Indians, and was then embraced by the Whig party. The Whigs saw in Crockett someone who could match Jackson's image as the common man's protector—and who might even be able to challenge Jackson for the presidency. They began ghostwriting his speeches and books, including his *Narrative of the Life,* which was in one sense a campaign biography.

The Whig propaganda made Crockett a national figure—a sort of western Poor Richard, uneducated but rich in common sense and experience. But Crockett's own constituents were less impressed by him. They noted his failure to pass a land bill protecting the rights of poor settlers and squatters; they noted that, in fact, in his entire congressional career he'd failed to get a single bill passed. With the Jacksonians mobilized against him, the 1835 congressional election promised to be a tight one. Crockett promised his followers that he'd serve them to the best of his ability if they elected him. And if they didn't? "You may all go to hell," Crockett answered, "and I will go to Texas."

They didn't—and so he did.

Crockett was not alone: by the early 1830s, although Texas was a province of Mexico, Americans made up 75 percent of its population. Americans flocked there for land that was available at one-tenth the price of land in the United States. For Crockett, who for all his fame was short on cash, the opportunity to buy cheap land was undoubtedly a factor in his decision to immigrate to Texas. And as a politician,

Fall of the Alamo—Death of Crockett.

The 1837 edition of Davy Crockett's Almanac *contained, along with this illustration, the following report: "Colonel Crockett's body was found . . . with his big dagger in his hand, and around him were lying seventeen dead Mexicans, eleven of whom had come to their deaths by his dagger and the others by his rifle and four pistols. . . ." But those who were actually at the Alamo told a very different story. Library of Congress.*

Crockett was also undoubtedly attracted by the possibility that Texas voters would appreciate him more than Tennesseans had.

The Mexican government, on the other hand, didn't like the idea of these Texans voting for anyone at all. Quite reasonably, Mexico saw these increasingly assertive immigrants as a threat to its authority, and decided to outlaw new immigration and ban slavery in the province. The more militant Americans responded by declaring Texas an independent nation and appointing Sam Houston as commander in chief. Like Crockett, Houston was an ex-Tennessean and an ex-congressman; unlike Crockett, Houston remained tied to the Jacksonians in the United States.

By the time Crockett arrived in San Antonio in early February 1836, tensions were near the breaking point. Not only were the Mexican general Santa Anna and his 2,400 troops on the march toward the fort but the Texans at the Alamo were themselves split between those who acknowledged Houston's authority and those who did not. Houston, recognizing that the 183 men in the Alamo could not hold the fort against Santa Anna's troops, ordered its commander, Colonel William Travis, to blow up the Alamo and retreat. But Travis, as part of the opposition to Houston, refused, thus setting up the fateful battle.

It is amidst these political maneuverings that Crockett's decision to stay at the Alamo—and the likelihood of his fighting to the death as opposed to surrendering—must be considered. Crockett had come to Texas because it was a land of economic and political opportunity, not so that he could fight and die. Moreover, Crockett was no soldier. (In his autobiography he readily admitted that he'd hired a substitute to finish out an earlier term of enlistment.) But once he got to Texas he found his past political affiliations threw him in with the anti-Houston, anti-Jackson forces, and these were the forces defending the Alamo. He was stuck there.

Of course, this doesn't prove that Crockett surrendered, or that his heroic death scene is mere myth. Many have died heroically on the battlefield with less evidence of previous heroism than Crockett's life provided. What Crockett's past life proved was merely that he was the type of person who easily *could* have surrendered. To determine whether he actually did so, historians needed some actual witnesses.

The obvious problem with witnesses, at least on the American side, was that they were dead.

Once Colonel Travis used his sword to draw his famous line in the sand, and all those willing to stay and fight to the death crossed the line, the fate of the Americans was sealed.* After 90 bloody minutes on the morning of March 6, 1836, they were all dead. (Not quite all: The Mexicans did spare the life of a slave, Joe, and a woman, Susannah

---

*The question of whether Travis really drew this line has intrigued historians almost as much as that of how Crockett died. The story went as follows: On March 3, Travis lined up his men and told them there was no escaping the Mexicans. He then drew a line with his sword and asked all those who would stand beside him and fight to the death to cross the line. Every man did so, but for one: Louis Rose, who would inevitably become known as "the yellow rose of Texas." Rose vaulted the walls of the Alamo and eluded the Mexicans.

The story was first written down in 1873, and by then it was at best thirdhand. Many historians have questioned not just the story, but whether Rose was even at the Alamo. Some have argued that the story didn't make sense: on March 3, Travis was still hoping reinforcements would reach the fort, so his heroic gesture would have been premature. But it's possible Rose was there, and it's also possible that the 1873 account got the story right but the date wrong. Perhaps Travis drew the line on March 5; by then it was all too clear that help could not arrive in time to save the Alamo.

Dickinson, and the latter's report of seeing Crockett's mutilated body has often been used to prove he died fighting. But she didn't see his body until well after the fighting had ended—and well after he might have been captured and executed.)

On the Mexican side, of course, there were many survivors. That their testimony was for so long ignored can only be attributed to American chauvinism. In 1975, however, Carmen Perry translated into English the narrative of José Enrique de la Peña, an aide to Santa Anna and an eyewitness to Crockett's death. According to de la Peña, Crockett most definitely did not go down fighting. Rather, he was captured along with six others and brought before Santa Anna. Drawing on his famous ability to tell tall tales, he attempted to talk his way out of his situation. He claimed that he'd merely been exploring the country around the Alamo when he'd heard of the Mexican advance. Then, "fearing that his status as a foreigner might not be respected," he'd sought refuge in the Alamo. But Santa Anna didn't buy it. He ordered Crockett and the others killed, and his officers (though not the horrified de la Peña) "fell upon these unfortunate, defenseless men just as a tiger leaps upon his prey."

Other Mexican witnesses offered briefer but similar versions of Crockett's death. Among them were Colonel Fernando Urissa, another aide to Santa Anna; General Martín Perfecto de Cos, Santa Anna's brother-in-law; Colonel José Sanchez Navarro, who led one of the assault columns against the Alamo; and Sergeant Francisco Becerra. Santa Anna's personal secretary also reported the capture and execution of some Americans (though he didn't mention Crockett). In spite of efforts to discredit the testimony of these Mexicans, the sheer number of witnesses to his surrender, and the lack of any reliable eyewitness to his death in battle, clearly favors the surrender story.

At the time, many U.S. newspapers reported the surrender, as did many nineteenth- and early twentieth-century histories. In fact, the story of Crockett's execution was often used as evidence of Santa Anna's barbarity, and it generated comparatively little controversy. Only after the Fess Parker/John Wayne versions were filmed did Crockett's death become a part of American mythology. But mythology, not history, is almost surely what it was.

The revisionist view of Crockett's death can be taken too far, however. Just because he wasn't Parker or Wayne didn't mean he died in vain. Even in its surrender and execution version, Crockett's death focused the attention of the United States on Texas, and money and volunteers rolled into the territory. Six weeks after the Alamo, Sam Houston's men, crying "Remember the Alamo!", overwhelmed the Mexicans. A day later Santa Anna surrendered.

Nor should Crockett's surrender be confused with cowardice: faced with insurmountable odds, Crockett made the only reasonable choice. De la Peña's account of the execution concludes by telling how "though tortured before they were killed, these unfortunates died without complaining and without humiliating themselves before their torturers." Or, to put it another way, Davy Crockett died like a hero.

☆ To investigate further:

Crockett, David. *A Narrative of the Life of David Crockett of the State of Tennessee*. Knoxville: University of Tennessee Press, 1987. This facsimile edition of Crockett's 1834 autobiography includes useful notes and an introduction by James Shackford and Stanley Folmsbee.

de la Peña, José Enrique. *With Santa Anna in Texas: A Personal Narrative of the Revolution*, translated and edited by Carmen Perry. College Station: Texas A&M University Press, 1975. Written soon after the battle, its translation and publication in 1975 set off the debate about Crockett's death.

Shackford, James. *David Crockett: The Man and the Legend*. Chapel Hill: University of North Carolina Press, 1956. Shackford was unaware of some of the Mexican sources on the Alamo; as a result, he argued that Crockett—who was certainly no coward—was likely to have been on the front lines and therefore was likely to have died very early on in the battle. Though he was wrong on this, he was right on most everything else, and his book remains the best biography of Crockett.

Kilgore, Dan. *How Did Davy Die?* College Station: Texas A&M University Press, 1978. A concise summary of the case that he was captured and then executed.

Lord, Walter. *A Time to Stand*. Lincoln: University of Nebraska Press, 1978. Originally published in 1961 and still the most dramatic history of the Alamo.

Lofaro, Michael and Joe Cummings, editors. *Crockett at Two Hundred: New Perspectives on the Man and the Myth*. Knoxville: The University of Tennessee Press, 1989. Most of the essays here are somewhat specialized but the ones by Kilgore and Hutton contain interesting descriptions of the backlash that followed the publication of Perry's translation of de la Peña's book.

Long, Jeff. *Duel of Eagles*. New York: Morrow, 1990. The most recent history of the Alamo; worth reading but not quite up to the standard set by Lord's 1961 book.

Derr, Mark. *The Frontiersman: The Real Life and the Many Legends of Davy Crockett*. New York: Morrow, 1993. The most recent biography of Crockett; worth reading but not quite up to the standard set by Shackford's 1956 book.

Groneman, Bill. *Defense of a Legend*, Plano, TX: Republic of Texas Press, 1994. Claims the de la Peña diary was a forgery, and that Crockett *was* killed at the Alamo.

Chapter 15

Why Did Lee
Order Pickett's Charge?

On July 3, 1863, just southwest of Gettysburg, Pennsylvania, Robert E. Lee met with James Longstreet, commander of the Confederate Army's First Corps and Lee's most trusted lieutenant. Lee ordered Longstreet to attack the center of the Union line on top of Cemetery Hill, about a half a mile away. Longstreet tried to dissuade Lee: the Union troops outnumbered the Confederates, were firmly entrenched behind stone walls, and had ample artillery to support them. The Confederates would have to get across more than half a mile of upward-sloping fields, during which time they would be completely exposed to Union fire. "General Lee," Longstreet later recalled telling his commander, "there never was a body of fifteen thousand men who could make that attack successfully."

But Lee overruled him. "The enemy is there," he said, "and I am going to strike him."

So Longstreet summoned General George Pickett and reluctantly ordered him to lead what has ever since been known as "Pickett's Charge." At about 3:00 P.M., Pickett led forward his men (probably 12,000–13,000—the exact number is not known). It was picture-book vision of the Civil War: a mile-wide parade of gray, flags waving, horses galloping, marching in perfect order across the gently rolling farmland. The elegant Pickett led the way, shouting: "Don't forget today that you are from old Virginia!"

When George Pickett stumbled back behind Confederate lines after surviving the disastrous charge that bears his name, Robert E. Lee ordered him to prepare his division to repel a Union counterattack. "General Lee," Pickett tearfully replied, "I have no division now." Lithograph by Currier and Ives. Library of Congress.

And then the Union forces opened fire. A few Virginians made it to the Union line but reinforcements quickly poured in and pushed them back. When the smoke cleared, nearly two-thirds of Pickett's division was gone—dead or captured. Gone, too, was the South's hope for independence. Lee would lead his army back to Virginia, and he would not surrender until almost two years later, but, most historians agree, Gettysburg was the high-water mark for the Confederacy. After Lee's defeat there and after the fall of the Confederate stronghold of Vicksburg, Mississippi, a day later, it was just a matter of time until the Union triumphed.

But a mystery remained. Why did Lee, against the advice of Longstreet, persist in ordering Pickett's charge? This was the same Robert E. Lee, after all, who a few months earlier had brilliantly masterminded the Confederate victories at Chancellorsville and Fredericksburg. Lee was renowned for his successes in drawing the Union forces into battle just when the conditions were most favorable to the

Confederacy. Yet at Gettysburg he abandoned the tactics on which he'd built his reputation and plunged ahead with the doomed attack at the Union's strongest point.

Why?

☆ ☆ ☆

To Southern historians (and, in sharp contrast to most wars, this one was chronicled to a significant degree by its losers), Pickett's charge presented a dilemma. On the one hand, Lee was virtually the patron saint of the South—a valiant and brilliant general who could do no wrong. On the other hand, Pickett's men had also come to symbolize the courage of Southern soldiers, soldiers who these same historians portrayed as capable of carrying out any reasonable order. So, if they failed—as they did at Gettysburg—those orders couldn't have been reasonable. Yet those orders came from none other than Lee himself.

What was needed, clearly, was someone else to blame. One convenient scapegoat was Major General James Ewell Brown (known as "Jeb") Stuart, commander of the Confederate cavalry. One of Stuart's major responsibilities was to act as a scout. When Lee's army crossed the Potomac and headed north into Pennsylvania, Stuart's cavalry was supposed to follow along his right flank. Stuart, however, found his path blocked by the Union army, and he had to cross the river much further east than he'd planned. Then, when he finally did get across, he couldn't resist the opportunity to raid the Union's supply wagons. As a result, Stuart did not arrive in Gettysburg until late in the afternoon of July 2, the day after the battle began and the day before Pickett's charge.

Lee greeted him coldly: "General Stuart, where have you been?" he asked. "I have not heard a word from you in days, and you the eyes and ears of my army."

Indeed, Stuart's absence had put Lee at a disadvantage. When Stuart had failed to report, Lee had assumed it was because the Union army was still south of the Potomac. The Confederate forces were therefore dangerously spread out when they first learned that the enemy was nearby. Perhaps, had Stuart arrived earlier, Lee would have chosen someplace other than Gettysburg for the fateful battle. Still, to blame Stuart for Pickett's charge seems unfair: by the time Stuart arrived, Lee could see the Union troops massed on Cemetery Hill—and he chose to attack nonetheless.

Many historians, therefore, looked elsewhere for someone to blame for the Confederate defeat, and a great many settled on Lieutenant General Richard Ewell. It was Ewell who commanded the first Confederate troops to take on the Union troops at Gettysburg. This was on July 1—still two days before Pickett's charge—and the first day's fighting seemed to favor the Confederacy. Ewell's troops pushed Union troops under General Winfield Scott out of the town of Gettysburg onto Culp's Hill and Cemetery Hill, just south of Gettysburg. But, having won the initial battle, Ewell failed to follow up with an attack on Cemetery Hill. This, in the view of some historians, was the critical error that cost the South the Battle of Gettysburg; had Ewell pushed on and taken the heights then, before the Union troops had time to regroup and organize their defenses, the battle would have been over and Pickett need never have charged.

This, however, is unfair to Ewell. His men had suffered heavy losses in taking the town and Southern reinforcements did not reach the scene until more than a half hour after the July 1 battle—during which time the Union forces also had the opportunity to regroup. By the time Ewell's forces were ready to attack, it was very doubtful they could have succeeded. Besides, even if Ewell acted slowly on July 1, he was still no more responsible for ordering Pickett's charge than Stuart was.

The man who actually ordered Pickett to charge—and the man at whom the harshest criticism of all has been directed—was James Longstreet. This is ironic, since you'll recall it was Longstreet who most strongly advised Lee *against* the attack. But, according to some historians, Longstreet did more than disagree with Lee's plan; he undermined its chance of success. Annoyed by Lee's rejection of his alternate plan—a flanking maneuver around the Union lines to set up a defensive position there—Longstreet sulked. Even though he knew Lee had planned an early morning attack, Longstreet didn't order Pickett's division to the front until after nine in the morning on July 3. This, some historians have argued, prevented Lee from coordinating Pickett's attack on the Union center with an early morning attack by Ewell's men on the Union right. Furthermore, it gave the Union troops additional time to fortify the center.

As with the criticism of Stuart and Ewell, the criticism of Longstreet was partly valid: Longstreet was slow to bring Pickett to the front, and even slower to order him to attack. But, again, as with Stuart and Ewell, it's by no means clear that quicker action on his part would have made any difference. The Union lines were almost certainly as strong at dawn as they were at three in the afternoon. Longstreet may have carried out Lee's orders reluctantly but he did carry them out; otherwise Lee would certainly have removed him from his command after Gettysburg. The closest Lee came to criticizing him was in a conversation on the evening of July 3, in which he said the charge could have succeeded if additional troops had been sent in to support Pickett's men. But it's difficult to see where Longstreet would have found enough men to make a difference. Besides, it just doesn't make sense to blame Longstreet for the failure of an attack he adamantly opposed.

Why, then, has Longstreet so often been portrayed by Southerners as the villain, even the Judas of Gettysburg? One reason was that he had the gall to criticize Lee openly, not just at Gettysburg but years later in his memoirs. Worse, Longstreet was one of the few Southern generals who after the war became a Republican (the party of Lincoln!); he even accepted a federal job under President Grant. To Southerners, this was treason—and if Longstreet was a traitor after the war, he was probably one during the war, too.

The South never forgave James Longstreet. In 1941, on hearing that the Japanese had bombed Pearl Harbor, one of the last living Confederate veterans commented: "If Longstreet hadn't bungled at Gettysburg, we wouldn't be in this mess now."

☆ ☆ ☆

In spite of the efforts of Southern mythmakers to blame Lee's subordinates, more objective historians recognized that the critical Confederate error at Gettysburg—the plan for Pickett's charge—was made by Lee himself. Stuart *was* late; Ewell *was* timid, Longstreet *was* slow to carry out Lee's order. But the decision to send in Pickett's men was Lee's alone, and the brunt of the blame had to fall on his shoulders.

To his credit, Lee never denied this. Immediately after the battle, Lee rode among the dazed survivors of Pickett's brigade, telling them they'd fought well and their defeat was all his fault. On returning to Virginia, Lee wrote Jefferson Davis, the Confederate president, offering to resign: "I cannot even accomplish what I myself desire. How can I fill the expectations of others?" (Davis refused to accept the offer.)

Simply blaming Lee, however, didn't solve the mystery. The question remained: why would a general—a general whose reputation had been built on maneuvering his opponents into attacking him where *he* wanted—now abandon those tactics and order so desperate and dangerous a charge?

One reason was that Lee's options in Pennsylvania were much more limited than they'd been in Virginia. Having made the bold decision to invade the North, Lee had shifted the time pressure from the Union troops to his own. Now it was Lee's men who were living off the land, cut off from their supplies. The Confederate food supplies were dangerously low—so Lee felt he couldn't afford just to wait until the Union generals erred.

He could, of course, have retreated to Virginia—accepting that the two days of battle preceding Pickett's charge were nothing but a bloody draw. But this would have been an admission that his invasion had failed, that the South could do no real damage to the North and was destined to spend the rest of its days fighting on its own soil, perhaps winning some additional battles but never winning the war.

As Lee saw it, he had to attack. He hadn't come to Pennsylvania to raid a few farmhouses; he'd come for a dramatic and decisive showdown that would convince the North, once and forever, to grant the South independence. Gettysburg, though it might not be the ideal site for such a victory, was the site fate had dealt him. He'd already pushed the Union troops out of the town and, he assumed, shaken their morale. He had enough artillery, he hoped, to knock out some Union guns before the charge. At last he had Stuart's cavalry present; it could sweep around the Union lines and cause chaos among the Union troops fleeing the scene. And, above all, he had Pickett's men, who had not been used in the previous days' battles and who were rested and raring to go. Lee had tremendous faith in the abilities of Confederate soldiers; they had won other battles against odds almost as overwhelming. This confidence—this overconfidence—fatally colored Lee's judgment.

What Lee failed to take into account was that the Union soldiers were just as brave and just as committed as those of the Confederacy. The Union army had been outgeneraled in previous battles but it had not been outfought. At Gettysburg, the Union army was under the command of a new leader, General George Gordon Meade. Lincoln had appointed Meade to the top spot only days before, on June 28, but Meade was not intimidated by Lee. When Pickett's men emerged on the valley before him, he did not retreat or panic; rather, he swiftly and calmly ordered reinforcements toward the center of his line.

This is not to say Meade was a great general. In fact, he was harshly criticized after the Battle of Gettysburg for failing to counterattack after Pickett's charge failed. Lincoln was especially displeased. "We had them within our grasp," lamented the president. "We had only to stretch forth our hands and they were ours." Still, the attacks on his post-Gettysburg actions should not obscure Meade's highly competent generalship during the battle. And the Southern historians' focus on Lee and his lieutenants should not obscure the fact that the Battle of Gettysburg was not just lost by the South, but won by the North.

Pickett, who survived the charge that bears his name, recognized this. Asked after the war why the attack failed, Pickett responded: "I believe the Union army had something to do with it."

☆ To investigate further:

The War of the Rebellion: A Compilation of the Official Records of the Union and Confederate Armies. Washington, DC: Government Printing Office, 1889. Volume 27 (there are 127 in all) includes a mass of reports and correspondence pertaining to Gettysburg.

Johnson, Robert Underwood and Clarence Clough Buel. *Battles and Leaders of the Civil War.* New York: Century Company, 1884. Volume 3 includes Gettysburg recollections of Union and Confederate officers.

Longstreet, James. *From Manassas to Appomatox.* Bloomington: Indiana University Press, 1960. Originally published in 1896, this was Longstreet's answer to his critics.

Freeman, Douglas Southall. *Robert E. Lee.* New York: Scribner's, 1935. Though Freeman's Lee is almost superhumanly noble, this 4-volume biography remains a classic. Volume 3 covers Gettysburg.

————. *Lee's Lieutenants,* New York: Scribner's, 1944. These three volumes complement Freeman's four on Lee. Volume 3, which covers Gettysburg, softens the unfair criticism of Longstreet in the Lee biography.

Stewart, George. *Pickett's Charge.* Boston: Houghton Mifflin, 1960. An objective and readable account of the charge.

Foote, Shelby. *The Civil War: Fredericksburg to Meridian,* New York: Random House, 1963. This second volume of Foote's three-volume history includes Gettysburg. Like the other two, it has been deservedly acclaimed for its narrative power and sweep, but equally deservedly criticized for its pro-South bias. Foote's 1994 book, *Stars in Their Courses: The Gettysburg Campaign,* is drawn from volume 2.

Catton, Bruce. *Never Call Retreat.* New York: Doubleday, 1965. This third and final volume of Catton's "Centennial History of the Civil War" covers Gettysburg. Along with the first volume, *The Coming Fury,* and the second, *The Terrible Sword,* it is among the most dramatic narrative histories ever written. Catton's 1974 book, *Gettysburg: The Final Fury,* draws from the larger work.

Coddington, Edwin. *The Gettysburg Campaign.* New York: Scribner's, 1968. A comprehensive study of the battle.

Shaara, Michael. *The Killer Angels.* New York: Random House, 1974. This novel about Gettysburg won a Pulitzer Prize and became a bestseller and the basis for the movie *Gettysburg.*

Connelly, Thomas. *The Marble Man.* New York: Knopf, 1977. Examines the evolution of Lee's image, replacing Freeman's saint with a more troubled and complex figure.

Piston, William Garrett. *Lee's Tarnished Lieutenant: James Longstreet and His Place in Southern History.* Athens: University of Georgia Press, 1987. A mostly favorable assessment of Longstreet.

McPherson, James. *Battle Cry of Freedom.* New York: Oxford University Press, 1988. The best one-volume history of the Civil War.

Waugh, John. *The Class of 1846.* New York: Warner, 1994. The West Point class of 1846 included, among other critical Civil War figures, Stonewall Jackson, George McClellan, and George Pickett. Pickett—not so incidentally, in the view of many historians—was ranked 59th in a class of 59 cadets. And here's another irony: the man whose pull got Pickett into West Point in the first place was his uncle's friend, an Illinois lawyer by the name of Abraham Lincoln.

Longacre, Edward G. *Pickett.* Shippensburg, PA: White Mane, 1995. Most historians have portrayed Pickett as an incompetent dandy: for example, Longstreet's chief of staff G. Maxey Sorrel described how Pickett's "long ringlets flowed loosely over his shoulders, trimmed and highly perfumed; his beard likewise was curling and giving out the scents of Araby." Longacre attempts, with only limited success, to portray him as a more complex and intelligent figure.

Thomas, Emory. *Robert E. Lee.* New York: Norton, 1995. A balanced biography, neither as hagiographic as Freeman's nor as cutting as Connelly's.

Chapter 16

Who Was to Blame for Wounded Knee?

In the year 1890, at a spot near Wounded Knee Creek in southwest South Dakota, Chief Big Foot and a band of about 120 Sioux warriors accompanied by 230 women and children, met up with 470 members of the Seventh Cavalry, commanded by Colonel James Forsyth. This was the same Seventh Cavalry that had met the Sioux at the Battle of Little Big Horn 16 years earlier; then the cavalry had been commanded by General George Armstrong Custer and the Sioux had wiped out an entire batallion.

At Wounded Knee, it was the Sioux who were almost wiped out. The battle left 25 soldiers and somewhere between 200 and 300 Indians dead, many of them women and children. It also left a number of disturbing questions: Who fired the first shot? Did the Sioux warriors conceal their weapons in order to ambush the soldiers, as many of the latter claimed? Or did the Seventh Cavalry take its revenge on a peaceful band of Sioux families? Was the Battle of Wounded Knee a battle at all—or a brutal massacre?

Eighty-five years later, while historians continued to investigate these questions, Wounded Knee was again the site of an armed confrontation between Native Americans and U.S. government forces. In 1975 two FBI agents found themselves in a shootout with members of AIM, a militant organization (its initials stand for American Indian Movement) devoted to Native American rights. When the shooting stopped this time, the two agents were dead. AIM member Leonard Peltier was convicted of murder. His supporters said he was framed by the FBI.

Once again Wounded Knee had become a symbol of Native American resistance. And once again there were disturbing questions to be answered.

The path which led Big Foot and his followers to Wounded Knee began about one hundred miles north of there, at a small Sioux village on the Cheyenne River. On the morning of December 23, 1890, the Sioux left their village, heading south toward the Pine Ridge Reservation. According to some accounts, Big Foot had been invited to Pine Ridge to settle some disputes between other Sioux factions; according to others, the Indians were going south to collect the payments due to them under the various treaties by which they'd ceded their land and moved into their reservations.

To Major General Nelson Miles, however, both Big Foot's destination and his motives were suspect. Miles was well aware that this was a period of intense unrest among the Sioux. Swarms of white settlers had killed off the buffalo, on which the Sioux depended for food. (In 1890 there were so many white settlers throughout the West that the U.S. Superintendent of the Census could no longer draw a line between those sections of the West that had been settled and those that were still wilderness; the frontier, he conceded, no longer existed.) The move to the reservations had completely disrupted Sioux institutions; major crop failures, epidemics of measles and whooping cough, and corrupt and incompetent government agents had further exacerbated their condition.

By 1890 the Sioux were near starvation. About three thousand had left the reservations and congregated in the Badlands, a stark region of plateaus and cliffs north of the Pine Ridge Reservation. There the Sioux danced the "Ghost Dance," a ritual meant to bring about a new world in which the white man would disappear and the buffalo, along with generations of past Indians, would return. The Ghost Dance was a strange mix of traditional Indian beliefs and messianic Christianity, but to a people feeling as helpless and hopeless as the Sioux, it was hard to resist.

In 1890, many whites saw the Ghost Dance as a war dance, but there's little evidence the Sioux that were killed that year at Wounded Knee were planning a battle. From an 1891 engraving by R. Taylor. Library of Congress.

In most of its forms the Ghost Dance religion, in spite of the apocalyptic images it called forth, did not call for violence against whites. Still, most whites—and Miles in particular—found it extremely threatening. Miles ordered the arrest of the leading Sioux chiefs who practiced the religion. On December 15, Indian policemen employed by the government arrived at the cabin of Sitting Bull—the chief who, along with Crazy Horse, had led the Sioux in the Battle of Little Big Horn. When Sitting Bull resisted, the police shot and killed him.

That left Big Foot as the most prominent Sioux chief who had taken up the Ghost Dance, and Miles ordered him arrested as well. But before the order could be carried out, Big Foot and his band slipped out of their village. The chief said he was heading to the Pine Ridge Reservation but, Miles was quick to note, the chief's destination might just as easily have been the Badlands, where he could join up with the Ghost Dancers most hostile to the whites. More disturbing still, some of Sitting Bull's most militant followers had fled after their chief's death and had reportedly joined Big Foot's band.

Miles ordered his forces to find Big Foot and bring him back. On December 28, a unit of the Seventh Cavalry intercepted the Indians. Big Foot surrendered, and the soldiers escorted the Indians to Wounded Knee. The next morning the Indians awoke to find themselves surrounded by even more soldiers, with cannons pointing down at them from a nearby hill. Colonel Forsyth ordered the Indians to disarm, and when the Sioux turned over only a few old guns, Forsyth sent his soldiers in to search the Indian tipis. With tensions running high on both sides, not much was needed to spark the conflagration.

Precisely what set off the fighting is unclear. According to some eyewitness reports, an Indian medicine man named Yellow Bird began walking among the warriors, telling them their sacred "ghost shirts" would protect them from the white man's bullets. Reportedly, as one of the soldiers lifted an Indian blanket to check for weapons, Yellow Bird threw a handful of dust into the air, signaling the warriors to draw their rifles and open fire. Other eyewitnesses told of how two soldiers grabbed Black Coyote, a deaf warrior who'd been carrying around his rifle, apparently without understanding what was going on. A struggle ensued, the rifle went off accidentally, and the soldiers then opened fire on the mostly disarmed Indians.

Which story did historians believe? It depended, at least partly, on where their sympathies lay. For historians predisposed to finding the Sioux deaths justifiable, the Yellow Bird story demonstrated that the Sioux warriors, or at least some of them, had started the fight. Moreover, it seemed as if they'd planned it in advance; witness the simultaneous appearance of the Indians' weapons upon the signal from Yellow Bird. And these were weapons that had been treacherously concealed after Big Foot had, supposedly, unconditionally surrendered.

For historians more sympathetic to the Indians, the Black Coyote story corroborated their suspicions. The soldiers must have honed in on an Indian who clearly didn't know what was going on, in order to provoke a fight. And, as these historians were quick to remind readers, these were soldiers of Custer's Seventh Cavalry; this was their chance to avenge Little Big Horn.

Viewed objectively, both of these interpretations are unfair: neither the Sioux nor the cavalry plotted in advance to start a fight. For the Sioux, a battle made no sense. They were vastly outnumbered and they had women and children in their midst; however desperate they were, they were not suicidal. Big Foot was suffering from pneumonia and was in no condition to plan a battle. True, he had once been one of the more ardent Ghost Dancers but he'd since lost faith in the religion; besides, he was always more of a peacemaker than a warrior. (Remember, at least according to some accounts, Big Foot was on his way to Pine Ridge to help work out a truce between Indian factions there.)

But if Big Foot and his warriors weren't looking for a fight, neither is there any hard evidence that Forsyth or his soldiers wanted trouble. Miles blamed Forsyth for deploying his troops in such fatal proximity to the Indians but this endangered the troops as well as the Indians; it was more an error of judgment on Forsyth's part than any indication that he was out for blood. Miles himself erred in his initial order to arrest Big Foot; had he left Big Foot alone, he and his followers probably would have ended up on the Pine Ridge Reservation, right where Miles wanted them. But, like Forsyth, Miles hoped to avoid a fight.

So, if neither side planned to fight, who is to blame for starting it? Probably no one. In an atmosphere as highly charged as that of December 29, either Yellow Bird throwing dust in the air or Black Coyote's gun going off could have set off the fight, without any advanced planning on either side. Perhaps both events occurred simultaneously; that would surely have sufficed.

This is not to say, of course, that no one is to blame in any sense. Whatever the immediate cause of the battle, there's no denying that it was preceded by decades of broken treaties, which drove Native Americans from their land. According to an 1868 treaty—the first treaty in which the Sioux agreed to any boundaries on their land—the "unceded Indian territories" would extend, forever, from the Missouri River west to the Big Horn Mountains in Wyoming and from just below the Canadian border south into Nebraska. By 1890, this had been whittled down to reservations comprised of fewer than 16,000 square miles. Moreover, the slaughter of so many women and children can't be attributed to the heat of battle alone; clearly the fighting released deep fears and prejudices and hatreds on the part of the soldiers. In this fundamental sense, then, the soldiers were to blame.

The fighting at Wounded Knee put an end to the Sioux uprising of 1890. Within two weeks, the remaining Ghost Dancers in the Badlands wandered back to the reservations and surrendered. Years later, a Sioux holy man, Black Elk, recalled the scene at Wounded Knee. "I can still see the butchered women and children lying heaped and scattered all along the crooked gulch as plain as I saw them with eyes still young," he said. "And I can see that something else died there in the bloody mud, and was buried in the blizzard. A people's dream died there."

In February 1973 Wounded Knee was back in the headlines. A few hundred Oglala Sioux Indians, joined by activists from AIM, seized the church at the tiny hamlet of Wounded Knee, right outside of which the bodies of Big Foot and his followers had been buried. For many of the Oglala, the occupation was a protest against the tribal council leader, Dick Wilson, whom they considered a puppet of the federal government. Wilson, they felt, was more interested in giving his cronies jobs and giving away mineral rights than in protecting the interests of the tribe. Wilson had organized vigilante squads that had terrorized his opponents. (He called his followers "Guardians of the Oglala Nation"; his opponents called them "goons.")

The leaders of AIM hoped to do more than oust Wilson. Fully aware that Wounded Knee remained a potent symbol of white injustice, they saw its occupation as a chance to publicize their broader grievances: against escalating white violence against Indians on the reservation, against exploitation of Indian lands, and against the federal government's Indian policies in general. In March, citing the long-ignored 1868 treaty, they declared Wounded Knee part of the Independent Oglala Nation.

As in 1890 the Indians of 1973 were vastly outnumbered and outgunned. Besides the Bureau of Indian police and Wilson's forces, the Justice Department sent in U.S. marshals, SWAT teams, and FBI agents. The occupiers held out for 71 days before agreeing to a peaceful settlement. Leaders of AIM had obviously failed to establish an independent nation, and in the end they were also unable to capitalize on the national attention the occupation had generated. Like other revolutionary movements of the '60s and early '70s, AIM soon fell apart under the weight of its own internal divisions and under relentless pressure from the FBI. The Wounded Knee occupation turned out to be the movement's high tide.

Compared to the 1973 occupation, the 1975 shootout, reputedly involving Leonard Peltier and other AIM members, was a sordid affair. It's unclear how the fight started, or what special agents Jack Coler and Ronald Williams were doing on the Pine Ridge Reservation, but it is clear that they were shot from very close range. This was an execution, not a battle that turned out to be fatal.

In response, the FBI launched the biggest manhunt in its history. Four men were eventually indicted; of these, one was released for lack of evidence, two were acquitted by a jury, and the fourth—Peltier—was convicted of murder in the first degree and was sentenced to two consecutive life terms in prison.

AIM claimed Peltier had been set up by the FBI. Supporting this claim was the testimony of a woman named Myrtle Poor Bear. In order to extradite Peltier from Canada, the FBI presented affidavits from Poor Bear in which she claimed to have witnessed Peltier commit the murders. But later she claimed that she'd never seen Peltier in her life and that the FBI had threatened to kill her unless she testified against him. Peltier's defenders also claimed the FBI fixed the ballistics reports to show Peltier's rifle was the murder weapon.

Peltier's case became a *cause célèbre* in the 1970s and 1980s. Novelist and naturalist Peter Matthiessen wrote a book about him and Robert Redford made a movie about him. He was compared to Sacco and Vanzetti, to Nelson Mandela, and to Crazy Horse, among others. Whether Peltier deserved this lionizing is unclear; though some of the government's evidence was tainted, not all of it was. Furthermore, the cold-blooded killing of the FBI agents was no act of heroism, and the 1975 killings ought not to be conflated—as they sometimes were in the rhetoric of Peltier's defenders—with either the 1890 massacre or the 1973 uprising.

Still, there's no denying that, even if he's guilty of murder, Peltier landed in jail (where he still is) because of a federal agency's abuses of Native American rights. In that sense, his story fits all too well into the history of Wounded Knee.

☆ To investigate further:

Mooney, James. *Ghost Dance Religion and Wounded Knee*. New York: Dover, 1973. Originally published in 1896, this remains a valuable study of the Ghost Dance phenomenon.

Utley, Robert. *The Last Days of the Sioux Nation,* New Haven, CT: Yale University Press, 1963. Though too charitable to the soldiers, this remains the best book on the period leading up to and including the 1890 battle.

Brown, Dee. *Bury My Heart at Wounded Knee.* Orlando: Holt, Rinehart & Winston, 1970. The history of the West from the Indians' perspective—so much so that it refers to whites by their Indian names (Custer is at first called "Hard Backsides" because he chased the Indians so long without getting out of his saddle; later he's called "Long Hair"). A best-seller, this was not quite so original in its approach as it claimed, but it is nonetheless a powerful indictment of America's treatment of Native Americans.

S.L.A.M. Marshall, *Crimsoned Prairie: The Wars Between the United States and the Plains Indians During the Winning of the West.* New York: Scribner's, 1972. Old-fashioned both in its highly entertaining narrative style and in its extremely forgiving attitude toward army actions.

Matthiessen, Peter. *In the Spirit of Crazy Horse.* New York: Viking, 1980. Though overly long, the book argues convincingly that Peltier was framed by the FBI. Publication was delayed for eight years because of libel suits by FBI agent David Price and former South Dakota governor William Jankow, two of the book's villains.

Jensen, Richard, R. Eli Paul, and John Carter. *Eyewitness at Wounded Knee.* Lincoln: University of Nebraska Press, 1991. Photographs from before and immediately after the 1890 massacre.

Smith, Paul Chaat and Robert Allen Warrior. *Like a Hurricane.* New York: The New Press, 1996. The rise and fall of the Indian Movement during the 1960s and 1970s.

Chapter 17

What Destroyed the *Maine?*

The U.S. battleship *Maine* arrived in Havana harbor in January 1898, amidst rising tensions between Spain and the United States. Spain was battling Cuban revolutionaries in an effort to hold on to some of its once great empire; the United States sympathized with the revolutionaries and was beginning to flex its own empire-building muscles. Officially the *Maine*'s mission to Cuba was a peaceful one, but both Spaniards and Americans recognized the ship was there as a show of U.S. naval strength and resolve.

So when the ship blew up at 9:40 P.M. on February 15 and 266 crew members were killed, jingoistic Americans had few doubts who was to blame. "The *Maine* was sunk by an act of dirty treachery on the part of the Spaniards," wrote the assistant secretary of the navy Theodore Roosevelt. The February 17 edition of William Randolph Hearst's *New York Journal* ran the headline: "Destruction of the Warship Maine Was the Work of an Enemy"; a front-page drawing was captioned: "The Spaniards, it is believed, arranged to have the *Maine* anchored over one of the harbor mines."

Others took a more cautious approach. President William McKinley told a friend: "We must learn the truth and endeavor, if possible, to fix the responsibility. The country can afford to withhold its judgment and not strike an avenging blow until the truth is known." (Roosevelt's response: "The president has no more backbone than a chocolate eclair.")

The navy quickly appointed a court of inquiry to determine the cause of the explosion, and in late March the court reached its verdict: the *Maine* was destroyed by a submerged mine. Though the court was unable to determine who placed or detonated the mine, the verdict released more pro-war sentiment than McKinley could resist. Even if the Spanish didn't set off the mine, it was clear to the president that most Americans considered them culpably negligent. The *Journal* had a new war cry: "Remember the Maine! To hell with Spain!" By mid-April the United States and Spain were at war.

Was the court's verdict correct? Was Spain to blame? Or did the United States go to war over what was nothing more than an accident—albeit a tragic one?

The 1898 court of inquiry was comprised of four naval officers, presided over by Captain William T. Sampson. The first to testify before them was Charles Sigsbee, the captain (and obviously, a survivor) of the *Maine*. Sigsbee testified that all required safety procedures had been followed on the ship. He said that prior to the explosion he had personally checked the coal bunkers in the forward part of the ship (where the explosion had taken place) and they had not been hot enough to set off an accidental fire. The implication was clear: if it hadn't been an onboard accident, it had to have been a mine.

What really swayed the court, however, was not Sigsbee's testimony but that of the next witness, Ensign Wilfred Van Nest Powelson. Powelson had studied naval architecture and he had been working on the scene, interviewing navy divers as they came up from the wreck. He described what the divers had seen. The shattered keel of the battleship appeared to have been bent in the form of an inverted V, where the explosion had been centered. Also, a section of bottom plating had been twisted up to within four feet of the surface.

The upward bending of the metal suggested that an explosion had pushed it up from *underneath* the ship. This was the first solid evidence of a mine. It was enough to convince the Sampson court.

Meanwhile, the Spaniards were conducting their own official investigation. Not surprisingly, they reached a very different conclusion. Had the explosion been caused by a mine, the Spanish report pointed

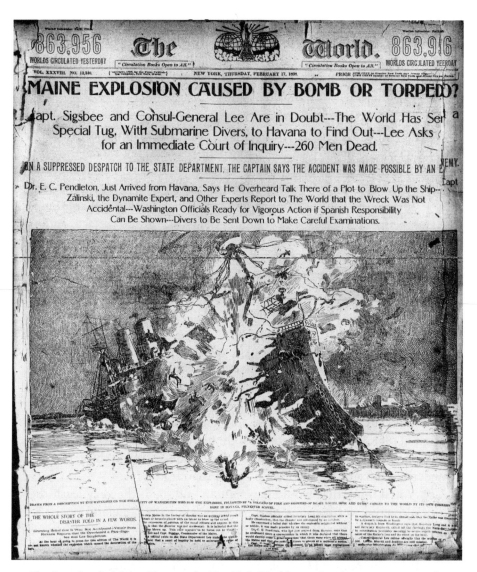

The day after the Maine blew up, the New York World *was already preparing to pin the blame on the Spanish, and it didn't take long for others in the press to call for revenge. In March 1898, before a navy court of inquiry had reached any verdict, illustrator Frederic Remington asked publisher William Randolph Hearst of the New York* Journal *if he could return home from Cuba. "Please remain," replied Hearst. "You furnish the pictures and I'll furnish the war." Library of Congress.*

out, witnesses should have heard a dull concussion rather than the sharp report most reported. Had a mine exploded, there should have been a visible geyser but no one reported seeing any upheaval of water. And had there been a mine, there ought to have been lots of dead fish in the harbor, but there were none.

Granted, the Spanish didn't have the same access to the ship's remains as did the Americans, and they also had an interest in seeing themselves cleared. But they raised some disturbing questions, and doubts about the Sampson court's conclusions lingered, even after the Americans rather easily won the 1898 war.

In 1910, therefore, Congress assigned the Army Corps of Engineers the formidable task of bringing the *Maine* to the surface, and in 1911 President Taft appointed a naval board of inspection to analyze the wreck and determine what caused the explosion. This second naval inquiry, with Rear Admiral Charles Vreeland as its most senior member, examined the evidence in far greater detail than could the first court, but their conclusions were much the same. They dismissed the arguments raised by the Spanish inquiry by noting that a few witnesses did hear a dull concussion and that a column of water might have been thrown up by the explosion but hidden by the dense clouds of fire and smoke that followed almost immediately. As for the dead fish, the Vreeland board suggested fish might only have been stunned by the explosion.

On only one issue did the 1911 Vreeland board differ from the original 1898 Sampson court. Though the second report agreed the explosion had been caused by a submerged mine, it placed the explosion underneath frame 27 of the ship rather than frame 18.

You'd think that would have put an end to, at the very least, the official navy investigations. But 62 years after the Vreeland board issued its report, the maverick Admiral Hyman G. Rickover, the navy's leading nuclear submarine expert, was intrigued by a newspaper article about the *Maine*. He took it upon himself to resolve the mystery once and for all, and he enlisted the aid of an engineer from the Naval Ship Research and Development Center and a physicist from the Naval Surface Weapons Center. After revisiting the 1898 and 1911 evidence, Rickover concluded that both courts had been wrong, and that there had been no mine under the *Maine*. The explosion, he believed, had been caused by an internal, accidental fire in bunker A-16.

Rickover put forth a number of arguments: among them that Sigsbee had taken only ordinary measures to guard against an accident (and, in fact, two other ships had been found to be dirty while under his command); that both the 1898 and 1911 boards had been under a great deal of pressure to exonerate the navy and to blame the Spaniards; and that the inner bottom plating was more mangled than the outer bottom plating at the point where the 1911 board thought the mine had been placed. In addition, Rickover cited his modern experts' findings that the upward folding of the bottom plating could have been caused by an internal explosion.

The response to the Rickover report was largely positive. Most historians were impressed by one of the navy's own admirals taking on the navy's official findings; remember, it was in 1976 that Rickover's report was first published and post-Vietnam mistrust of the military was rampant. A few historians took issue with his technical analysis, arguing that just because Rickover's experts demonstrated the upward folding *could* have been caused by an internal explosion, that didn't prove it *couldn't* have been caused by an external one. And some questioned whether all of this nuclear-age expertise was relevant to an examination of the workings of antique musket powder. But most considered Rickover's analysis admirable, if not definitive.

Yet, amidst all the technical analysis, what often seemed lost was the question of motive.

If we assume for the moment that it was a mine that blew up the *Maine,* must we therefore assume that it was the Spaniards who placed and detonated it? The Spaniards were desperate to avoid war with the United States; as they fought to hold on to their colony, the last thing in the world they wanted to see was the United States intervening on behalf of the Cuban revolutionaries. In fact, only a few days before the explosion, the Spanish commander in Havana had taken Sigsbee to the bullfights as his guest. And after the explosion the Spaniards appeared as horrified, if not more so, than the Americans.

In the near century since the explosion, a number of other suspects have been put forward. Though the Spanish government may have been eager to avoid war with the United States, there were many in the Spanish military, especially followers of the hardline General Valeriano Weyler, who resented the presence of the *Maine* in their harbor. In November 1897 Weyler had been replaced by the more moderate General Ramón Blanco y Eranas, who was actively pursuing some form of autonomy for Cuba. To Weyler's followers, therefore, the *Maine*'s destruction was a double cause for celebration: it was a blow against both the Yankee meddlers and the spineless moderates.

Who else had reason to want the United States in the war? The rebels themselves, perhaps. Their military position had not improved during the two months previous to the explosion and could only be helped by the Spaniards having to defend themselves against the Americans. In addition, the more moderate Spanish government presented a political threat to them as well as to the Weylerites. The limited autonomy offered by the moderates was unacceptable to revolutionaries bent on full independence—and the *Maine*'s destruction guaranteed that compromise would never come to pass.

Who else? Could an American eager to get us into the war be responsible? Ferdinand Lundberg, one of William Randolph Hearst's biographers, pointed a finger at the publisher. Hearst had been involved in other intrigues in Cuba, and a few days before the explosion, when his illustrator Frederic Remington asked permission to return home from Cuba, Hearst wired back: "Please remain. You furnish the pictures and I'll furnish the war." And Hearst certainly profited from the war: two days after the explosion, the *Journal*'s circulation rose to over a million.

But Hearst's blustering and profiting amounted to circumstantial evidence, at best. Without question the most likely culprits were extremists, either of the Spanish or the rebel variety. Both had reason to want to see the ship destroyed. And while it seems unlikely historians will ever know for sure whether it was Spaniards or revolutionaries—or fate—that blew up the *Maine,* almost all do agree that the forces unleashed by that explosion not only propelled us into war with Spain but into a prominent role in world affairs from which we have never retreated.

☆ To investigate further:

Message from the President of the United States Transmitting the Report of the Naval Court of Inquiry Upon the Destruction of the United States Battle Ship Maine in Havana Harbor. Washington, DC: Government Printing Office, 1898. Includes the testimony taken before the court as well as the court's report and the president's response to it.

Wilson, Herbert W. *The Downfall of Spain*. New York: Little, Brown, 1900. Wilson was the first historian to tackle the mystery; his book is a thorough examination of what was then known.

Weems, John Edward. *The Fate of the Maine*. New York: Henry Holt and Company, 1958. Leans toward a mine, but doesn't rule out the possibility of an accident.

Thomas, Hugh. *Cuba: The Pursuit of Freedom*. New York: Harper & Row, 1971. Leans toward an accidental explosion, but considers the Cuban revolutionaries the most likely candidate to have detonated a mine.

Rickover, H. G. *How the Battleship Maine Was Destroyed*. Washington, DC: Department of the Navy, 1976. Rickover's case against a mine, along with the report of his technical experts.

O'Toole, G. J. A. *The Spanish War*. New York: Norton, 1984. One of the most recent and readable histories of the war.

Blow, Michael. *A Ship to Remember*. New York: Morrow, 1992. A balanced presentation, which concludes that the *Maine*'s destruction remains an unsolvable mystery.

Samuels, Peggy and Harold. *Remembering the Maine*. Washington, DC: Smithsonian Institution Press, 1995. The case that Weyler's followers set off a mine.

Chapter 18

Were Sacco
and Vanzetti Guilty?

No murder case—with the possible exception of O. J. Simpson's—has so sharply divided the country as that of Sacco and Vanzetti. To their supporters, Sacco and Vanzetti were, in the words of the latter, "a good shoemaker and a poor fish peddler." They were prosecuted and ultimately executed because they were radicals and immigrants in a society that would tolerate neither. That view was shared by Governor Michael Dukakis of Massachusetts, the state in which Sacco and Vanzetti lived and died. In 1977, 50 years after Sacco and Vanzetti had been executed, Dukakis declared that "any stigma and disgrace should be forever removed from the names of Nicola Sacco and Bartolomeo Vanzetti."

Revisionists have argued that Sacco and Vanzetti were indeed guilty and by the late 1960s the consensus among historians seemed to be that Sacco, at least, was probably guilty, though Vanzetti was probably not. That consensus proved shortlived, however. In the late 1980s both sides uncovered new evidence, and both sides claimed their new evidence proved they'd been right all along.

☆ ☆ ☆

The murders for which Sacco and Vanzetti were executed took place on April 15, 1920, in the town of South Braintree, 12 miles south of Boston. In the course of stealing the Slater and Morrill shoe factory's

$15,776 payroll, robbers shot and killed the paymaster, Frederick Parmenter, and his guard, Alessandro Berardelli. The crime followed a similar but unsuccessful holdup that took place in nearby Bridgewater a few months earlier; in the Bridgewater attempt, it was the L. Q. White shoe factory's payroll that the criminals were after. Both crimes took place in daylight, in front of dozens of witnesses who told police the criminals looked Italian.

Italians were on the mind of Chief Michael Stewart of the Bridgewater police for other reasons as well. The country was in the midst of what came to be known as the Red Scare. In response to the Bolshevik success in Russia as well as a series of strikes, riots, and bombings that took place in America during 1919, local police forces across the country were cracking down on radical immigrant groups. On January 2, 1920, more than four thousand foreigners were arrested, of whom more than five hundred were ultimately deported.

Among those just deported was a local anarchist named Furrucio Coaccio. Stewart recalled that Coaccio's deportation had been very easy; too easy, it now seemed. Was it possible, Stewart wondered, that Coaccio had seen his deportation as an opportunity to get out of the country quickly—with the loot from the South Braintree robbery? Stewart's suspicions were further aroused when he discovered that Mike Boda, who was now living in Coaccio's house, was an employee of the L. Q. White Shoe Company. He went to see Boda but Boda was gone.

Boda, however, had left his car behind at the local garage. Stewart asked the garage owner to let him know right away if Boda came to pick it up. Boda came by on May 5, but, before the police could get there, he took off. Left behind for the police were the two men who had accompanied him to pick up the car: Sacco and Vanzetti.

Soon the police had more reasons to suspect Sacco and Vanzetti. Both were armed, Sacco with a .32 caliber Colt automatic pistol and Vanzetti with a .38 caliber Harrington and Richardson revolver. What's more, both lied to the police; they denied knowing Boda and they denied being involved with any radical groups. Each of these claims was easily shown to be false, since the garage owner had told police they arrived with Boda and since Sacco had on him an announcement of an anarchist meeting at which Vanzetti was to speak.

The trial of Sacco and Vanzetti began on May 31, 1921. The prosecution made much of the lies the defendants had told the police, arguing that it revealed their "consciousness of guilt." More damning, perhaps, was the testimony of seven witnesses who identified Sacco as having been in South Braintree before, during, or after the shooting. No one placed Vanzetti at the shooting, but two witnesses said they saw him in the getaway car and two others said they saw him in or around South Braintree earlier in the morning of the crime.

Most damning of all was the physical evidence against the two. Not only was Vanzetti armed when he was arrested but the Harrington and Richardson revolver was the same kind of gun that the slain guard, Alessandro Berardelli, had owned; the prosecution argued that Vanzetti had taken it from him during the robbery. For Sacco, the situation was worse still: two expert prosecution witnesses, William Proctor and Charles Van Amburgh, testified that one of the bullets taken from Berardelli's body, known as Bullet III, had been fired through the Colt .32 automatic found on Sacco on the night of his arrest.

To all of the prosecution's evidence, the defense had an answer.

To the "consciousness of guilt" argument, Sacco and Vanzetti answered that, yes, they had lied to the police—but the guilt they had been conscious of was that they were radicals and foreigners. In fact, on the night they were arrested, they now admitted, they had planned to pick up Boda's car and use it to move some incriminating radical literature to a safer hiding place. No wonder they had lied to the police; in the midst of a massive roundup of radical foreigners, they assumed that's what they were being arrested for. They were concealing their involvement in a radical anarchist group, not their involvement in a murder.

As for the eyewitnesses, the defense had plenty of its own. A total of eleven eyewitnesses had placed either Sacco or Vanzetti at or near the crime scene, but plenty of other eyewitnesses had seen one or more of the robbers and failed to identify either of the defendants. The defense also attempted to impeach the testimony of the prosecution's witnesses, pointing out, for example, that one of those who identified Vanzetti stated he had spoken in clear English while in fact Vanzetti had a heavy Italian accent. Finally, the defense put on the stand witnesses who claimed to have been with Sacco and Vanzetti at the time of the crime—and nowhere near the crime scene (though the prosecution attempted to discredit the alibis by pointing out that these witnesses were friends of the defendants and fellow anarchists).

On the whole, the eyewitness testimony probably cancelled itself out. For every prosecution witness, there was a defense witness to contradict his or her story; for every defense witness, a prosecution wit-

SACCO FLAYS CAPITALISTS IN FIERY SPEECH IN COURT

Holds Courtroom Spellbound by Address---Went to Mexico to Escape War Service, He States--- Proud of Having Been a Slacker

A cap found at the murder site didn't fit Sacco, but—in contrast to those who watched O. J. Simpson struggle to get his hand into a glove—this jury was unmoved. From the Boston Post, *July 8, 1921.*

ness told otherwise. That made the physical evidence all the more crucial, and though the defense also had its own experts, the testimony of
Proctor and Van Amburgh was persuasive. On July 14, seven weeks after the trial began, the jury found Sacco and Vanzetti guilty of murder
in the first degree.

☆ ☆ ☆

But the defense had just begun to fight. Defense attorneys submitted a
series of motions for a new trial. One included an affidavit from Proctor, whose testimony had been instrumental in securing a conviction.
In the affidavit, Proctor stated: "Bullet number III, in my judgment,
passed through some Colt automatic pistol, but I do not intend by that
answer to imply that I had found any evidence that the so-called mor-
tal bullet had passed through this particular Colt automatic."

This was a far cry from his trial testimony, where he had clearly
implied that it was Sacco's specific gun that had fired the fatal bullet.
Furthermore, Proctor admitted to arranging the careful phrasing of
the trial testimony with the DA in order to leave the jury with the
wrong impression. This was virtually an admission that he'd conspired
with the DA to commit perjury; it cast doubts not only on Proctor's
credibility but on the integrity of the DA. Nevertheless, on October 1,
1924, Judge Webster Thayer denied the defense's motion for a new trial.

The next bombshell came in November 1925. Celestino Madeiros, who was being held in the same prison with Sacco while appealing a conviction for murder during a bank robbery, came forward
and confessed to participating in the shoe company robberies.
Madeiros would not name his confederates, but he did say that neither
Sacco nor Vanzetti had anything to do with the crimes. Defense attorney Herbert Ehrmann undertook his own investigation and determined that Madeiros had been working with a Providence gang under
the leadership of Joe Morelli. The gang had been charged with other
robberies of the same Slater and Morrill shoe company that Sacco and
Vanzetti had supposedly robbed. More remarkable still was the striking resemblance between Sacco and Joe Morelli: when Ehrmann
showed prosecution and defense witnesses a picture of Morelli, a
number of them identified him as Sacco.

Again, however, Thayer was unmoved. In October 1926, after ob-
serving that Madeiros, when questioned, seemed unfamiliar with the
scene of the crime, Thayer dismissed the defense motion for a new

trial. In April 1927, he sentenced Sacco and Vanzetti to die, and on August 23, 1927 the sentence was carried out.

☆ ☆ ☆

Still, the case would not die. Writers on each side continued to research and publish, with defenders of Sacco and Vanzetti especially prolific. These tended to emphasize the prejudices of the judge or jury, and of the country as a whole during the Red Scare.

Then in 1962, Francis Russell published one of the most influential of the revisionist studies of the case. Originally convinced that Sacco and Vanzetti were innocent, Russell came to believe that Sacco, at least, was guilty. Russell's change of heart began after he learned that Fred Moore, the primary defense lawyer during the first four years of the case, thought that Sacco was guilty. He was further persuaded when he learned that Carlo Tresca, a leading Italian-American anarchist, also thought Sacco was guilty.

But Russell still had to resolve the question of Bullet III. In 1961 he set up new tests during which ballistics experts found that Bullet III had indeed come from Sacco's gun. For Russell, this clinched the case.

But the defense had some new evidence of its own. After the Massachussets State Police released an enormous file on the case in response to a freedom of information act suit, William Young and David Kaiser discovered that Vanzetti's gun was *not* that of the guard, Berardelli, as the prosecution had claimed. More shocking still, the prosecution knew this and concealed its findings from the defense. As for Bullet III, Sacco's defenders conceded the bullet came from his gun, but noted that, according to the autopsy report and eyewitness reports in the newly released police files, the same assailant had fired all four bullets into Berardelli. How, then, could only one of the four bullets have come from Sacco's gun? To Young and Kaiser, there could only be one explanation: a bullet was shot from Sacco's gun *after the murder,* and then was substituted for one of the real bullets.

In short, according to this latest evidence, Sacco and Vanzetti were framed. Whether because they were convinced of their guilt, or just because they wanted to get rid of a couple of troublesome Italian radicals, the district attorney and his assistant used evidence they knew to be false in order to convict Sacco and Vanzetti.

For most historians, the Young/Kaiser conclusions were more convincing than Russell's. Russell assumed Moore and Tresca knew enough to determine whether Sacco and Vanzetti were guilty, but there's no way to test that evidence. Even Russell couldn't question these witnesses; he heard what each said through intermediaries. At best, Russell's evidence is hearsay; at worst, mere rumor.

The new evidence tending to exonerate Sacco and Vanzetti, in contrast, came directly from the prosecution and police files. Even before Sacco and Vanzetti were executed, the defense had questioned the state's credibility on such matters as Proctor's testimony and the reluctance to pursue the Madeiros lead. Now it became even more difficult to trust the state. The new evidence may not have proven Sacco and Vanzetti were innocent, but it certainly leaves us with reasonable doubts.

So, too, do recent studies of the pair's anarchist backgrounds. The radical organizations in which both Sacco and Vanzetti were involved were committed to violent insurrections. There's even some circumstantial evidence that Sacco and Vanzetti may have been involved in some of the 1919 bombings that led to the Red Scare (and, indirectly, to their arrest). When Sacco and Vanzetti lied to the police after their arrest, they may have been covering up more than their membership in a radical organization; it's very possible they were planning to use Boda's car to transport some explosives, rather than the radical literature they talked about at their trial. Ironically, however, this violent background also attested to the pair's innocence. Anarchists were committed to violence—but for the sake of revolution, not robbery. And there has never been any sign that the Bridgewater and South Braintree robberies were motivated by anything other than greed.

☆ To investigate further:

Frankfurter, Felix. *The Case of Sacco and Vanzetti.* New York: Little, Brown, 1927. The future Supreme Court Justice's passionate argument that the trial was unfair and that Sacco and Vanzetti were innocent.

Frankfurter, Marion and Gardner Jackson, editors. *The Letters of Sacco and Vanzetti.* New York: Viking, 1928. After reading Vanzetti's eloquent and moving letters, it's easy to see why so many believed so strongly that he could not be guilty of murder.

Fraenkel, Osmond. *The Sacco-Vanzetti Case.* New York: Knopf, 1931. Includes extensive selections from the court records.

Ehrmann, Herbert. *The Untried Case*. New York: Vanguard, 1933. How Ehrmann, one of the attorneys for the defense, put together the case against the Morelli gang.

Joughin, Louis and Edmund Morgan. *The Legacy of Sacco and Vanzetti*. New York: Harcourt Brace, 1948; reissued in 1971 by Princeton University Press (Princeton, NJ). A balanced case for the defense, which also traces how the case was represented in the press and in the arts.

Montgomery, Robert. *Sacco-Vanzetti: The Murder and the Myth*. Greenwich, CT: Devin-Adair, 1960. The first of the revisionist studies.

Russell, Francis. *Tragedy in Dedham*, New York: McGraw-Hill, 1962. Sacco was guilty, Vanzetti innocent.

Felix, David. *Protest: Sacco-Vanzetti and the Intellectuals*, Bloomington: Indiana University Press, 1965. A somewhat shrill and unfocused revisionist effort.

Ehrmann, Herbert. *The Case That Will Not Die*. New York: Little, Brown, 1969. The case for the defense, by one of the defense attorneys.

Feuerlicht, Roberta. *Justice Crucified*, New York: McGraw-Hill, 1977. A passionate case for innocence, though it adds little evidence to previous studies.

Young, William, and David Kaiser. *Postmortem*. Amherst: The University of Massachusetts Press, 1985. The latest evidence and one of the best cases for innocence.

Russell, Francis. *Sacco and Vanzetti*. New York: Harper & Row, 1986. In 1982, Russell received a letter from Ideala Gambera, the son of a radical who had known Sacco and Vanzetti. Gambera said his father had told him that everyone in the anarchists' circle knew Sacco was guilty; for Russell, this was yet more proof that both were guilty. But it's still just hearsay, and except for this letter Russell had little to say that wasn't in his 1962 book, *Tragedy in Dedham*. That first book remains the better of the two, and the best of all the revisionist studies.

Avrich, Paul. *Sacco and Vanzetti*. Princeton, NJ: Princeton University Press, 1991. Though it takes no final position on the pair's guilt or innocence, this is unique and important for its investigation of the political movement of which they were a part.

Chapter 19

Who Kidnapped
the Lindbergh Baby?

Of the most famous trials of the twentieth century—those of Sacco and Vanzetti, Alger Hiss, the Rosenbergs, and O. J. Simpson—the Lindbergh kidnapping trial stands out for its lack of political significance. No one could say the accused, Bruno Richard Hauptmann, was being tried because of his politics or his race. Yet the 1932 crime and trial gripped the American press and public at least as firmly as any of these others. In the days and months following the kidnapping, sightseeing planes circled the scene of the crime, hot dog vendors lined up along the road where the body was found, and among the many thousands of letters the Lindbergh family received were 12,000 just from people eager to recount their dreams about the case.

Partly, of course, this was sheer voyeurism. The father of the kidnapped child was Charles Lindbergh, the first man to fly solo across the Atlantic. In a country which celebrated both individualism and technology, the 1927 flight guaranteed Lindbergh heroic status. This was only enhanced by his 1929 marriage to Anne Morrow, the daughter of a prominent banker and ambassador, and then by the birth of their blond-haired, blue-eyed baby, Charles Jr., a year later. But Lindbergh's status alone cannot explain the fascination with the kidnapping of Charles Jr. In the early years of the Depression, the crime tapped into deeper fears about what the future held for America's children. No wonder that Maurice Sendak, author and artist of some of the spookiest children's stories of any time, once said: "All of my books are really about the Lindbergh kidnapping."

For most Americans, therefore, the arrest, conviction, and execution of Hauptmann brought some satisfaction. But it was distinctly less satisfying that Hauptmann went to his death proclaiming his innocence. In the years since then, others have taken up his cause, contending that in their eagerness to solve such a highly publicized crime, the police arrested—and the state of New Jersey put to death—an innocent man.

☆ ☆ ☆

The kidnapping took place the evening of March 1, 1932, at the Lindbergh's newly finished house near Hopewell, New Jersey. Normally the family stayed there only on weekends, living the rest of the time at the Morrow family estate. But this particular week they decided to stay on. About eight o'clock Anne Lindbergh and her nursemaid Betty Gow put the baby to bed; at ten Gow went to check on him and found he was gone.

Instead, the Lindberghs found a note that read:

> Have 50,000 $ redy 25000 $ in 20 $ bills 15000 $ in 10 $ bills and 10000 $ in 5 $ bills. After 2–4 days we will inform you were to deliver the Money. We warn you for making anyding public or for notify the Polise the child is in gut care.

At the bottom of the note were two intersecting circles, with the oval intersection colored red. This, the note said, was a "singnature" by which the Lindberghs would be able to recognize that future notes were from the actual kidnappers and not some other extortionist trying to cash in without actually having the child.

Indeed, the Lindberghs were soon besieged by a variety of shady characters. One was the recently jailed gangster Al Capone, who offered his services as an intermediary between the Lindberghs and the kidnappers—in return for Capone's freedom. The offer was declined.

Others were more successful in convincing the Lindberghs they could help. A former justice department agent, Gaston Means, claimed to know the kidnappers and convinced Evalyn Walsh McLean, the owner of the Hope diamond, to donate $100,000 to save the baby's

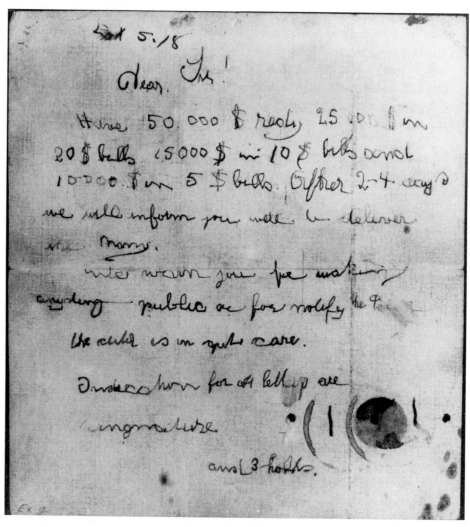

This ransom note was found on the windowsill of the Lindbergh baby's nursery. The handwriting matched Bruno Richard Hauptmann's, and the fact that it was clearly written by someone of German background (note the use of "anyding" instead of "anything" and "gut" instead of "good") was also held against the German-born defendant. Courtesy of the New Jersey State Police.

life—after which the money and Means promptly disappeared. (Means was eventually tracked down and convicted of embezzlement.) Another con artist, named Mickey Rosner, moved into the Lindbergh house and spent more than a week there, monopolizing their phone lines with calls to his supposed intermediaries, before the Lindberghs gave up on him and had the police throw him out.

Of all those who offered help, perhaps the most unlikely connection to the kidnappers turned out to be the most legitimate. This was Dr. John Condon, a retired schoolteacher from the Bronx. Condon was in the habit of writing eccentric letters to the Bronx *Home News,* and in one of his letters he offered his services to the kidnappers as an intermediary. Remarkably, they responded: on March 9 he received a letter with the telltale intersecting circles. This ultimately led to a rendezvous with the kidnappers at St. Raymond's Cemetery on the night of April 2. While Lindbergh remained in the car, Condon met with a man who identified himself as "John"; in return for $50,000, John gave Condon a note telling where to find the baby. Alas, a thorough search of the area described in the note turned up nothing. Seven weeks later the baby's body was found, just a couple of miles from the Lindbergh house.

Though the efforts to save the baby had been in vain, the search for the kidnappers went on. The police had noted all the serial numbers on the ransom notes Condon had given to John; moreover, the ransom was paid largely in gold certificates that, because of new currency regulations, were increasingly rare, and the police hoped this would make them easier to track. Sure enough, about two and a half years later, a gas station attendant was handed a ten-dollar gold certificate. Suspecting it might be counterfeit, he wrote down the car's license number on the certificate. And when a bank identified the certificate as ransom money the police tracked down the car's owner, Bruno Richard Hauptmann. A search of Hauptmann's garage uncovered a shoebox with $13,760 more of Lindbergh ransom money.

The evidence against Hauptmann seemed overwhelming. Handwriting experts identified Hauptmann's handwriting as the same as that on the ransom note. Condon, after some initial hesitation, identified Hauptmann as the "John" to whom he'd given the ransom money in the graveyard. Lindbergh himself identified John's voice as the same voice he'd heard from the car, as he sat waiting for Condon near the graveyard. Above all, there was the ransom money found in Hauptmann's possession.

Hauptmann's background didn't help his case. He was a German immigrant, and the spelling errors in the ransom note ("gut" for "good," "anyding" for "anything") were consistent with what might be expected from a native German speaker. Worse, Hauptmann had fled Germany to avoid sentencing for crimes that included using a ladder to enter a second-floor bedroom window (as had been the case in the kidnapping), and robbing two women who were pushing baby carriages down the street.

It seemed an open-and-shut case. Certainly the jury thought so: though five jurors favored life imprisonment instead of the death penalty, none doubted his guilt. Hauptmann was electrocuted on April 3, 1936.

☆ ☆ ☆

And yet, to his death, Hauptmann proclaimed his innocence. Even when New Jersey's governor offered to convert his sentence to life imprisonment in return for a confession, Hauptmann refused.

Revisionists took up his cause. Anthony Scaduto in 1976 and Ludovic Kennedy in 1985 published books contending the evidence against Hauptmann was at best flimsy. Handwriting analysis was a notoriously subjective science, not the basis for a conviction, they argued. And Condon, though an impressive courtroom witness, had been extremely hesitant about picking Hauptmann out of a police lineup. To revisionists, this was best explained as the result of pressure from the authorities: the police might have threatened Condon that if he didn't identify Hauptmann decisively, they'd prosecute him as an accomplice. As for Lindbergh, he admitted he'd only heard "John" say a couple of words at the graveyard; that he identified the voice as Hauptmann's with such certainty could be another sign that the authorities had inappropriately pressured a witness, perhaps by playing on a father's fear that if he didn't come through at the trial his son's murderer would go free.

According to Scaduto and Kennedy, the case against Hauptmann was based on this kind of trumped-up evidence. The police and prosecutors—under tremendous pressure to solve the most widely talked about crime of the age—had railroaded through a conviction. Scaduto also claimed that the police had interrogated Hauptmann mercilessly, even beaten him, in a vain effort to elicit a confession.

But what about the ransom money? Even if we concede that the authorities trampled on Hauptmann's rights as a defendant, how could revisionists explain the money in his possession? Well, Hauptmann himself always maintained that a friend, Isidor Fisch, had asked him to hold on to the shoebox with the money while Fisch returned to Germany to visit his parents. Only accidentally did Hauptmann discover the box was full of money, and only because Fisch owed him money had Hauptmann spent some of it. Fisch, alas, had died shortly before the arrest.

To revisionists like Scaduto and Kennedy, this was as good an explanation as any. To most historians, however, the Fisch story was just that—a fish story, made up by Hauptmann in a desperate attempt to save himself. A 1987 book by Jim Fisher, a former FBI agent who'd gone through the newly opened New Jersey State Police archives, concluded that, although the police might have violated some of Hauptmann's rights, there was no evidence that they'd cooked up any evidence against him. Most historians have agreed with Fisher—and with the jury—that Hauptmann was guilty.

Many, however, have questioned whether he acted alone. Might Fisch have been a co-conspirator? Or was there another conspirator somewhere inside the Lindbergh house? If not, how could Hauptmann have known the layout of the house? More tellingly, how could he have known that the Lindberghs would be staying there on that particular Tuesday, contrary to their usual custom?

All this pointed to inside help, perhaps from one of the Lindbergh servants. Colonel Norman Schwarzkopf of the New Jersey State Police (the father of the Desert Storm commander) suspected an inside job from the start, but Lindbergh refused to let Schwarzkopf question the servants. He steadfastly maintained they were entirely trustworthy.

Lindbergh's motives for standing in Schwarzkopf's way are unclear. Perhaps it was because he'd been taken in by the various con men claiming to know the kidnappers. One can understand how a desperate parent would want to believe in anyone offering hope. Perhaps, too, it was reassuring to Lindbergh to think that his son was in the hands of professional gangsters—if they were in it just for the money, they would be less likely to harm the child. Or perhaps, as Joyce Milton suggested in her 1993 biography, Lindbergh couldn't bear to think that he'd been betrayed by servants he'd trusted.

Whatever his motives, the restrictions Lindbergh placed on Schwarzkopf frustrated not only police but historians. Because questions about inside help were not asked then, they cannot be answered now. And so, though we can be fairly sure Hauptmann was guilty, we must also suspect that others, equally guilty, went free.

☆ To investigate further:

Whipple, Sidney. *The Trial of Bruno Richard Hauptmann*. New York: Doubleday, 1937. Includes a complete transcript of the trial.

Lindbergh, Anne Morrow. *Hour of Gold, Hour of Lead*. New York: Harcourt Brace Jovanovich, 1973. A mother's heartbreaking diaries and letters.

Scaduto, Anthony. *Scapegoat*. New York: Putnam's, 1976. Even if it doesn't convince you Hauptmann was framed, it will convince you his rights were violated.

Kennedy, Ludovic. *The Airman and the Carpenter*. New York: Viking, 1985. Kennedy's three previous books resulted in the posthumous pardon or release of convicted murderers; this one didn't succeed in overturning Hauptmann's conviction but it is the most persuasive argument for his innocence.

Fisher, Jim. *The Lindbergh Case*. New Brunswick, NJ: Rutgers University Press, 1987. The most recent and most thorough case against Hauptmann.

Milton, Joyce. *Loss of Eden*. New York: HarperCollins, 1993. A dual biography of Charles and Anne Morrow Lindbergh, including the best statement of the case that Hauptmann was the kidnapper—but not the only one.

Behn, Noel. *Lindbergh: The Crime*. New York: Atlantic Monthly Press, 1994. Contends the baby was killed in a fit of envy by Anne Morrow Lindbergh's sister, after which—to prevent a scandal—the family concocted the kidnapping story. Though an intriguing explanation for Lindbergh's refusal to let the police question the servants, it's ultimately unconvincing.

Chapter 20

Did Babe Ruth Call His Shot?

By 1932 Babe Ruth was already past his prime; at 38, his years of eating and drinking too much were catching up with him. No longer was he the best hitter in baseball, let alone the greatest player ever, as he once had been. Still to come, however, was the single most dramatic—and most disputed—moment of his career: his "called shot."

The setting was Chicago, the third game of the World Series between the Chicago Cubs and the New York Yankees. The Yankees had won the first two in New York and the Cub players and fans were restless and surly, tossing insults and lemons onto the field. In the fourth inning, with the score tied, Ruth came to bat; from the Chicago stands came cries that Ruth was old, he was fat, he was washed up. The Chicago pitcher, Charlie Root, threw two strikes and the jeering intensified.

Here's how Ruth recalled what happened next, in his autobiography:

> I stepped back again and pointed my finger at those bleachers, which only caused the mob to howl that much more at me. Root threw a fast ball . . . I swung from the ground with everything I had and as I hit the ball every muscle in my system, every sense I had,

told me that I had never hit a better one, that as long as I lived nothing would ever feel as good as this.

I didn't have to look. But I did. That ball just went on and on and on and hit far up in the center-field bleachers in exactly the spot I had pointed to.

A crucial home run in the World Series is itself a guarantee of at least temporary fame; this "called shot"—a home run before which the batter predicted not just the exact pitch he'd hit but the exact place it would land—was a story destined for immortality.

But did it actually happen?

You'd think this mystery would be a cinch to solve. After all, more than 51,000 people were in Chicago's Wrigley Field when Ruth came to bat. Sportswriters from across the country witnessed the game, and the next few days' newspapers were filled with reports of the home run. In the *New York World-Telegram,* Joe Williams wrote that "with the Cubs riding him unmercifully from the bench, Ruth pointed to center field and punched a screaming liner to a spot where no ball ever had been hit before."

A couple of days later, Paul Gallico wrote in the *New York Daily News* that "Ruth pointed like a duellist to the spot where he expected to send his rapier home." A day after that, Bill Corum wrote for the Hearst newspapers that Ruth "pointed out where he was going to hit the next one, and hit it there."

Given Ruth's history as a great hitter and showman, the story seemed credible. This wasn't even the first time Ruth had called his shot. Back in 1926, another story went, he'd visited a dying boy in the hospital and promised to hit a home run for him; the next day he hit a home run and the boy miraculously recovered. The facts in that case were not quite so dramatic: in reality, the boy had been hospitalized after falling from a horse and was by no means dying, and Ruth didn't visit him in person until after he hit the home run. But he had sent the boy an autographed baseball along with a promise to hit one for him, and then he did hit the home run the next day. Not so fantastic, when you think about it: for a hitter with 714 lifetime home runs and a tremendous love of the spotlight, it was to be expected that some of the home runs were going to come after some of the promises.

Did Ruth point to the center-field bleachers before the most famous home run of his career? Depends who you ask. Courtesy of Thomas L. Carwile.

Still, the 1932 World Series called shot was in a class by itself. In this instance Ruth had called the specific pitch and the specific spot to which he'd hit it. The odds against success were astronomical; even Ruth, in an interview with the sportswriter John Carmichael, once admitted there was an element of luck involved.

Inevitably, there were skeptics.

Foremost among them were the two Chicago Cub players nearest the action. Gabby Hartnett, the catcher, was the only player near enough to hear what Ruth said; according to Hartnett, Ruth's words were "It only takes one to hit," referring to the one strike he had left. But Hartnett said Ruth pointed his finger at the Chicago players riding him from the dugout, *not* at the center-field bleachers.

Charlie Root, the pitcher, vehemently denied Ruth pointed to center field. Root even turned down the opportunity to play himself in a movie version of Ruth's life that included the called shot. "Ruth did not point at the fence before he swung," said Root. "If he had made a gesture like that, well, anybody who knows me knows that Ruth would have ended up on his ass."

So, it seemed, the eyewitness testimony cancelled itself out. For every witness who saw Ruth call his shot, there was one to swear he didn't. More objective evidence, in the form of a 16-millimeter home movie taken by spectator Matt Kandle Sr., was tantalizing but inconclusive: Ruth is definitely seen pointing—but whether at the pitcher, or the Cub bench, or the center-field bleachers is impossible to say.

Among serious baseball historians, however, the consensus that emerged was that Ruth did *not* point to center field. These historians pointed out that, of all the sportswriters present at the game, only one—Joe Williams, whose *World-Telegram* article is quoted above—mentioned the called shot in an article written that day. One other, John Drebinger of the *New York Times,* said Ruth "notified the crowd that the nature of his retaliation would be a wallop right out of the confines of the park," but this story didn't specify that Ruth pointed to center field. According to Ruth's premier biographer, Robert Creamer, the story that Ruth pointed to center field originated with Williams and then was picked up by Gallico and Corum and other writers who either respected Williams or who just couldn't resist such a good story.

Over time, Williams himself backed away from his initial story. It was Williams, in a February 1950 column, who quoted Gabby Hartnett's story and—though Williams still said he had "a distinct memory that [Ruth] did motion in the general direction of the stands in right center"—he admitted he now had doubts as to what that gesture meant. Fifteen years after that column, a 1965 Williams column recalled a conversation in which the sportswriter casually asked Ruth whether the called shot was the greatest thrill of his career. No, Ruth replied (according to Williams), his greatest thrill had been striking out Cobb, Crawford, and Beach with the bases full. Williams surmised that Ruth had deliberately ducked the question; Ruth couldn't bring himself to debunk his own legend, but he also didn't want to lie to Williams.

Not that Ruth had anything to be ashamed of. If, as Hartnett reported and as seems most likely, Ruth merely predicted he was going to hit a home run but didn't point to where it would land, this would still be a fitting capstone to his career. George Washington deserves to be a legendary figure, even if he never chopped down a cherry tree; so does Babe Ruth, even if he never pointed to center field.

☆ To investigate further:

Meany, Tom. *Babe Ruth*. New York: A. S. Barnes, 1947. An old-fashioned, anecdotal sports biography, but still fun; Meany, who once worked for Joe Williams, was an eyewitness to the called shot and a true believer.

Babe Ruth as told to Bob Considine, *The Babe Ruth Story*. New York: Dutton, 1948. A conventional sports autobiography for an unconventional sports figure.

Mrs. Babe Ruth with Bill Slocum, *The Babe and I*. Prentice-Hall, 1959. A loyal but surprisingly candid and often touching portrait by Ruth's second wife.

Creamer, Robert. *Babe: The Legend Comes to Life*. New York: Simon & Schuster, 1974. Not only the best biography of Ruth but one of the best biographies of any sports figure.

Wagenheim, Kal. *Babe Ruth: His Life and Legend*. Westport, CT: Praeger, 1974. A fine biography, though it had the misfortune of being published at the same time as Creamer's definitive work.

Sobol, Ken. *Babe Ruth and the American Dream*. New York: Random House, 1974. Some cynicism is called for in any biographer—and certainly in biographers of legendary figures like Ruth—but Sobol just doesn't seem to like his subject very much.

Smelser, Marshall. *The Life That Ruth Built*. New York: Quadrangle, 1975. A meandering and overly long biography that was the last and the least of the spate of mid-seventies biographies. (The rush of Ruth bios can probably be attributed to the fact that Hank Aaron was then challenging Ruth's lifetime home-run record.)

Ritter, Lawrence and Mark Rucker. *The Babe*. New York: Ticknor & Fields, 1988. An elegant pictorial biography, including stills from Matt Kandle's home movie.

Williams, Peter, editor. *The Joe Williams Baseball Reader*. Chapel Hill, NC: Algonquin, 1989. A collection of Williams' columns through which you can trace the birth, growth, and abandonment of the called-shot story.

Chapter 21

Was Amelia Earhart a Spy?

We must be on you but cannot see you. Gas is running low."

This ominous message from Amelia Earhart reached the coast guard cutter *Itasca* in the early morning hours of July 3, 1937. The cutter was cruising off the coast of Howland Island, a tiny speck in the middle of the South Pacific that was to be one of the final stops on Earhart's record-breaking, round-the-world flight. But Earhart never reached Howland Island and soon lost contact with the *Itasca*. President Franklin Roosevelt ordered a massive naval search. It lasted one week, cost four million dollars (no mean sum back then), and covered approximately 250,000 miles—to no avail. Earhart, her navigator Fred Noonan, and her Lockheed Electra aircraft had disappeared.

Officials concluded Earhart had run out of gas and gone down somewhere in the ocean. In the years since then, however, the official story has been repeatedly challenged. One of the most persistent and intriguing of the alternative scenarios recasts Earhart and Noonan as spies for the United States. Their round-the-world adventure was merely cover, with their actual mission being to take pictures of Japanese installations in the Pacific. But the Japanese forced them down and (in some versions) took them prisoner or (in other versions) executed them.

The Earhart-as-spy story originated in 1943, in *Flight for Freedom,* a movie starring Rosalind Russell as a famous aviator named Tonie Carter and Fred MacMurray as the navigator she falls in love with. They plan to get lost over the Pacific to give the navy a pretext for searching the area and checking out Japanese fortifications. Just before taking off on the last leg of the journey, Carter learns that the Japanese are on to her, and that they plan to take her prisoner. So she takes off alone and ditches the plane in the ocean, sacrificing her life so the search can go on.

The movie was pure fiction. But it captured the imagination of the public and of generations of journalists, historians, and aviation buffs—some of whom set out to prove it was more than fiction.

Among the leading proponents of the Earhart-as-spy story was CBS reporter Fred Goerner. In 1960 Goerner came across a newspaper article about Josephine Blanco Akiyama, who said that while she was a girl on Saipan Island she'd witnessed a plane crash in the harbor, after which a white woman and man were taken into Japanese custody. Soon after, Akiyama recalled, she had heard shots fired.

Goerner spent six years investigating the matter, interviewing hundreds of islanders who claimed to have seen Earhart and Noonan. He concluded that the two landed somewhere in the Marshall Islands, were picked up by a Japanese fishing boat, and were then taken to Japanese Pacific military headquarters on Saipan. Some of Goerner's evidence didn't stand up on closer investigation: the remains in an un-marked grave turned out to be of non-Caucasian origin and parts of a twin-engine airplane he recovered turned out to be made in Japan. Equally problematic were that the islanders' stories about the fliers of-ten contradicted each other: some claimed to have seen just a woman, others a man and woman; some saw the plane wrecked, others virtually undamaged; some saw the fliers summarily executed, others in jail; and the crash itself was apparently witnessed on a whole range of islands.

Still, so many islanders claimed to have seen Earhart and Noonan that their stories couldn't be dismissed out of hand. It is certainly pos-sible, though by no means proven, that two white fliers were captured by the Japanese sometime before the war. But were these two Earhart and Noonan? And were they on a spy mission?

To answer these questions, investigators turned from the Pacific to Washington, D.C. One of these, Randall Brink, spent thirteen years analyzing documents obtained through the Freedom of Information Act. His conclusion was similar to Goerner's: Earhart was a spy. In Brink's account, Earhart's trip started as a publicity stunt but evolved into a spy mission. As a personal friend of the Roosevelts, Earhart did not hesitate to approach the president for help in arranging for refueling stops during her trip. And the president couldn't risk the temptation to use the trip for military intelligence.

To begin with, Brink pointed out, there wasn't even an airstrip on Howland Island until Roosevelt ordered the Coast Guard to build one for Earhart. This was a major construction job—at taxpayers' expense—and it would be hard to justify it as nothing more than a favor for a friend.

Brink interviewed a Lockheed technician who told him he'd cut holes in the plane so that special cameras could be installed to take pictures of Japanese installations. Brink also argued that Earhart's last-minute change in flight direction, from westward to eastward, could only be explained if hers was a spying mission. According to the original itinerary, Earhart would have flown westward over the Pacific and landed in Lae, New Guinea. There she would have been surrounded by civilians, in foreign territory, and any number of things could have gone wrong, including the discovery of the bulky camera. But by going from west to east, she would land on the isolated, U.S.-controlled Howland Island immediately after photographing Japanese installations. On Howland the film could easily be handed over to U.S. agents before she flew on to meet the crowds at Hawaii, her next stop. Earhart's explanation that she was changing the flight direction because of a seasonal change in wind patterns made no sense, Brink said; by flying from west to east she was *bucking* the prevailing wind.

In addition, Brink uncovered evidence in the files of naval intelligence that, prior to her flight, the navy had secretly installed powerful engines in Earhart's plane that would enable it to take a different, longer flight path than had been announced. This path, Brink concluded, would take her over the Japanese-controlled Marshall and Caroline Islands.

Finally, Brink found that Earhart was heard by radio operators for days after she supposedly disappeared and died. Some of these reports may have been unreliable, but as with the testimony of the islanders gathered by Goerner, there were too many to dismiss them

Those who thought Amelia Earhart was a spy for the United States pointed to her close friendship with Franklin and Eleanor Roosevelt. Here she is on a night flight over Washington with the first lady. (Eleanor Roosevelt always wanted to take flying lessons, but never did.) Courtesy of the National Air and Space Museum.

out of hand. Brink believed that Roosevelt was well aware of all the evidence that Earhart had survived, and that he ordered it covered up so that her spying activities, too, would be buried.

Brink's detractors argued that his evidence was circumstantial and that he'd overstated his case. For example, Brink cited a document in which FDR's treasury secretary, Henry Morgenthau Jr., stated that if the full story of Earhart's last flight were made public, her reputation would be ruined. Brink read that as evidence that the administration wanted to cover up Earhart's spying; Tom Crouch of the National Air and Space Museum, however, pointed out that it could just as easily be read to mean that Earhart made some errors in judgment that could have undermined her reputation as a great flyer.

Some of Brink's speculation was, indeed, a bit off the wall. He gave serious consideration, for example, to a longstanding but completely unsubstantiated theory that after being captured by the Japanese, Earhart had become "Tokyo Rose," the infamous wartime disc jockey who beguiled American troops in the Pacific. At one point, Earhart's husband had made a special trip to the front lines to listen to a Tokyo Rose broadcast and had said he would stake his life that it was *not* his wife's voice.

And though Franklin Roosevelt died without ever publicly discussing Earhart's flight, Eleanor Roosevelt repeatedly denied any spy plot, stating: "Franklin and I loved Amelia too much to send her to her death." So, in the end, the spy theorists had lots of evidence, but all of it circumstantial, and lots of speculation, some of it wild.

While Brink was searching through files in Washington, other researchers continued to scour the Pacific for evidence of Earhart's landing. The best funded of them was Richard Gillespie, executive director of The International Group for Historic Aircraft Recovery (TIGHAR). In 1989 and 1991, with $750,000 of TIGHAR money, Gillespie led expeditions to the uninhabited island known as Nikumaroro. It was there that, during the initial search for Earhart, a navy pilot had reported "signs of recent habitation." But after repeated circling and zooming failed to elicit any answering wave, the pilot concluded no one was there.

Gillespie thought the pilot might have missed something, and what he found there convinced him he was right. He returned with a number of objects, among them part of a woman's size nine shoe, consistent with the style Earhart wore; a mid-thirties cigarette lighter, which might have belonged to Noonan (who was a smoker); and an aluminum navigator's bookcase with screwholes that suggested it might have been installed on an airplane. Gillespie believed he'd solved the Earhart mystery: Earhart and Noonan had crashed on Nikumaroro.

This did not prove, of course, that Earhart died on Nikumaroro; she might still have been captured by the Japanese and she might still have been a spy. But, Gillespie claimed, here at last was some hard evidence to replace the circumstantial evidence and wild speculations of the spy theorists.

But how hard was Gillespie's evidence?

His detractors were quick to point out that even though Niku-maroro may be uninhabited now, it had been at times colonized by is-landers and military personnel. Shoes might have traveled there by some means other than Earhart's feet, and the same could be said for all the flotsam and jetsam Gillespie collected. Besides, the navy pilot who'd flown over the island was a trained professional on the lookout for any signs of Earhart, Noonan, or their plane—and he'd concluded they weren't there.

So it seems, barring some yet to be discovered evidence, Amelia Earhart is destined to remain a missing person. We simply cannot say for sure where she landed, or whether she was a spy.

But what if we put aside the relics of Earhart's trip and look instead at Earhart herself? What clues might be found in her past behavior? Was she the type of person likely to be a spy?

Certainly no one could doubt she had sufficient courage to be a spy. This was, after all, the first woman to fly across the Atlantic as a passenger (in 1928), the first woman to fly solo across the Atlantic (in 1932), the woman who broke her own transcontinental speed record (in 1933), the first person to fly solo from Honolulu to the mainland (in 1935). And her relationship with the Roosevelts was sufficiently close that they might very well have felt comfortable discussing top secret matters with her.

But Earhart was an ardent pacifist, likely to have resisted any-thing to do with the military. Besides, there were plenty of other moti-vations for the trip besides spying. Money, for one: Earhart's husband, the publisher George Putnam, was a master publicist with visions of lucrative endorsement contracts for his wife. Indeed, the trip gener-ated more attention than he could have dreamed; alas, without Earhart, there was no way for Putnam to cash in.

Nor need we be so cynical to explain why Earhart took off. This was a woman who loved flying, and a flight around the world was the ultimate aerial adventure. In her journal of the flight (which she cabled to Putnam from various stops along the way so that it would be ready for publication right after the trip was over), Earhart recounted her reasons for the trip: "Here was shining adventure, beckoning with new experiences. . . . Then, too, there was my belief that now and then women should do for themselves what men have already done—and occasionally what men have not done . . . perhaps encouraging other women toward greater independence of thought and action." So feminism, too, propelled Earhart.

Her disappearance, like her motivations for the trip, can be explained without resorting to spy stories. Strictly as an aviation challenge, the trip from New Guinea to Howland Island was plenty dangerous. Howland was tiny and remote and barely above sea level; under the best of circumstances it would be difficult to find. Earhart and Noonan planned to reach it after approximately 18 hours in the air—18 hours that came after having already flown much of the way around the world, in a noisy, vibrating plane with barely room to stretch. To say that Earhart and Noonan were unlikely to be at their most alert under these conditions is no insult to either. And there is also a possibility that Noonan was drunk or hung over; though there's absolutely no evidence that this was the case, he was an alcoholic who'd been fired by by Pan American, and suspicions linger.

None of this proves that Earhart wasn't a spy. Nor does it preclude the possibility that, even if Earhart had nothing to do with it, the navy saw her disappearance as an opportunity to survey the Japanese military build-up in the region. But it's worth noting that most of Earhart's biographers have concluded she wasn't a spy. And though other investigators might have looked more carefully at the particulars of Earhart's disappearance, it was her biographers who looked most carefully at the woman herself.

☆ To investigate further:

Earhart, Amelia. *Last Flight*. New York: Harcourt, Brace, 1937. Earhart's journal, which was originally to be called "World Flight." Though it was much embellished by Putnam and other editors, and though it obviously ended before the end, it's still the closest we come to Earhart's own account of the trip.

Goerner, Fred. *The Search for Amelia Earhart*. New York: Doubleday, 1966. The story of Goerner's six-year investigation and the reasons he concluded Earhart was a spy.

Rich, Doris. *Amelia Earhart*. Washington, DC: Smithsonian, 1989. A thorough, workmanlike biography.

Lovell, Mary. *The Sound of Wings: The Life of Amelia Earhart.* New York: St. Martin's, 1989. In spite of its title, this is actually a dual biography of Earhart and Putnam.

Gillespie, Richard. "The Mystery of Amelia Earhart." *Life,* April 1992. Gillespie's own account of his Nikumaroro expeditions.

Wilkinson, Stephan. "Amelia Earhart: Is the Search Over?" *Air & Space,* September 1992. A more objective analysis of Gillespie's expedition.

Ware, Susan. *Still Missing.* New York: Norton, 1993. A feminist biography: the title refers not just to the unsolved mystery surrounding Earhart's disappearance but to her still unfulfilled goal of equality for women.

Brink, Randall. *Lost Star.* New York: Norton, 1994. Though some of Brink's speculation about what might have happened after Earhart was captured is farfetched, this presents the most thorough case that she was a spy.

Chapter 22

Who Was to Blame for Pearl Harbor?

When FDR declared December 7, 1941, "a date that will live in infamy," he left no question about who the infamous party was—the perpetrators of the "unprovoked and dastardly attack" on Pearl Harbor, the Japanese empire.

For many, though, Roosevelt's explanation didn't wash. The world was already at war, all diplomatic efforts to resolve tensions with Japan had failed, the entire Pacific Ocean was ready to boil over. How, with all of this going on, could our army and navy be caught sleeping?

To some revisionists, a more sinister explanation than Roosevelt's seemed called for. They've argued that the infamy belonged to Roosevelt himself. They've claimed that Roosevelt knew in advance of the attack on Pearl Harbor and deliberately withheld information about it from the U.S. commanders in Hawaii. His motive: to get the United States into the war. Eager to fight the Japanese and Germans, frustrated by isolationists in Congress and the American public, this Roosevelt was a warmonger who would stop at nothing, not even betraying his own forces, to get his way.

Among the earliest to point fingers at Roosevelt were his commanders at Pearl Harbor: Admiral Husband Kimmel, the Commander in Chief

150

If FDR didn't know in advance about Pearl Harbor, he was nonetheless actively involved in the war effort. Here he is consulting with Churchill aboard the HMS Prince of Wales—*four months before the attack. Courtesy of the FDR Library.*

of the U.S. Pacific Fleet, and Lieutenant General Walter Short, Commanding General, Hawaii Department of the Army. Both, admittedly, had a strong incentive to blame Roosevelt—or, for that matter, anyone but themselves. The humiliation of the defeat at Pearl Harbor had been compounded by a presidential committee that found both Kimmel and Short guilty of "dereliction of duty."

Neither officer took this verdict lying down. Most frustrating of all was that the committee had not considered what they—and all future revisionists—considered the key evidence against Roosevelt. Namely, Magic. Magic was the code name used to refer to the brilliant work of Lieutenant Colonel William Friedman, who in August 1940 cracked the most secret of Japanese codes. From 1940 on, as a result of Friedman's breakthrough, U.S. intelligence officers were reading all of Japan's diplomatic messages.

One of these messages, which U.S. intelligence intercepted on September 24, 1941, was a "strictly secret" message from the Japanese foreign ministry to its Honolulu consulate. This came to be known as the "bomb plot" message. It read:

> With regard to warships and aircraft carriers, we would like to have you report on those at anchor. . . , tied up at wharves, buoys, and in docks.

That the consulate was spying on American ships at Pearl Harbor was no surprise to anyone; the Japanese had been following U.S. fleet movements for quite a while. Now, however, they were suddenly interested in the locations of the ships in the harbor.

Why the sudden change in the Japanese spies' focus? To many who analyzed it later, including Kimmel and Short, the answer was obvious: the Japanese wanted to know the locations of ships at the harbor because they were planning to attack them there.

Yet no one in the navy or army in Pearl Harbor received a copy of the intercepted message.

Kimmel and Short felt somewhat vindicated when the navy and the army conducted their own investigations and concluded that their commanders had not been derelict. But that satisfied few. For one thing, a lot of people suspected the military was covering up the truth to protect its own people and image. And even for those who did trust the military, the question remained: if Kimmel and Short weren't to blame, who was?

This was a question too pressing to be left to historians. In 1945 a joint congressional committee opened its own investigation.

☆   ☆   ☆

Testifying about the bomb plot message, Short told the committee:

> While the War Department G-2 may not have felt bound to let me know about the routine operations of the Japanese in keeping track of our naval ships, they should certainly have let me know that the Japanese were getting reports of the exact location of the ships in Pearl Harbor . . . because such details would be useful only for sabotage, or for air or submarine attack on Hawaii. . . . This message, analyzed critically, is really a bombing plan for Pearl Harbor.

Kimmel agreed that "knowledge of these intercepted Japanese dispatches would have radically changed the estimate of the situation made by me and my staff."

The testimony mesmerized the nation. How could U.S. intelligence have failed to pass on such a critically important message to Kimmel or Short?

In the 39 volumes of testimony and documents gathered by the congressional committee, there is no definite answer. Various officers confirmed that the bomb plot message was definitely intercepted yet never reached Kimmel or Short. It *may* have reached the Washington desk of Admiral Harold Stark, chief of naval operations. Stark told the committee he didn't remember seeing the message, but he admitted that even if he had seen it he would have considered it "just another example of their [Japan's] great attention to detail." Also, he assumed (incorrectly) that Kimmel was receiving the same messages directly from Naval Communications.

The congressional committee's verdict was split.

The majority report, signed by six Democrats and two Republicans, blamed the military, both in Washington and in Hawaii. It blamed army and navy intelligence in Washington for failing to pass on this and other intercepted Japanese messages to Kimmel and Short; it blamed Kimmel and Short for failing to appreciate the considerable intelligence and other information that was available to them.

The minority report, signed by two Republicans, blamed not only the military but the administration, including Roosevelt, for failing to put the Pearl Harbor commanders on a full alert for defensive actions, given the increasing tension with Japan. Even the Republicans, however, stopped short of accusing Roosevelt of having known about the attack in advance.

Given the political pressures to which Congress was subjected, a split verdict was hardly surprising. But as time passed, most Americans came to accept the opinion of the majority report. World War II, it was generally agreed, was "the good war." So, just as Republicans dropped their prewar isolationism, they put aside their suspicions about the war's origins. As for Kimmel and Short, they continued to proclaim their innocence, but even in the military fewer and fewer cared.

And, in retrospect, the preponderance of evidence did support the majority opinion of the committee. No one conspired to keep

Kimmel and Short in the dark. Instead, a great many people in Washington and Hawaii—including Roosevelt but also including most other top American officials—grossly underestimated the Japanese. Everyone expected that some skirmish would eventually draw the United States into war; what no one foresaw was that the Japanese would strike so suddenly and decisively. Far from being Roosevelt's pawns, the Japanese military leaders were bold tacticians. They realized war was inevitable and they determined—probably correctly—that a preemptive strike was their best chance to win it.

It was the general underestimation of the Japanese—abetted by bad communication, bad coordination, and bad luck—that was to blame for Pearl Harbor.

Yet the case against Roosevelt has popped up again and again, and it's made for some strange bedfellows. Revisionists have included both anti-communists, who felt the United States should have been fighting the Soviet Union instead of Germany and Japan, and leftist historians of the sixties, who saw sinister parallels between how Roosevelt ensnared the country into World War II and how Johnson and Nixon trapped us into Vietnam.

And in one sense, the case against Roosevelt has stood the test of time. Most historians now agree that, in his eagerness to get the United States into the war, Roosevelt was guilty both of provoking the Japanese and of overstepping his constitutional powers. In early 1941, well before Pearl Harbor and in violation of its own neutrality acts, the United States was providing covert aid to China in its war against Japan. In addition, Roosevelt's "lend-lease" plan, by which he was lending arms to the British and allowing them to pay later, was pure fiction: no one in the administration expected Britain to return the arms or to pay for them. One Republican senator, cutting through the pretense, commented: "Lending arms is like lending chewing gum. You don't want it back."

Roosevelt had no choice. Given the still-prevailing isolationism of the Congress and the public, his deceptions and manipulations were the only means he had to act against Japan and Germany. Still, there's no question that when Roosevelt described the attack on Pearl Harbor as "unprovoked," he was not telling the whole truth.

But did he know about the attack in advance? No.

After all—and this is perhaps the strongest defense of Roosevelt that can be made—Roosevelt wanted America in the war so that we could *win* the war. And it's a hell of a lot easier to win a war if your Pacific fleet is floating on, and not under, the waters of Pearl Harbor.

☆ To investigate further:

Hearings Before the Joint Committee on the Investigation of the Pearl Harbor Attack, Congress of the United States, Seventy-ninth Congress, Government Printing Office, 1946. Still the *primary* primary source.

Beard, Charles A. *President Roosevelt and the Coming of the War, 1941.* New Haven, CT: Yale University Press, 1948. Accuses Roosevelt of manipulating the American public and the Japanese, but not of actually knowing in advance about the attack.

Morison, Samuel E. *By Land and By Sea.* New York: Knopf, 1953. Includes a clear refutation of Beard's arguments.

Barnes, Harry E. *Perpetual War for Perpetual Peace.* Caldwell, ID: The Caxton Printers, 1953. Goes the whole way: not only does it claim Roosevelt wanted the attack, but that he knew about it in advance and then covered that up.

Kimmel, Husband E. *Admiral Kimmel's Story.* Washington, DC: Regnery, 1955. Kimmel's own defense.

Wohlstetter, Roberta. *Pearl Harbor: Warning and Decision.* Stanford, CT: Stanford University Press, 1962. How and why American intelligence organizations failed to understand the Japanese messages they intercepted.

Prange, Gordon W. *At Dawn We Slept.* New York: McGraw-Hill, 1981. The most thorough statement of the orthodox position and of the Japanese side of the story. This essay is much indebted to the book.

Toland, John. *Infamy.* New York: Doubleday, 1982. Asks some provocative questions but ultimately not a convincing revisionist statement.

Prange, Gordon W. *Pearl Harbor: The Verdict of History,* New York: McGraw-Hill, 1986. Refutes Toland's arguments but is otherwise a largely unnecessary reorganization of the arguments made quite well in *At Dawn We Slept.*

———*Dec. 7, 1941.* New York: McGraw-Hill, 1988. The third, and least necessary, of Prange's Pearl Harbor trilogy.

Thompson, Robert S. *A Time for War.* New York: Prentice Hall Press, 1991. A compelling account of Roosevelt's efforts to get the United States into the war.

Rusbridge, James and Eric Nere, *Betrayal at Pearl Harbor.* New York: Summit, 1991. Argues that Churchill knew of the attack in advance and, in order to lure the United States into the war, withheld the information from Roosevelt.

Clausen, Henry C. *Pearl Harbor: Final Judgment.* New York: Crown, 1992. Recapitulating his 1945 investigation for the Army, Clausen argues against any conspiracy. Instead, he blames uncoordinated intelligence and serious errors on the part of Kimmel, Short, and others.

Costello, John. *Days of Infamy.* New York: Pocket, 1994. Accuses Roosevelt of gross strategic miscalculations but *not* of knowing about the attack in advance.

Chapter 23

Why Did Truman Drop the Bomb?

In his 1955 memoirs, Harry Truman devoted only a few pages to his decision to drop an atom bomb on the city of Hiroshima.

"I regarded the bomb as a military weapon and never had any doubt that it should be used," wrote Truman. "The top military advisers to the President recommended its use, and when I talked to Churchill he unhesitatingly told me that he favored the use of the atom bomb if it might aid to end the war."

To end the war: this was Truman's clear and succinct rationale for using the bomb. Its devastating strength would convince the Japanese that an unconditional surrender was their only option, thus saving the lives of the American soldiers who would otherwise have to force that surrender on Japan's home ground. General Marshall had told him that an invasion might cost half a million American lives, Truman added.

Truman's secretary of war, Henry Stimson, wrote a somewhat lengthier defense of the decision to drop the bomb. Published in the February 1947 issue of *Harper's* magazine, Stimson's article recounted his activities as the chief adviser on atomic policy to both Franklin Roosevelt and Truman. In April 1945, as scientists prepared the bomb's final testing, Truman appointed Stimson head of a committee to consider the scientific, political, and military aspects of the bomb. In June,

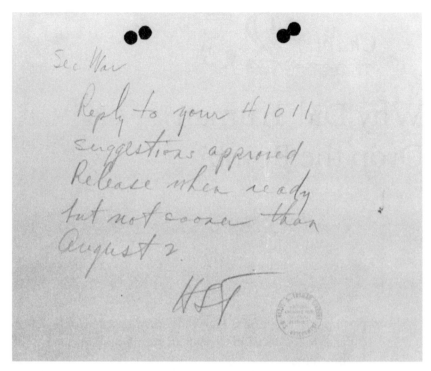

Truman's order, written in pencil to Secretary of War Stimson, to drop the bomb. Courtesy of Harry S. Truman Library.

the committee recommended using the bomb as soon as possible. The committee reported that scientists could envision no technical demonstration, such as dropping a bomb over a deserted island, that would convince the Japanese of its power.

On July 26, after meeting with Churchill and Stalin at Potsdam, a suburb of Berlin, Truman issued an ultimatum to the Japanese. This came to be known as the Potsdam Proclamation. Though it didn't mention the atom bomb specifically, the Proclamation warned Japan that it must surrender or face "prompt and utter destruction." Two days later, the Japanese premier responded that the ultimatum was "unworthy of public notice." That left Truman with no choice but to show he'd meant what he'd said. "For such a purpose," Stimson wrote, "the atomic bomb was an eminently suitable weapon."

From that point on, events unfolded exactly according to plan: on August 6 the first atom bomb fell on Hiroshima; on August 9 the second fell on Nagasaki; on August 14 the Japanese surrendered. Truman's and Stimson's accounts of the decision-making process seemed unimpeachable; not only had they explained clearly why they'd used the bomb, but history had proved their analysis to be correct.

Yet in the fifty-plus years since Hiroshima, revisionist historians have argued that Truman's decision to use the bomb was not nearly so straightforward as his memoirs or Stimson's article indicated. Revisionists have claimed that nowhere near 500,000 Americans would have died in an invasion; that Japan was at the brink of surrender even before the bomb was dropped; that Truman knew all of this and used the bomb anyway. His motive, according to some revisionists, was not to demonstrate American power to its Japanese enemies, but to its Russian allies. By these accounts the bomb was not the final blast of World War II, but the first blast of the Cold War.

The first to question the official explanation were hardly leftists or pacifists. Among them was Admiral William Leahy, who presided over the U.S. Joint Chiefs of Staff and was chief of staff to the commander in chief of the army and navy, serving Roosevelt in that capacity from 1942 to 1945 and Truman from 1945 to 1949. A few years after the bombs were dropped, Leahy stated: "It is my opinion that the use of this barbarous weapon at Hiroshima and Nagasaki was of no material assistance in our war against Japan. The Japanese were already defeated and ready to surrender."

Dwight Eisenhower, too, went public with his doubts. He recalled telling Stimson, before the bomb was used, "of my belief that Japan was already defeated and that dropping the bomb was completely unnecessary."

And as early as 1945, the U.S. Strategic Bombing Survey, an extensive and official study established by Stimson, published its findings that conventional bombing would have forced a Japanese surrender by the end of the year.

A variety of scholars have challenged Truman's contention that 500,000 Americans would have died in an invasion of Japan. They've pointed to U.S. military planning documents indicating that an initial landing on the island of Kyushu would have resulted in between 20,000 and 26,000 dead; the highest estimate found in these documents (based on a full-scale invasion of all Japan) was 46,000. Moreover, Truman himself used a variety of figures, with the 500,000 being only the latest and highest.

The debates over these numbers, however, only obscured the revisionists' main point: if the Japanese were at the brink of surrender, there need never have been an invasion—or an atom bombing.

In presenting their evidence, the revisionists turned to an unlikely source: a memo written by the leading defender of the decision to drop the bomb, Stimson himself. For though the secretary of war had undeniably recommended that the bomb be dropped, his proposed draft of the ultimatum to be issued to the Japanese differed in one significant point from the final Potsdam Proclamation.

In a July 2 memo to the president, reprinted right in his *Harper's* defense of the bomb, Stimson called for the ultimatum and then added: "I personally think that if in saying this we should add that we do not exclude a constitutional monarchy under her present dynasty, it would substantially add to the chances of acceptance." In other words, if the ultimatum held out the hope that the Japanese could keep their emperor, they might be more willing to surrender.

Stimson urged Truman to clarify the surrender terms to hold out the possibility of some continuing role for the emperor. So did others, including Acting Secretary of State Grew on May 28, Admiral Leahy on June 18, the State Department in a formal recommendation on June 30, Churchill on July 18, and the Joint Chiefs of Staff, also on July 18. Many pointed to intercepted Japanese documents and peace feelers the Japanese had sent out to neutral countries as evidence that Japan's leaders knew they were nearing defeat and sought only to assure that the emperor would be protected. Of the major administration figures consulting with the president on the bomb, only Secretary of State James Byrnes consistently and adamantly opposed any clarification of the surrender terms.

In the actual Potsdam Proclamation, Byrnes got his way: there was no mention of the emperor. Why did Truman go along with Byrnes—against the advice of so many of his other advisers? And why did the ultimatum not mention specifically that a new and phenomenally powerful weapon would be unleashed on Japan's cities? Wouldn't this, too, have made Japan's surrender more likely?

To some revisionists, the answer to these questions was clear: dropping the bomb was a show of force aimed not at Japan but at Russia. As further support for this thesis, revisionists noted the difference between Truman's behavior toward the Russians before and at Potsdam. Prior to the Potsdam meeting between Truman, Churchill, and Stalin, American policy had been aimed at getting Russia to go to war with Japan. On numerous occasions Truman stated that this was the primary reason he wanted to meet Stalin at Potsdam. In this, he succeeded: Stalin agreed that by the middle of August he'd declare war on Japan. In a letter home to his wife, Truman gloated: "I've gotten what I came for—Stalin goes to war . . . I'll say that we'll end the war a year sooner now, and think of the kids who won't be killed!"

But on July 16, once Truman received word that the atom bomb had been successfully tested in the New Mexico desert, American strategy suddenly changed. No longer did the president see any need for Russian help against the Japanese; no longer, in fact, did he see Russia as a wartime ally. In his mind, the Communists were now a postwar rival to be kept out of Japan and anywhere else. On July 17, Byrnes rejected Stimson's advice about including assurances about the emperor in the Potsdam Proclamation. The same day, the newly aggressive Truman faced Stalin across the Potsdam conference table and dismissed the latter's demand for bases in Turkey and the Mediterranean.

As Churchill put it, upon being told of the successful test of the bomb: "Now I know what happened to Truman yesterday. When he got to the meeting after having read this report he was a changed man. He told the Russians just where they got on and off and generally bossed the whole meeting."

The revisionist claims did not go unchallenged. Defenders of the orthodox explanation of the decision countered by arguing that Japan's peace feelers and other evidence that they might consider surrendering were a far cry from an actual surrender, and that the Japanese cabinet was at best divided on the subject. Others pointed out that even if the 500,000 figure was inflated, the cost of an invasion of Japan's home islands would still be considerable. At Okinawa, the equivalent of just three Japanese divisions had held out for one hundred days against a much larger U.S. ground force that was supported by heavy naval and air bombardment. The Okinawa campaign had left 12,520 Americans dead and another 36,631 injured and, along with kamikaze suicide raids, had left American soldiers and policy makers alike with a very vivid image of the ferocity of Japanese resistance. Under these circumstances, any American president would have to be concerned about the casualties an invasion would bring.

As for the decision not to mention the emperor in the Potsdam Proclamation, Truman may have felt bound by American public opinion. Since Pearl Harbor, Americans had sought revenge; to settle for anything less than unconditional surrender would have seemed a failure of nerve or will. Ironically, dropping the bomb may very well have allowed Truman to offer the surrender terms he couldn't beforehand. With America's mastery so completely established, he could let the emperor stay on. Hirohito remained the titular head of the Japanese nation until his death in 1989.

The debate over the bomb came to a head in 1994 when the Smithsonian Institution in Washington, D.C., prepared an exhibit commemorating the fiftieth anniversary of the Hiroshima bombing. The projected exhibition was fairly evenhanded: it stated that the war *might* have ended without the bombings if the Potsdam Proclamation had guaranteed the emperor's position, but this was by no means a strong revisionist position. Still, it was too strong for organizations like the American Legion, whose protests led the Smithsonian to remove any text from the exhibit. Instead, the *Enola Gay,* the plane that dropped the bomb, was displayed without any explanation or context.

That veterans' organizations were so offended by the exhibit is ironic, given that top military leaders such as Marshall, Eisenhower, and Leahy were among the earliest to argue against the bomb's necessity. Indeed, the veterans' organizations didn't seem to realize that their insistence that the bomb had won the war shifted the credit for that victory away from their own heroic efforts. But all this was lost in a debate that had become so politicized that the traditionalists could only see the revisionists as unpatriotic, and the revisionists could only see the traditionalists as callous and immoral.

What extremists on both sides have too often lost sight of is that the traditionalist and revisionist positions aren't irreconcilable. The traditionalists' claim that the bomb was dropped *solely* to save American lives was untrue—but that doesn't mean that saving lives wasn't a major concern. Conversely, though revisionists have demonstrated Truman's decision was made with an eye on Russia as well as Japan, that certainly doesn't mean he dropped the bomb *solely* to position America for the Cold War.

Truman did not drop the bomb for any single reason, traditionalist or revisionist. Many factors pushed him toward his decision—a desire to avenge Pearl Harbor and an ignorance of the bomb's full dangers, to name two more. For an inexperienced and as yet unelected president, the sheer momentum of a $2-billion project must also have been difficult to resist. "He was like a little boy on a toboggan," recalled Major General Leslie Groves, who headed up the project to build the bomb.

Might he have changed course? Perhaps. There were certainly opportunities. But the forces pushing that toboggan downward were very powerful indeed.

☆ To investigate further:

Stimson, Henry. "The Decision to Use the Atomic Bomb." *Harper's* magazine, February 1947. Written by Truman's secretary of war, this was one of the earliest and most influential of the official explanations.

Truman, Harry. *Memoirs*. New York: Doubleday, 1955. Volume One includes Truman's own account of his decision.

Sherwin, Martin. *A World Destroyed*. New York: Knopf, 1975. An account of the interaction between scientists and policymakers and of the origins of the arms race prior to the end of World War II.

Wyden, Peter. *Day One*. New York: Simon & Schuster, 1984. An excellent general history of the bomb, before and after Hiroshima.

McCullough, David. *Truman*. New York: Simon & Schuster, 1992. A masterful biography.

Allen, Thomas B. and Norman Polmar. *Code-Name Downfall*. New York: Simon & Schuster, 1995. A history of America's secret plans to invade Japan, and the latest defense of the traditional position.

Alperovitz, Gar. *The Decision to Use the Atomic Bomb*. New York: Knopf, 1995. The most recent and most comprehensive statement of the revisionist position, this supercedes Alperovitz's influential but more limited 1965 book, *Atomic Diplomacy*.

Nobile, Philip, editor. *Judgment at the Smithsonian*. New York: Marlowe and Company, 1995. Includes the script of the aborted fiftieth anniversary exhibit.

Chapter 24

Were the Rosenbergs Guilty?

L ike Sacco and Vanzetti a generation before, Julius and Ethel Rosenberg became a symbol to those on the left of how the American government was ruled by those on the right. To the left, the conviction and execution of the Rosenbergs for "stealing the secret of the atomic bomb" revealed a society caught in the thrall of hysterical McCarthyism. So, when the Rosenbergs' sons sued the government under the Freedom of Information Act, and in 1980 obtained the FBI files on the case, those on the left assumed the couple would be finally and fully vindicated. What the files revealed, however, was not nearly so clearcut.

When the Soviet Union successfully tested its atom bomb in August 1949, the United States immediately set out to find those responsible for stealing the classified information. The search led to the British atomic scientist Klaus Fuchs, who was arrested and who confessed that he had given information to the Soviets while working on the bomb at Los Alamos in 1945. Fuchs led the FBI to his American courier, Harry Gold, who was also arrested and also confessed. Gold, in turn, led agents to David Greenglass, an Army corporal who had worked in the laboratory at Los Alamos.

It was Greenglass who fingered Julius Rosenberg, his own brother-in-law. According to Greenglass, Rosenberg had dropped out of the Communist Party in 1943 in order to take on a role as Soviet spy. When Greenglass was sent to Los Alamos, Rosenberg arranged for him to pass on atomic information to Harry Gold. In fact, according to Greenglass, Rosenberg headed up a spy ring whose activities extended well beyond the theft of the atomic information.

At the 1951 trial of the Rosenbergs, the star witnesses were Gold and Greenglass. Gold testified that during the first weekend of June 1945, he traveled to New Mexico, where he met with Greenglass and gave him five hundred dollars in exchange for information on the atomic bomb. Greenglass testified that he was following instructions from his brother-in-law. The defense counsel, Emanuel Bloch, focused his efforts on discrediting Greenglass: he charged him with accusing the Rosenbergs to win leniency for his own crimes and to settle some old family grudges. Bloch did not cross-examine Gold at all since, as he explained in his summation to the jury, Gold had not claimed any direct contact with the Rosenbergs.

Later defenders of the Rosenbergs, primarily Walter and Miriam Schneir in their 1968 history of the case, were convinced that Bloch's failure to question Gold's story was a serious error. The Schneirs argued that, apart from the confessions of Gold and Greenglass, the government's sole proof that Harry Gold even met David Greenglass, when the latter supposedly passed on information to the former, was a registration card from the Albuquerque Hilton with Gold's name on it. The card had been placed in evidence during the trial. Yet, when the Schneirs examined it years later, they were shocked to find that the dates on the front and back of the card did not match. Furthermore, when the Schneirs showed the card to a handwriting expert, she expressed "some very real doubts" about whether the initials on the card were actually written by the clerk on duty at the Hilton. The Schneirs could come up with only one explanation for the discrepancies in the date and the handwriting: the card had been forged by the FBI to substantiate a Gold-Greenglass meeting that never actually took place.

Those historians who believed in the Rosenbergs' guilt were not convinced. Handwriting analysis was a notoriously imprecise science. Also, they argued, a simple hotel error could account for the different dates on the back and front of the card as easily as a botched forgery.

The Rosenbergs' supporters marching in front of the White House on June 15, 1953, four days before the couple's executions. UPI/Corbis-Bettman.

After all, if the FBI was going to forge a registration card, it would probably have managed to forge one without any error.

So, it seemed, the evidence submitted at the trial could not change anyone's mind. Those who believed in the Rosenbergs' guilt continued to maintain that David Greenglass was telling the truth; it was inconceivable to them that Greenglass would send his own sister and brother-in-law to the gas chamber—not to mention ending up with a 15-year prison term himself—unless he and the Rosenbergs were spies. For those who believed in the couple's innocence, the Rosenbergs were scapegoats for America's anger over the loss of its nuclear monopoly. Greenglass had accused them out of fear or vindictiveness or naivete, and the government was persecuting them because they'd been members of the Communist Party.

And so matters stood until Robert and Michael Meeropol, the Rosenbergs' two sons (they'd taken on their adoptive parents' name after their parents' execution) sued the government for the release of the FBI files on the case. When they won that case, some 250,000 pages of FBI and other government documents pertaining to their parents' case were suddenly open to the public.

Supporters of the Rosenbergs celebrated. Among those who assumed the new documents would vindicate the Rosenbergs were historians Richard Radosh and Joyce Milton, both of whom believed the couple had been framed. Their study of the new evidence, released in a 1983 book, convinced them otherwise.

One startling revelation in the documents was that the government had not relied exclusively on Greenglass for reports of the Rosenbergs' spying activities. Another informer, Jerome Tartakow, had supplied a great many details about the Rosenbergs, though he never testified in court. Tartakow, who was serving a two-year sentence for interstate auto theft, was Rosenberg's closest companion in jail; like Rosenberg, he was a former communist and the two spent a great deal of time playing chess together. In return for a reduction of his sentence, Tartakow regaled the FBI with stories of Rosenberg's spy rings. Tartakow reported that Rosenberg had admitted to him that "he played the game and lost." He also tipped off the FBI about a photographer who had taken some passport photos of the Rosenbergs soon after Greenglass's arrest, and whose testimony at the trial was particularly damning. Defenders of the Rosenbergs were quick to assail Tartakow's character (and even his FBI contacts were suspicious about some of his reports). Still, it was no longer just Greenglass's word on which the Rosenbergs' guilt depended.

The newly opened FBI files revealed other evidence against the Rosenbergs as well, including interviews with more reliable informants who claimed to have heard, albeit indirectly, of the Rosenbergs' spy ring. And the files traced the very suspicious disappearances of three of Julius Rosenberg's closest friends soon after his arrest. One, Morton Sobell, was caught in Mexico and tried and convicted (though not executed) with the Rosenbergs. Two others, Joel Barr and Al Sarant, later turned up in the Soviet Union.

Taken together, this new evidence, though circumstantial, convinced Radosh and Milton that the Rosenbergs were indeed spies. The Schneirs continued to defend the Rosenbergs; they issued a revised edition of their book in which they argued that additional evidence from FBI files was meaningless since the FBI was perfectly capable of manufacturing or destroying evidence. But most mainstream historians sided with Radosh and Milton and now accepted the guilty verdict. In 1995, the Rosenbergs' remaining defenders received another blow, when the army released Russian cables it had intercepted and decoded in 1943. Among the Russian agents referred to was one identified as JR.

Still, the government did not emerge from the new investigations with clean hands, either. For one thing, though the new evidence against Julius Rosenberg was damning, the evidence against Ethel Rosenberg was much flimsier. David Greenglass, notably, accused only his brother-in-law and never his sister. Worse, the FBI files made clear that the only reason Ethel Rosenberg was arrested was to put pressure on her husband to confess and name names. When this strategy failed, the government upped the ante, hoping that the threat of executing Ethel would break Julius. Perhaps the most shocking document in the files revealed that FBI agents standing by at Julius Rosenberg's execution had ready a number of questions, should he choose to talk at the last moment. Among the questions was: "Was you wife cognizant of your activities?" Even as it executed her, it was clear the government remained uncertain of her guilt.

This is not to say that Ethel Rosenberg was innocent. The Rosenbergs were a very close couple, and Ethel almost certainly was aware of what her husband was up to. But there was no evidence she participated in his spying, and the government's cynical behavior in executing a wife in order to pressure a husband can hardly be considered a triumph of justice.

Furthermore, the FBI files make clear that even if the Rosenbergs were guilty of spying, the death penalty was a gross injustice. The information they were convicted of passing on to the Russians simply wasn't that important. A few months after describing the case as "the crime of the century," J. Edgar Hoover privately acknowledged to FBI agents that Soviet scientists had undoubtedly developed their bomb independent of any information they'd received through espionage. And a year after the Rosenbergs' execution, General Leslie Groves, the military chief of the Manhattan Project, told a closed meeting of the Atomic Energy Commission that "the data that went out in the case of the Rosenbergs was of minor value."

What David Greenglass passed on to Harry Gold—a crude drawing of part of the plutonium-fired implosion device—could hardly
have condensed the results of the Manhattan project in any technolog-
ically meaningful way. At most, the sketch confirmed a small part of
what the Russians had already learned from Klaus Fuchs's far more sophisticated information (Fuchs, after all, was an atomic physicist) and
from their own research. David Greenglass was a spy and so was Julius
Rosenberg, but both were small-time amateurs. Rosenberg couldn't
even hold a job, let alone run a major spy ring. To accuse him of having "stolen the secret of the atomic bomb" was either a cynical move
on the part of the government, playing to the anticommunist hysteria
of the period, or a sign that the government was itself caught in the
grips of that hysteria.

The irony of the Rosenberg case, then, is this: the accusers and
defenders of the Rosenbergs were both right. The Rosenbergs were
spies, and they were also scapegoats. The Rosenbergs were not innocent, but they certainly did not deserve to die.

☆ To investigate further:

Schneir, Walter and Miriam. *Invitation to an Inquest.* New York: Doubleday,
1965. Revised edition Pantheon, 1983. The case for the Rosenbergs' innocence.

Nizer, Louis. *The Implosion Conspiracy.* New York: Doubleday, 1973. A day-by-
day account of the trial, somewhat biased in favor of the prosecution.

Meeropol, Robert and Michael. *We Are Your Sons.* Boston: Houghton Mifflin,
1975. The Rosenbergs' sons own stories, including very moving letters from
and between their parents, and a much less compelling argument for their innocence.

Milton, Joyce and Ronald Radosh, *The Rosenberg File.* Orlando: Holt, Rinehart
and Winston, 1983. The definitive case for the Rosenbergs' guilt.

Philipson, Ilene. *Ethel Rosenberg.* New York: Franklin Watts, 1988. Although a
biography and not an investigation of the case, this portrait of the Rosenbergs as struggling working-class parents makes it difficult to believe they
could have managed to do much more than just get by.

Sharlitt, Joseph. *Fatal Error.* New York: Scribner's, 1989. Concludes that the
Rosenbergs were spies but that they were tried and executed unfairly.

Carmichael, Virginia. *Framing History.* Minneapolis: University of Minnesota Press, 1993. How the Rosenberg case has been portrayed in the arts; interesting more as a work of criticism than history.

Weiner, Tim. "U.S. Tells How It Cracked Code of A-Bomb Spy Ring." The *New York Times,* July 12, 1995. The latest revelations.

Chapter 25

Who Killed JFK?

No event, save perhaps Pearl Harbor, traumatized the nation as much as the assassination of President John F. Kennedy on November 22, 1963. Not surprisingly, in both cases the public responded by questioning the official version of what happened. But while the controversy over who was to blame for Pearl Harbor has faded with time, the mystery of who killed JFK is by no means resolved in the minds of most Americans. In the more than two thousand books and tens of thousands of articles on the subject, investigators have argued that Kennedy was killed by, to mention just the main culprits: the CIA, the KGB, the FBI, the Mafia, Fidel Castro, anti-Castro Cubans, and the Joint Chiefs of Staff. Not to mention Lee Harvey Oswald.

Confronted by so much confusing and often contradictory evidence, historians have been tempted to throw up their hands and say that this is one mystery that just can't be solved. Most Kennedy scholars, in fact, have shied away from his death. But they're wrong to do so, for not only is the subject too important to ignore, but the massive accumulation of evidence has moved us a great deal closer (though not all the way) to the mystery's solution.

☆ ☆ ☆

The first official investigation into the assassination was that of the Warren Commission, headed by the Chief Justice of the Supreme Court, Earl Warren. The commission's report, released just ten months after Kennedy's death, offered a clear and simple answer to the question of who killed the president: Oswald did it, and he did it alone.

The Warren Commission concluded that Oswald had shot Kennedy from the sixth-floor window at the southeast corner of the Texas School Book Depository Building in Dallas. A construction worker across the street from the Depository saw Oswald shoot and described him to police. Forty-five minutes later, Dallas policeman J. D. Tippit stopped Oswald, who pulled out his revolver and killed Tippit. Oswald fled into a movie theater, from which he was dragged out by Dallas police. Two days later, as Oswald was being transferred from the city jail to a county jail, Jack Ruby broke through the crowds and fired a fatal shot into Oswald.

The Warren Report painted a picture of Oswald as a crazy loner, driven partly by a commitment to Marxism and partly by his own personal madness. Sent by his mother to an orphanage when he was just three, he was committed to a youth center for troubled boys when he was fifteen. He joined the marines, was twice court-martialled, went to Russia, tried to defect, and attempted suicide when the Russians decided to send him home. The Russians then relented and sent him to Minsk, where he spent two years building radios. But Oswald envisioned himself as a revolutionary leader, not a factory worker; he became as disillusioned with communism as with capitalism, and he returned to America. Back home his violent nature manifested itself in beatings of his Russian wife and in his attempted murder of right-wing General Edwin Walker. (Evidence of this previous assassination attempt only surfaced after Oswald's arrest for Kennedy's murder.)

Why did Oswald kill Kennedy? Not because of any long-felt animosity or planning. It was merely chance that Oswald happened to work in the School Book Depository Building. But when he learned that the president's limousine would pass within rifle range, he seized his opportunity. Convinced he was destined for greatness, yet a failure at everything he'd tried, Oswald grabbed his place in history.

As for Ruby, he was a failed night club and strip joint owner who, like much of the country, was griefstricken at the assassination. But, like Oswald, Ruby loved the spotlight and, on an impulse, he too seized the chance to take center stage.

This, at least, was the scenario presented by the Warren Report.

☆ ☆ ☆

It didn't take long for skeptics to start chipping away at the commission's credibility.

Early critics pointed out that the commission had been under tremendous pressure, both to issue its report quickly and to assure the country that Oswald acted alone. Reports of Soviet and Cuban involvement in the assassination could lead to war, after all. Besides, Lyndon Johnson didn't want any lingering questions about the assassination clouding his reelection prospects. So, though the Commission supposedly worked tirelessly to find the truth, it held its hearings in secret and relied heavily on the FBI and Secret Service reports. Most witnesses appeared before staff members, rather than the commission itself; in fact, not once were all seven commission members present during questioning.

With faith in the Warren Report waning, Jim Garrison, the New Orleans district attorney, undertook his own investigation in 1966. Garrison was convinced that while Oswald was in New Orleans—where he lived before moving to Dallas—he'd hooked up with two local figures, David Ferrie and Clay Shaw. According to Garrison, all three worked for the CIA, which was behind the plot to kill Kennedy. But Ferrie died before Garrison could learn more from him, and Shaw was acquitted a mere 45 minutes after a jury retired for deliberations. And rightly so: Garrison's case against Shaw depended heavily on the testimony of a witness who admitted he had no conscious memory of anything to do with a conspiracy; only after prosecutors had drugged and hypnotized him did his story come out.

Though Garrison's conspiracy theory proved unfounded, more responsible investigators continued to undermine the credibility of the Warren Report. In March 1975 ABC aired, for the first time, the Zapruder film (film footage of the assassination taken by a spectator at the Dallas motorcade). Besides shocking the nation with its graphic detail, its image of Kennedy's head snapping back and to the left seemed to indicate a bullet fired from in front, rather than from the rear (where the School Book Depository was located).

Also in 1975, a Senate committee was shocked to learn that the CIA, with the assistance of the Mafia, had repeatedly tried to assassinate Castro during the early 1960s. Immediately this raised questions as to whether the Kennedy assassination might have been Castro's revenge, and what other information the CIA might have withheld from the Warren Commission.

In July came another bombshell: Oswald had been in contact with the FBI *before* the assassination. FBI agent James Hosty admitted he'd received a note from Oswald shortly before the assassination and had been ordered to destroy it right after the assassination. In addition, the FBI had deleted Hosty's name, address, and telephone number when information from Oswald's address book was sent to the commission.

By 1977 the Warren Commission's credibility was in shreds, and Congress took it upon itself to launch a new full-scale investigation. In contrast to the Warren Report, the House Select Committee on Assassinations took its time, almost three years, and it explored the darkest recesses of the CIA, FBI, and other government agencies. In addition, the committee appointed panels of independent experts who used technology unavailable in 1964. These experts resolved many of the questions about autopsy reports, ballistics matches, firearms tests, and photographic evidence that critics of the Warren Report had raised over the previous 15 years.

After all this, the committee seemed convinced that, though the Warren Commission's investigation was seriously flawed, its conclusion was essentially correct: Oswald alone had killed Kennedy. Then, just before the Committee was to issue its report, it heard from three acoustics experts who had analyzed the dictabelt of a Dallas policeman's motorcycle. These experts informed the committee that they'd enhanced the recording and were 95 percent certain that they could detect four distinct shots. Because two of these shots came too close to each other for Oswald's rifle to have fired both, there must have been two riflemen. The experts also said that this additional shot came not from the Depository building behind Kennedy but from a grassy knoll in front of him.

The committee quickly revised its conclusion. In July 1979 it announced that since there were two gunmen, there must have been a conspiracy to kill JFK. But soon after the committee reached its conclusion, Dallas policeman H. B. McClain, whose radio was supposed

to be the source of the dictabelt recordings, came forward with information that indicated that the recording hadn't been from his radio.
He'd raced along with the president's limousine to the hospital, sirens
blaring all the way—yet on the recording there are no sirens to be
heard. So, it seemed, the testimony on which the committee had based
its conclusion had been based on the careful analysis of a tape which
might have been recording a scene nowhere near and having nothing
to do with the assassination.

This latest twist had only a minor impact on public opinion. Overwhelmed by revelations that government agencies and officials had
lied—not only to the Warren Commission but about Vietnam and Watergate as well—the vast majority of the American public had become
convinced of a conspiracy. A 1983 *Newsweek* poll showed only 11 percent believed Oswald had acted alone. This conviction was hardened
with the release of Oliver Stone's 1991 movie, *JFK,* in which Jim Garrison reemerged in the form of actor Kevin Costner.

Yet, as reporters and a few historians continued to investigate the
case, their reports were increasingly less sensationalist. Though the
CIA and FBI clearly had covered up information relevant to the assassination, their primary interests had been, in the case of the CIA, to
conceal its efforts to assassinate Castro, not Kennedy; and in the case
of the FBI, to make sure its reputation wasn't tarnished by its failure to
recognize the threat Oswald posed. Gerald Posner's 1993 book, *Case
Closed,* was enthusiastically embraced, at least by the mainstream
press, for its thorough refutation of much of the evidence conspiracy
theorists had gathered over the past 30 years.

Posner was extremely effective in marshalling technical expertise,
some but by no means all of which had been presented to the House
committee. He presented, for example, a convincing explanation of the
"magic bullet." This bullet, identified as having been shot from Oswald's rifle, was found on the stretcher of Texas Governor John Connally, who'd been riding in the presidential limousine and who'd been
injured by one of the shots aimed at Kennedy. After analyzing the Zapruder film, the Warren Commission had determined that the time between when Kennedy was first hit and when Connally was first hit was
not sufficient for a single gunman to have fired two shots. Therefore,
the commission concluded, a single bullet had hit both.

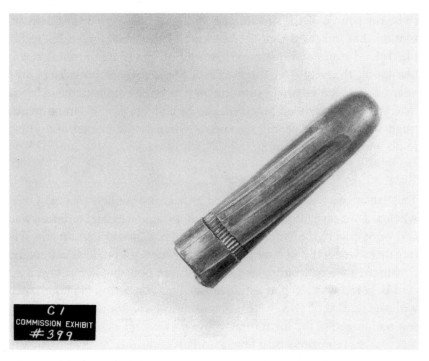

The "magic bullet," which the Warren Commission determined killed Kennedy and also went through Texas Governor John Connally. Critics of the commission couldn't believe a bullet could pass through two people and come out in such near-perfect condition. Courtesy of National Archives.

Critics of the commission wondered how a single bullet could have gone through both Kennedy and Connally and emerged, in nearly pristine condition, on Connally's stretcher. To conspiracy theorists, the mysterious appearance of a whole bullet from Oswald's gun smacked of a setup. A more likely explanation of how both Kennedy and Connally were hit one right after the other, they argued, was that a second bullet had been fired by a second gunman. But Posner's experts employed new technology to show that Connally's wounds and the intact bullet were the likely result of a bullet slowed by its passage through both Kennedy and Connally.

More than any technical evidence, however, what has undermined many conspiracy theories are flaws in their own logic. Consider the main candidates:

The CIA. The agency was capable of assassination—it had already admitted its attempts to kill Castro. And some high up in the agency could have feared that Kennedy, embarrassed by the CIA's bungling of the invasion of Cuba at the Bay of Pigs, might try to interfere with other CIA operations and curtail the agency's independence. *But:* This was the same Kennedy who had approved the CIA's plan to invade Cuba at the Bay of Pigs, who brought the world to the brink of nuclear war during the Cuban missile crisis, and who escalated U.S. involvement in Vietnam. Hardly a president likely to close down the Cold War or the CIA.

The KGB. Oswald was a Marxist who'd defected to Russia. *But:* Recently released KGB files indicate the Russians considered Oswald nothing but a nuisance and were delighted to be rid of him. Besides, Khrushchev would have been crazy to risk nuclear war for the sake of replacing Kennedy with the more hardline Lyndon Johnson.

Castro. Castro was aware that the CIA had tried to kill him, and in September 1963 he'd threatened revenge. *But:* Castro himself later insisted that it would have been "tremendous insanity" for him to order Kennedy's assassination and risk the full fury of all America. And, though he undoubtedly hated Kennedy, Castro wasn't insane. It is possible, however, that Oswald read of Castro's threat in the New Orleans *Times-Picayune* and took it upon himself to carry it out.

Anti-Castro Cubans. Many Cubans were unhappy Kennedy had backed away from stronger support during the Bay of Pigs fiasco; some extremists among them may have wanted the president dead. *But:* Oswald was a communist and an admirer of Castro. It's hard to imagine him working with Castro's enemies.

The Mafia. As attorney general, Robert Kennedy was cracking down on organized crime and a number of dons were undoubtedly incensed. Plus Jack Ruby had plenty of mob connections, albeit low-level ones. So, this theory went, Oswald had been hired to kill Kennedy and then Ruby had been hired to make sure Oswald didn't talk. Robert Blakey, chief counsel for the House Select Committee on Assassinations, thought the Mafia was behind the murder and the committee went so far as to discuss particular mobsters—in particular, teamster boss Jimmy Hoffa, Tampa godfather Santo Trafficante, and New Orleans godfather Carlos Marcello. All had spoken of hitting the president (at least according to witnesses of questionable reliability). *But:* There was no evidence that they'd done more than talk. Besides, couldn't the Mafia have found more reliable hitmen than Oswald and Ruby?

Of course, none of this *proves* there was no conspiracy. And, even if none of the above groups conspired with Oswald, there remains the possibility of a conspiracy between Oswald and other disaffected amateurs, some of whom may have had connections with the CIA, the Cubans, or the mob. For many Americans, Kennedy's death was so traumatic that it seemed *unfair* that he be the victim of Oswald alone; at least a conspiracy would imbue his death with some greater meaning. And, indeed, there are still too many unanswered questions about the assassination to rule out such a possibility.

But against the illogic of each particular conspiracy theory must be held up the logic, albeit twisted, of Oswald's own mind. Desperately ambitious and deeply tortured, Oswald may have seen the assassination as his chance to punish both America and Russia for not recognizing that he was a great man, destined to change the course of history—which, whether alone or with others, he most definitely did.

☆ To investigate further:

Report of the President's Commission on the Assassination of President John F. Kennedy, Washington, DC: United States Government Printing Office, 1964. Even those who disparage the findings of the Warren Commission have found its 26 volumes of testimony and evidence an invaluable source.

Weisberg, Harold. *Whitewash.* New York: Dell, 1966. The first in-depth attack on the Warren Report, this was originally self-published in 1965.

Lane, Mark. *Rush to Judgment.* Orlando: Holt, Rinehart and Winston, 1966. Another early attack on the Warren Report, this established a tradition of best-sellers on the subject. Lane also authored a 1991 book, *Plausible Denial,* which argued that the CIA killed Kennedy.

Epstein, Edward Jay. *Inquest.* New York: Viking, 1966. Of the early attacks on the Warren Report, this stands up best. Epstein presents a convincing case that the commission was unable to insulate itself from political and national security considerations. Epstein's 1968 book, *Counterplot* (Viking, NY), is also useful as a refutation of Garrison's theories, and his 1978 book, *Legend* (Readers Digest Press, NY), is an intriguing investigation of the CIA's efforts to establish whether Yuri Nosenko, a KGB officer who defected to the U.S. and who claimed to have supervised Oswald's case in Russia, was telling the truth. All three books were republished in a single volume, with new material, in a 1992 Carroll & Graf (NY) edition.

Ford, Gerald and John Stiles. *Portrait of the Assassin.* New York: Ballantine, 1966. Consisting largely of reprints of testimony before the Warren Commission, this was the first book to defend the Warren Report. Then-Representative Ford was a member of the commission.

Summers, Anthony. *Conspiracy.* New York: McGraw-Hill, 1980. Claims that a conspiracy involved Oswald, anti-Castro exiles, Mafia members, and CIA renegades.

Lifton, David. *Best Evidence.* New York: Macmillan, 1980. Claims that Kennedy's body was stolen and surgically altered in order to eliminate evidence of a shooter in front of the president.

Blakey, G. Robert and Richard Billings. *The Plot to Kill the President.* New York: New York Times Press, 1981. Claims that the conspiracy involved organized crime and anti-Castro exiles. Blakey was counsel to the House Select Committee on Assassinations.

Davis, John. *Mafia Kingfish.* New York: McGraw-Hill, 1988.

Scheim, David. *Contract on America.* Silver Spring, Maryland: Argyle Press, 1983. Both Scheim & Davis (see above) claim the Mafia did it.

Garrison, Jim. *On the Trail of the Assassins.* New York: Sheridan Square Press, 1988. The New Orleans D.A.'s story, which was the basis of Oliver Stone's movie *JFK.*

Posner, Gerald. *Case Closed.* New York: Random House, 1993. A thorough and compelling presentation of the case that Oswald acted alone.

Mailer, Norman. *Oswald's Tale.* New York: Random House, 1995. More a novelist's portrait of Oswald than an analysis of the evidence; nonetheless, the Oswald who emerges from the (often brilliant, if overly long) portrait is clearly a man capable of shooting the president, by himself.

Chapter 26

What Happened at the Gulf of Tonkin?

Within hours of succeeding the slain John Kennedy, President Lyndon Johnson vowed: "I am not going to lose Vietnam."

That was easier said than done: the situation that Johnson inherited was already bleak and rapidly deteriorating. By early 1964 about 40 percent of South Vietnam was under Vietcong control, South Vietnamese soldiers were deserting at alarming rates, and the North Vietnamese were in the process of turning the Ho Chi Minh trail into a modern logistical system through which thousands of troops, weapons, ammunition, and other equipment were pouring south. The new regime in Saigon—the result of an assassination which preceded Kennedy's by three weeks—appeared to be even more corrupt and inept than its predecessors. Without a significant increase in U.S. support (there were currently just over 16,000 American troops there, none of whom were directly involved in the fighting), a communist victory seemed inevitable.

On the home front, Johnson was doing much better. His opponent in the upcoming election, Barry Goldwater, was talking about how satisfying it would be to lob a nuclear missile "down into the gents' room in the Kremlin." Voters panicked by Goldwater's extremism were flocking to the Democratic camp in droves, especially after the president promised that "we are not about to send American boys nine or ten thousand miles away from home to do what Asian boys ought to be doing for themselves."

But this presented a problem for Johnson. Unless he did something, Vietnam would fall. Yet, as the peace candidate, how could he escalate American involvement in the war?

Then, in the Gulf of Tonkin, off the coast of North Vietnam, came the solution to Johnson's problem. The administration reported that on August 2 and then again on August 4, while the U.S. destroyer *Maddox* was on a routine patrol mission in the Gulf, it was ambushed by North Vietnamese patrol boats. After the first attack, Johnson was restrained, promising only that patrols in the Gulf would continue and that U.S. forces would destroy any attackers. But a second attack called for a tougher response, which Johnson could now give without undermining his moderate image. He ordered planes from the nearby USS *Constellation* and USS *Ticonderoga* to attack the base of the North Vietnamese patrol boats and a supporting oil complex, and on August 5 they carried out this mission by dropping the first U.S. bombs on Vietnam. The mission was a success: eight boats were destroyed and twenty others damaged, and 90 percent of the oil depot was destroyed.

Still, Johnson and his advisors felt they might need more authority to respond quickly and decisively to the situation in Vietnam. On August 6, the president submitted to Congress legislation officially titled "Joint Resolution to Promote the Maintenance of International Peace and Security in Southeast Asia." The legislation, which was soon dubbed the Gulf of Tonkin Resolution, authorized the president "to take all necessary steps, including the use of armed force, to assist any member or protocol state of the Southeast Asia Collective Defense Treaty requesting assistance in defense of its freedom." On August 7, after Secretary of Defense Robert McNamara appeared before the Senate Committees on Foreign Relations and the House Foreign Affairs Committee to describe the unprovoked aggression against U.S. ships in the Gulf of Tonkin, the House approved the resolution by a vote of 416 to 0 and the Senate by a vote of 88 to 2.

Everything seemed to be going Johnson's way. The election was a landslide, with Johnson receiving 61.1 percent of the vote to Goldwater's 38.5 percent. And, in the Gulf of Tonkin Resolution, Congress had signed a blank check—a check which Johnson cashed in January 1965, when he ordered 100,000 ground troops to Vietnam.

The U.S.S. Maddox in 1947, seventeen years before it was involved in the battle—or rather, the alleged battle—that led to the escalation of the Vietnam War. AP/Wide World Photos.

But, as the United States became mired in the Vietnam War, questions arose, not only about whether we ought to be there, but also about how we got there. Some critics of the war claimed the U.S. ships had been the aggressors in the Gulf of Tonkin; others claimed that the battle there had never even taken place. Worse, some contended the administration knew these facts and intentionally misled Congress in order to extract from that body the power to go to war.

Historians of the Vietnam War, and of the Gulf of Tonkin incidents in particular, are fortunate that one of those who came to doubt the administration's story was Senator William Fulbright who, as chair of the Foreign Relations Committee, was in a position to investigate the matter.

Initially, Fulbright was one of the administration's most useful supporters, shepherding the Gulf of Tonkin resolution through the Senate. When Senator Gaylord Nelson proposed amending the resolution to require congressional approval before the dispatch of troops to Vietnam, Fulbright convinced him that Johnson had no intention of sending the troops and that the amendment was therefore unnecessary. But as the war widened so did the breach between Johnson and Fulbright and by 1966 Fulbright was openly critical of the president's foreign policy.

His suspicions about the Tonkin incidents were heightened in May of that year, when Assistant Secretary of State William Bundy, in secret testimony before the committee, said he'd written a draft similar to the Tonkin resolution in May or June 1964—several months before the incidents in the gulf. Bundy called the drafts "normal contingency planning," but it was clear that the administration had been preparing to escalate the war well before anything happened in the Gulf of Tonkin.

In September 1967 Fulbright authorized the committee staff to begin an inquiry into the Tonkin incidents, and he requested copies of the official logbooks of the *Maddox*. What emerged from the staff's investigations and the 1967–1968 hearings before the Foreign Relations Committee was a very different story from the one Johnson and McNamara had presented to the committee in 1964.

First, it became clear that the administration's claim that the *Maddox* was engaged in a routine patrol was at best misleading, if not downright false. Cables to and from the *Maddox* repeatedly referred to something called "34-A Operations," which, the Pentagon eventually admitted, included South Vietnamese raids on the islands in the vicinity of the U.S. ship. During the brief 1964 hearings before the passage of the resolution, McNamara had stated that "our Navy played absolutely no part in, was not associated with, was not aware of, any South Vietnamese actions, if there were any." Yet the cables indicated that the captain of the *Maddox,* John Herrick, had been aware of the operations and that his superiors might very well have been using the *Maddox* as a decoy to draw the North Vietnamese patrol boats away from the area of the 34-A Operations.

Second, though the *Maddox* had been pursued by North Vietnamese patrol boats on August 2, it was the *Maddox* that first opened fire. The North Vietnamese held their course and then did fire torpedoes at the destroyer. The torpedoes missed the destroyer but the destroyer's guns were on target; one of the North Vietnamese patrol boats sunk and the others retreated back to port, briefly pursued by aircraft from the *Ticonderoga*.

It was the revelations about the August 4 incident, however, that most shocked the committee. It was this attack, remember, that had supposedly prompted Johnson to retaliate. Yet what the committee found was that the second battle almost certainly did not take place at all.

True, the *Maddox* and *Turner Joy* (another destroyer that had joined the *Maddox* after the August 2 attack) had fired four hundred rounds into the black night, dropped depth charges, and at one point tried to ram their attackers. *But not a single sailor on either vessel had actually seen or heard North Vietnamese ships or gunfire.* Nor had the pilots of the planes summoned from the *Constellation* seen the enemy. And though the *Maddox*'s sonars counted a total of 26 enemy torpedoes, none scored a hit. Even more suspicious, the sonar man on the *Turner Joy* hadn't reported any torpedoes.

Aboard the *Maddox,* Captain Herrick began to have doubts about the incident even before it ended. So once the shooting stopped, he conducted an experiment, putting the ship into high-speed turns. After each, the sonar man reported hearing torpedoes. Herrick concluded that most, if not all, of the *Maddox*'s torpedo reports were probably caused by the echo of outgoing sonar beams hitting the ship's rudders. He wired his superiors that the "entire action leaves many doubts" and suggested a "complete evaluation" before any further measures were taken.

But by then Johnson was in no mood to wait. Even as the Pentagon was sending urgent messages asking the Pacific commanders for evidence substantiating the attack, American bombers were already en route to their first North Vietnamese targets.

☆ ☆ ☆

The navy did not invent the battle of August 4; as Herrick suggested soon after, the weather and an "overeager sonar man" might have accounted for the confusion. Nor did Johnson or McNamara invent the battle, as some later critics of the war contended; both may very well have thought the *Maddox* was attacked. But in their eagerness to use the incident to push through the congressional resolution, both ignored a good deal of evidence that the attack never took place, and both undeniably misled the public and the Congress when they described a complex and ambiguous incident as a clear, unprovoked attack. Only days after the resolution had passed, Johnson admitted he knew more than he'd told. In a private comment to George Ball, his undersecretary of state, he said: "Hell, those dumb, stupid sailors were just shooting at flying fish."

Some of the blame for what followed, however, must be shared by Congress. The Gulf of Tonkin resolution was only the latest in a series of congressional abdications of its constitutional power to declare war. Congress had stood by as Truman sent troops to Korea without any congressional authorization; it had given permission for Eisenhower to deploy U.S. forces "as he deems it necessary" to protect Taiwan against a communist assault. Like Johnson, many Democrats in Congress were positioning themselves for the upcoming elections, and they feared Republicans would portray a vote against the resolution as unpatriotic or weak.

Later, Fulbright and others contended that they'd never intended to authorize a full-scale war in Asia. As the 1967 Senate Foreign Relations Committee report commented, "the prevailing attitude [in 1964] was not so much that Congress was granting or acknowledging the executive's authority to take certain actions but that it was expressing unity and support for the President in a moment of national crisis." Even hawks such as Senator John Stennis became disillusioned by the administration's broad use of the resolution, and in August 1966 Stennis told Secretary of State Dean Rusk that he thought the administration's deceptions might have invalidated the resolution. But Rusk dismissed the argument and Stennis's legal position was never tested. And, however much Fulbright and Stennis and others in Congress might have later regretted it, they could not deny that they'd voted for a resolution giving Johnson very broad powers; so broad, Johnson later quipped, that it was "like grandma's nightshirt—it covered everything."

☆ To investigate further:

Goulden, Joseph. *Truth Is the First Casualty.* Chicago: Rand McNally, 1969. The first of the revisionist accounts of the incident.

Galloway, John. *The Gulf of Tonkin Resolution.* Cranbury, NJ: Fairleigh Dickinson University Press, 1970. Especially useful for its inclusion of relevant documents such as the resolution itself, Johnson's addresses to the nation and to

Congress, and the transcripts of the Committee on Foreign Relations' 1968 hearings.

Windchy, Eugene. *Tonkin Gulf.* New York: Doubleday, 1971. A thorough reconstruction of the incidents.

Karnow, Stanley. *Vietnam.* New York: Viking, 1983. Given its broad scope, this cannot go into detail about the Tonkin gulf or many other aspects of the war; still, it remains the best general, balanced history of the war.

Stockdale, Jim and Sybil. *In Love and War.* New York: Harper & Row, 1984. Before becoming Ross Perot's 1992 running mate, Stockdale was a navy pilot who took off from the *Ticonderoga* to aid the *Maddox;* his book tells what he saw and what he didn't see—"no boats, no boat gunfire, no torpedo wakes—nothing but black sea and American firepower."

McNamara, Robert. *In Retrospect.* New York: Times Books, 1995. In retrospect, McNamara admits the escalation of the Vietnam War was an error, but he continues to deny (unconvincingly) that he or anyone in the administration deliberately misled Congress about the Gulf of Tonkin incidents.

Moïse, Edwin. *Tonkin Gulf and the Escalation of the Vietnam War.* Chapel Hill: University of North Carolina Press, 1996. The most recent and most thorough history of both the events and nonevents.

Chapter 27

Who Killed Malcolm X?

To most mainstream historians, the assassination of Malcolm X in February 1965 was the work of the Nation of Islam, the black nationalist religious group from which Malcolm had defected a year earlier. In the alternative presses, however, many black writers have questioned this explanation, arguing that U.S. intelligence forces played a role in the conspiracy. Compounding the problem has been the lack of extensive scholarship on Malcolm. In contrast to Martin Luther King Jr., whose life and times have been the subject of a number of major works, Malcolm is still best known through his own autobiography. And while *The Autobiography of Malcolm X* well deserves its place in the back pockets of radicals and rappers—and of any serious student of the period—it is by no means a definitive history of Malcolm's life. Nor, of course, could Malcolm cover his own death.

Does this mean Malcolm's death is destined to remain a mystery? Not entirely.

Whatever else its critics may say about the mainstream account of Malcolm's death, no one can question that the leadership of the Nation of Islam hated Malcolm X. To the Nation, Malcolm was not just an enemy but an apostate and traitor. Malcolm had originally converted to the Nation of Islam in 1949, while serving a term in prison for burglary. The Nation redeemed him from a life of crime: no longer was he Malcolm Little (as he'd been born) or "Detroit Red" (as he'd called himself when he became a pimp and con artist); now he was Malcolm X. "The Muslim's 'X,' " he explained in the *Autobiography,* "symbolized the true African family name that he never could know [and] replaced the white slave master name . . . which some blue-eyed devil named Little had imposed upon my paternal forebears."

What the Nation offered Malcolm (and hundreds of thousands of other blacks) was a radical alternative theology. The Nation's leader, Elijah Muhammad, asserted that all whites were devils (created by an evil black scientist) whose world would be destroyed in the coming racial Armageddon. Malcolm's brilliant rhetorical skills propelled him to the forefront of the Nation, first as the minister of Harlem's Mosque Number 7, the largest in the country, and then as the Nation's National Minister. He became the voice of black nationalism, the angry counterpoint to Martin Luther King Jr.'s preachings about Christian love.

So successful was Malcolm in his role as the Nation's mouthpiece that he became much better known to the press and public than Muhammad himself. This provoked the envy of others in the Nation, including its leader.

Doctrinal disagreements, too, were tearing apart Muhammad and Malcolm. Muhammad's apocalyptic vision provoked fears among whites but what he actually called for was not violence against white society but a complete withdrawal from it. Malcolm's impulses, on the other hand, were more activist. When Martin Luther King led the 1963 civil rights "March on Washington," for example, Muhammad, as part of his nonengagement policy, prohibited his followers from attending. Malcolm went along with Muhammad, *part* of the way: he derided the integrationists, branding the March the "Farce on Washington" and calling it more of a picnic than a protest. But, in blatant disregard of Muhammad's ban, Malcolm couldn't resist attending the March.

Malcolm's faith became even shakier when he learned that Muhammad had fathered a number of illegitimate children. Malcolm called a meeting of New York Muslim leaders, supposedly in order to prepare them in case the adulteries became public. In the eyes of many around Muhammad, however, this was just another example of Malcolm trying to undermine Muhammad's position.

The rift between Malcolm and Muhammad became public after John Kennedy's assassination. Muhammad had ordered all Muslims to refrain from commenting on the assassination. Malcolm, however, couldn't resist: asked for his comments, he first mentioned the many Third World leaders who'd been killed as a result of American intervention and concluded by saying that Kennedy's assassination was "a case of chickens coming home to roost."

Muhammad was outraged. Not that Muhammad was a fan of Kennedy (who was, after all, the president of a nation of white devils), but Malcolm had disobeyed his direct order. Muhammad suspended his chief minister for 90 days, and before the period was up Malcolm had formally broken with the Nation and started his own rival organization, the Muslim Mosque, Inc.

Now Malcolm presented an even greater danger to the Nation. Not only was he preaching heresy, but he was heading a rival group and appealing to the Nation's own members. Nation ministers denounced Malcolm; he retaliated by going public with the stories of Muhammad's adulteries. So the Nation pushed up its rhetoric another notch. In a three-part series in the organization's newspaper, *Muhammad Speaks,* Minister Louis X of Boston—who had been recruited to the Nation by Malcolm and who later became known as Louis Farrakhan—condemned the "unbelievable treachery" of his former mentor. The December 4, 1964, issue of *Muhammad Speaks* contained the most suggestive attack of all: "Only those who wish to be led to hell, or to their doom, will follow Malcolm," Farrakhan wrote. "The die is set, and Malcolm shall not escape. . . . Such a man as Malcolm is worthy of death."

During the final year of his life, between his March 1964 break with the Nation and his February 1965 assassination, Malcolm was continually harassed by death threats. In his autobiography, he wrote: "Wherever I go . . . black men are watching every move I make, awaiting their chance to kill me. . . . I know that they have their orders. Anyone who chooses not to believe what I am saying doesn't know the Muslims in the NOI [Nation of Islam]."

Hostile, armed Muslims chased Malcolm in New York, Los Angeles, and Chicago. Just a week before his assassination, Malcolm's house in Queens was firebombed. Finally, on February 21, as he began to speak before his followers at the Audubon Ballroom in Harlem, he

Outside the Audubon Ballroom in Harlem, February 21, 1965. UPI/Corbis-Bettman.

was shot to death by at least three and possibly (according to some witnesses in the crowd) five assassins.

☆ ☆ ☆

One of those assassins, Talmadge Hayer, was caught at the scene. The police subsequently arrested two other suspects, Norman 3X and Thomas 15X. Both Norman 3X and Thomas 15X were members of the Nation's mosque in Harlem; both had been accused of shooting Benjamin Brown, another Muslim minister who'd strayed from the fold; and both were placed at the Audubon by eyewitnesses. In March 1966 a jury found all three defendants guilty of murder.

Twelve years later, in 1978, Hayer confessed that he had, indeed, killed Malcolm, along with four fellow Muslims from the Nation's Newark Mosque Number 25. He'd stayed silent so long, he said, to protect Elijah Muhammad; since Muhammad had died in 1975, Hayer could now tell the truth. And, he emphasized, Norman 3X and Thomas 15X were completely innocent.

What to make of Hayer's story? The prosecution didn't buy it, nor did Judge Harold Rothwax, who decided that Hayer was merely trying to get his accomplices off the hook.

But many historians have found Hayer's story convincing. Clearly, Hayer was guilty—and now that he'd admitted he'd done it for the sake of the Nation, his motive was equally clear. As for Norman 3X and Thomas 15X, the case against them had never been as strong as that against Hayer. No physical evidence placed them anywhere near the Audubon on the night of Malcolm's murder and, of the hundreds at the Audubon, only a handful had identified them—this in spite of the fact that Norman 3X and Thomas 15X were well-known members of the Nation (and thus just the type of person for whom Malcolm's followers and bodyguards would have been on the lookout). Hayer's confession swayed Peter Goldman, author of the best biography of Malcolm written to date. In the original 1973 edition of his book, Goldman argued that Norman 3X and Thomas 15X were guilty but in the 1979 revision he admitted it was likely they were innocent.

All three men convicted of the murder—Hayer, Norman 3X, and Thomas 15X—have now been paroled and, barring some deathbed confessions, it seems likely that history's verdict will overturn that of the jury. Hayer was certainly guilty; Norman 3X and Thomas 15X were probably not. But more pressing historical questions remain: Who ordered the assassination? Was it Elijah Muhammad? Was it Louis Farrakhan? Or, as Hayer maintained, did he and his accomplices act for the sake of the Nation but without direct orders from any higher-ups?

Elijah Muhammad always denied giving any order to kill Malcolm. So, too, has Louis Farrakhan, though he has acknowledged that his rhetoric contributed to the atmosphere that led to the assassination. But, Farrakhan and others in the Nation have stressed that investigators wanting a full understanding of Malcolm's death should look beyond the Nation. The Nation of Islam, they argue, was not the only organization that wanted Malcolm dead.

The FBI's history of harassing Martin Luther King Jr.—which included secretly recording his extramarital affairs and threatening to send the tapes to his wife unless he committed suicide—was well documented by the 1975 Senate Select Committee on Intelligence Activities. Unfortunately the bureau's campaigns against the Nation and against Malcolm have not been as fully investigated. Many of the files remain classified, and those that have been released include critical deletions.

But from the files that have been released, a great deal has been learned. FBI surveillance of the Nation dates back to 1956, and its actions included some of the same types of dirty tricks used against King. Between 1959 and 1962, the bureau channeled embarrassing information about Elijah Muhammad's finances and sex life to journalists. When this failed to slow the Nation's growth (perhaps because its members were not quite so puritanical or voyeuristic as J. Edgar Hoover and his agents), the bureau sent anonymous letters with additional information on Muhammad's sex life to "selected individuals" in the Nation hierarchy. Who these individuals were has been deleted from the files, but it's reasonable to assume that Malcolm was among them, and that some of the details about Muhammad's sex life that so upset him came from the FBI.

The files also indicate that at least one and possibly two FBI agents had infiltrated the Nation's top leadership, and that their job was to "plant the seed of dissension" within the organization. A February 1964 memo suggested a move that "could possibly widen the rift between Muhammad and Little and possibly result in Little's expulsion from the NOI." Again, the specifics are deleted from the file, so it's impossible to know what the plan was or even whether it was enacted. But we do know that, as the FBI desired, the rift between Muhammad and Malcolm widened.

Until more FBI files are declassified, it's impossible to say exactly what role the bureau played in Malcolm's assassination. Some, like Farrakhan, have speculated that it was an FBI agent planted in the Nation who gave the order to murder Malcolm. At this point, such speculation remains just speculation; there is no proof that anyone in the FBI actually participated in any way in the murder plot. But—and the revelations about the FBI's campaign against King and others may make this seem less shocking and appalling than it ought to be—it's quite clear that, from J. Edgar Hoover down to his agents in the field, the FBI considered its mission to be one of escalating the feud between Malcolm and the Nation. That the FBI might instead have used some of its intelligence and manpower to save Malcolm's life seems never to have occurred to anyone in the bureau.

An odd epilogue to this sordid tale must have brought at least some satisfaction to Farrakhan. Both Betty Shabazz, Malcolm's widow, and Quibilah Shabazz, his daughter, had blamed Farrakhan for Malcolm's death. In 1995 the FBI arrested Quibilah Shabazz, charging that she had tried to hire a hit man to kill Farrakhan and avenge her father's death. The key witness was a long-time government informant of dubious reliability, and prosecutors and defense lawyers ultimately struck a deal that spared them a trial and let Quibilah Shabazz off with a two-year probation.

Before the deal was struck, however, Farrakhan and Betty Shabazz spoke out together against the government's case. Ironically, this latest federal intervention in the life and death of Malcolm X had brought about what the 30 years since the assassination had not—a reconciliation between Malcolm's family and the Nation of Islam.

☆ To investigate further:

X, Malcolm, as told to Alex Haley. *The Autobiography of Malcolm X.* New York: Grove Press, 1994. A classic of African-American letters.

Goldman, Peter. *The Death and Life of Malcolm X.* Champaign: University of Illinois Press, 1979. Though Goldman is a little too reluctant to accuse the authorities of wrongdoing, this is nonetheless the best biography of Malcolm. In the original 1973 edition, Goldman argues that Norman 3X and Thomas 15X were guilty; in the 1979 edition, confronted by Hayer's second confession, he concedes the others were probably innocent.

Garrow, David. *The FBI and Martin Luther King, Jr.* New York: Norton, 1981. The revelations about the FBI's war against King had come out during Senate hearings, so this book added little in the way of facts. But Garrow's analysis of the FBI's motives are provocative and convincing.

Carson, Clayborne. *Malcolm X: The FBI File.* New York: Carroll & Graf, 1991. Though it *is* missing a lot of files that have been released (as well as many still classified), what *is* here is at least suggestive of the mass of intelligence and gossip collected by the FBI.

Breitman, George, Herman Porter, and Baxter Smith. *The Assassination of Malcolm X.* New York: Pathfinder, 1991. Originally published in 1976, this is a Marxist view of the assassination. The authors argue that, after leaving the Nation, Malcolm was evolving toward socialism (for which there is some evidence) and that this provoked the CIA into some role in the assassination (for which the evidence is very circumstantial).

Perry, Bruce. *Malcolm.* Barrytown, NY: Station Hill Press, 1991. A controversial psychobiography that interprets Malcolm's life and politics as a response not to white racism but to an abused childhood. Though his analysis is often simplistic, Perry raises many issues ignored by other scholars.

Evanzz, Karl. *The Judas Factor*. New York: Thunder's Mouth Press, 1992. The Judas of the title is John Ali, a top-level Nation figure who Evanzz thinks conspired with the CIA and FBI to murder Malcolm. Evanzz raises some valid questions but doesn't answer them convincingly.

Friedly, Michael. *Malcolm X: The Assassination*. New York: Carroll & Graf, 1992. The most thorough statement of the position that the Nation of Islam was responsible for Malcolm's death, and that the FBI (though actively working to discredit the Nation and Malcolm) did not in any way participate in the plot.

Lee, Spike with Ralph Wiley. *By Any Means Necessary*. New York: Hyperion, 1992. Lee's account of the making of his film about Malcolm includes his tantalizingly suggestive but ultimately frustrating interviews with Farrakhan and others involved in the case.

Gardell, Mattias. *In The Name of Elijah Muhammad*. Durham, NC: Duke University Press, 1996. The fullest account of the Nation of Islam's ideology and theology, this also includes the best account of how the FBI attempted to incite the Muslims to violence against one another.

Chapter 28

Who Was to Blame for the Kent State Killings?

In spite of its 20,000 students, Kent State University in early 1970 was virtually unknown outside Ohio. All that soon changed. On May 4 of that year, national guardsmen who'd been called in to control antiwar protests opened fire on a crowd of students, killing four and wounding nine others. From then on, the name Kent State would instantly conjure up images of slain students and horrified onlookers.

The tension that culminated in the shootings began building on Thursday, April 30, when President Richard Nixon announced on national television that he was sending American troops into Cambodia. This infuriated opponents of the war, who felt Nixon was escalating a war he'd promised to end. On Friday students threw rocks and bottles through storefronts in downtown Kent, and police had to use tear gas to disperse the crowd. On Saturday word spread around the campus of a plan to burn the Army ROTC building, and a large crowd gathered there. That evening the building was burned to the ground.

Students awoke on Sunday to find the campus occupied by armed soldiers of the Ohio National Guard. Governor James Rhodes arrived in Kent for a press conference where he promptly increased the general tension by calling the protesters "worse than the brownshirts and the communist element . . . the worst type of people that we harbor in America." And Adjutant General Sylvester Del Corso of the

National Guard added that "we will apply whatever degree of force is necessary to provide protection for the lives of our citizens and their property."

By Monday, May 4, student anger about Cambodia had been transferred to the national guardsmen. A noon rally attracted about two thousand students, though the vast majority just wanted to see what was going on. Guardsmen ordered the crowd to disperse; demonstrators responded by chanting "Pigs off campus" and "One, two, three, four, we don't want your fucking war." Some also started throwing rocks at the soldiers. At 12:25 a group of guardsmen crested a hill and suddenly turned, rushed back to the top of the hill, and opened fire.

To those in the antiwar movement, this was the ultimate escalation of the Vietnam War; American soldiers had branched out from killing Vietnamese to killing Americans. Hundreds of thousands of students across the country went on strike. To them, the guardsmen were murderers, guilty of conspiring with each other or their higher-ups (in some theories, as high up as the White House) to kill innocent students who were peacefully exercising their constitutional rights. Many Americans, however, thought the students got what they deserved. Richard Nixon's "silent majority" saw the students as a dangerous threat to American society and an immediate threat to the guardsmen. The guardsmen, in their view, acted in self-defense.

To cut through the heightened rhetoric of both sides, historians had to answer some fundamental questions. Were the guardsmen in danger when they opened fire, or did they just want to teach the protesters a lesson? Did someone order them to fire, or did they fire on their own? Most fundamentally of all: *Why did the guardsmen shoot?*

A series of court cases did little to answer these questions. A state grand jury indicted 25 people, mostly students, and issued a report blaming students, faculty, and the Kent State administration for the violence. But in September 1971 the state dropped almost all the charges for lack of evidence. Then a federal grand jury indicted eight guardsmen but they, too, were not convicted: in November 1974, before the case went to a jury, the judge dismissed the charges on the grounds that the government had failed to prove its case beyond a reasonable doubt.

Meanwhile, the students injured in the shootings and the parents of the slain students sued the guardsmen, the governor, and the university's president. But the civil suit was also inconclusive. The parties settled out of court, with the state of Ohio agreeing to pay a total of $675,000 to the parents and students. The defendants also signed a statement of regret about the shootings, but it was carefully worded to avoid any admission of guilt.

Among those who sympathized with the students, many suspected that these legal processes had been tainted by political considerations. Those suspicions were confirmed in May 1978, when NBC-TV revealed the existence of a 1970 memorandum from John Ehrlichman, Nixon's chief domestic advisor, to Attorney General John Mitchell. The memo, marked EYES ONLY, referred to a previous memo in which Nixon had ordered Mitchell not to convene a federal grand jury to investigate the case.

Why would Nixon try—unsuccessfully, it turned out—to squelch a grand jury investigation? With Watergate still fresh in everyone's mind, it seemed that this, too, was part of a cover-up. But what was he covering up?

One theory was that Nixon had ordered the National Guard to get tough with the students, and that he didn't want the administration to be blamed for the shootings. This seems unlikely: the National Archives has no record of a conversation between the president and Governor Rhodes or General Del Corso or anyone else connected with the killings. Nixon's sympathies undoubtedly lay with the guards, not the students, but it's hard to imagine how, sitting in the White House, he could have arranged the chaotic sequence of events that led to the killings.

Another theory, less far-fetched, was that Nixon feared a federal grand jury would find out that the government had planted its agents among the student demonstrators. The presence of government agents on campus would explain a number of other mysteries as well: for one, why the state had so suddenly dropped its case against the demonstrators, and for another, the strange circumstances surrounding the burning of the ROTC building. That the building was going to burn Saturday night was common knowledge; a large crowd had gathered to watch it by 8:00. Yet the police didn't show up until 9:15. Even more mysteriously, the blaze was under control when the police arrived; it did not burn out of control until *after* the police had finally chased away the demonstrators and taken custody of the building.

If government agents played some role in the fire—perhaps setting the blaze in order to give the authorities an excuse to call in the National Guard and crack down on the demonstrators—it would make sense of these strange goings-on. Still, it must be emphasized, there's no hard evidence that there were government agents on campus, let alone involved in the fire. And there are other ways to explain Nixon's interference with the Justice Department; perhaps he just didn't want to see the guardsmen prosecuted for the murder of students who were, after all, demonstrating against Nixon's policies. So, reluctantly, most historians have admitted that they cannot say for sure why Nixon tried to stop a grand jury investigation. Nor are they sure who set fire to the ROTC building; it might have been government agents, but it might also have been student or outside radicals.

☆ ☆ ☆

But, to return to the events of May 4: Were the guardsmen in any immediate danger when they opened fire?

Spokesmen for the Guard initially claimed that the troops were retaliating to sniper fire. This was almost certainly not true. An extensive investigation by the FBI found no evidence of any bullets other than military ones.

The next and main claim made by the guardsmen was that the troops fired to protect themselves against a wild, onrushing crowd of demonstrators who were pelting them with rocks and bricks. This claim, too, was dubious. No guardsman had to be treated for any injuries after the incident. Nor were the guardsmen trapped; in fact, just before they turned and fired, they seemed about to pass out of the demonstrators' sight. Most of the witnesses interviewed by the FBI said the main body of the crowd was at least 60 yards away from the guardsmen, and photographs and television film confirmed that only a few students were any nearer. The nearest of the victims was 60 feet away, not the 20 or 30 claimed by some guardsmen.

Might the guardsmen have panicked, even if they were in no immediate danger? Possibly. Many had been on duty for nearly a week with little sleep; they'd had at least some stones thrown at them and a great many insults. But the majority of evidence contradicts this supposition as well. There were 67 shots fired—a lot more than you'd expect from a few panicked guardsmen. And dozens of witnesses told the FBI that, right before the shooting began, the guardsmen turned

The National Guard claimed it had been under attack by demonstrators at Kent State, but no photo showed any student within 60 feet of the guardsmen. Courtesy of Kent State University.

together to face the crowd. All this would seem to indicate the decision to shoot was just that: a decision, not a panicky accident.

So we come to the final question. Who made that decision? Some witnesses thought they saw officers on the scene giving hand signals which might be construed as an order to fire, but every officer denied giving any such order. Other witnesses reported that, just prior to the shooting, a number of guardsmen went into what they described as a "huddle." It may have been there that an officer gave the order, or that some guardsmen just decided among themselves that they'd taken enough from the students and that it was time to teach them a lesson.

No "smoking gun" was ever found at Kent State. Unless one of the guardsmen involved comes forward with some additional information, we're unlikely to learn precisely how the decision to open fire came about. But there's no question, as the president's commission on campus unrest concluded in its September 1970 report, that "the indiscriminate firing of rifles into a crowd of students and the deaths that followed were unnecessary, unwarranted, and inexcusable."

☆ To investigate further:

Eszterhas, Joe and Michael Roberts. *Thirteen Seconds.* New York: Dodd, Mead, 1970. A quickie by two Cleveland *Plain Dealer* reporters, but with some interesting profiles of key figures, including the slain students.

The Report of the President's Commission on Campus Unrest. Washington, DC: U.S. Government Printing Office, 1970. An unbiased and authoritative report, though it leaves unanswered many crucial questions.

Michener, James. *Kent State: What Happened and Why.* New York: Random House, 1971. As always, Michener has accumulated an extraordinary quantity of information. Some of it is useful and compelling, though his narrative is colored by his strong dislike of the protesters.

Davies, Peter. *The Truth About Kent State.* New York: Farrar Straus Giroux, 1973. Davies was an insurance broker who became obsessed with one of the slain students, and who saw conspiracies everywhere. Nonetheless, it was his investigation that forced the very reluctant federal government to prosecute the guardsmen. Davies also deserves credit for his altruism: when NBC commissioned a docudrama on Kent State, it paid Michener $400,000 for the rights. Davies, on whose book NBC relied heavily, didn't ask for a cent.

Kelner, Joseph and James Munves, *The Kent State Coverup.* New York: Harper & Row, 1980. Kelner, the chief counsel for the victims during the first civil trial, argues (self-servingly but convincingly) that the judge and jury were prejudiced against his clients.

Gordon, William A. *The Fourth of May.* Buffalo, NY: Prometheus Books, 1990. Balanced and thorough—and as close to the last word as anyone has come so far.

Chapter 29

What Did Nixon Know About Watergate?

Soon after the Watergate break-in of June 17, 1972, it became obvious this had been some sort of political operation. The burglars were caught, after all, in the Democratic National Committee (DNC) headquarters, in the Watergate office complex, and they had on them bugging devices—hardly the tools needed for a simple burglary. And then police traced the money in the burglars' possession to the Committee to Reelect the President, the aptly acronymed CREEP.

Still, no one in the White House revealed any particular concern. The president's press secretary smugly labeled the incident a "third-rate burglary." Other Republicans were equally quick to point out that no one involved in the president's campaign had any motive for being involved in such a crime. At the time of the burglary, Richard Nixon's political position seemed completely secure. Just eleven days before the break-in, Nixon had delightedly watched George McGovern win the California primary, virtually clinching the Democratic presidential nomination. Nixon realized McGovern was perceived as an ultraliberal, far to the left of the majority of voters, and his nomination made the president's reelection seem inevitable.

With Nixon's reelection virtually in the bag, what could he or anyone associated with him possibly want from the Democratic headquarters? As Nixon himself wrote in his 1978 memoirs: "The whole thing made so little sense. *Why?* I wondered. Why then? Why in such a blundering way?"

Why, indeed?

To Nixon's question, some historians and journalists have answered that, indeed, neither Nixon nor anyone with his interests in mind had anything to do with the break-in. Some were convinced that the break-in was arranged by the Democrats to frame Nixon. Somewhat more plausibly, others seized on the CIA connections of some of the burglars. According to this theory, the agency felt threatened by the president's policy of détente with the Soviet Union. So its agents planned—and then sabotaged—the burglary in order to embarrass Nixon. Still others believed the Joint Chiefs of Staff were behind the crime, for much the same reason.

Of the theories exculpating Nixon, the latest was presented in a 1991 best seller, *Silent Coup,* by journalists Len Colodny and Robert Gettlin. According to Colodny and Gettlin, it was the president's counsel, John Dean, who masterminded the break-in. Why did Dean do it? Because his girlfriend (and future wife) was linked to a call-girl ring supposedly being used by the DNC.

All these theories grew out of the entirely false assumption that the DNC held nothing of interest to Nixon. True, when the break-in was planned in June he was way ahead in the polls. But the operation was planned and approved earlier in the year; at that point the front-runner for the Democratic nomination was not George McGovern but Edmund Muskie—and Muskie was ahead of Nixon in the polls.

Besides, even if the election was secure, Nixon still might have wanted to find some dirt on his opponents. According to some reports, he was especially interested in what might be found from bugging the phone of DNC chairman Lawrence O'Brien. Nixon had disliked O'Brien ever since O'Brien's days as an adviser to President Kennedy, and he'd come to hate him when O'Brien became an adviser to Howard Hughes. Nixon, too, had a relationship with Hughes, including a questionable loan from the industrialist to the president's brother that had been a big embarrassment to the president. Nixon found it galling that the O'Brien/Hughes relationship had never cost O'Brien and the Democrats politically. Nixon was so obsessed with getting O'Brien that in early August, some seven weeks after the

"He says he's from the phone company..."

Courtesy of the Los Angeles Times.

Watergate break-in (when it was obviously risky for Nixon to continue to go after him), the president ordered his chief of staff H. R. Haldeman to use the IRS to embarrass O'Brien.

The Watergate break-in might also have revealed how much the Democratic campaign managers knew about a Republican deal with

ITT, a corporation which had allegedly offered cash in return for a favorable antitrust ruling. Or it might have been linked to Republican efforts to find out how much the Democrats knew about illegal contributions from Thomas Pappas, a prominent businessman and Nixon supporter. Still another possibility was that the burglars were after evidence linking the Democrats to left-wing radicals.

By his own admission, the plans for the break-in were drawn up by G. Gordon Liddy, an ex-FBI agent and right-wing ideologue who was now CREEP's general counsel. On January 27 he presented his plans to John Mitchell, who was at that time the attorney general of the United States but who was preparing to resign from that office in order to run Nixon's campaign committee. Also present at the meeting was John Dean. The plans that Liddy presented included more than just wiretapping the DNC; they also called for kidnapping antiwar demonstrators and sabotaging the air-conditioning system at the Democratic convention.

According to all three present at that meeting, Mitchell rejected the plans: they were unrealistic and too expensive, he told Liddy. (That they were also blatantly illegal seemed never to have crossed the attorney general's mind.)

On March 30 Mitchell met with his deputy at CREEP, Jeb Magruder. Again, the subject was what to do about Liddy's plans. Liddy had revised them, cutting the budget from $1 million to $250,000 but still including the break-in. This time, according to Magruder, Mitchell approved the plan. Mitchell always denied he had done so, but the evidence is against him—for he soon began authorizing large payments to Liddy.

But what of Nixon himself? Did he approve the plan—or even know about it in advance?

☆ ☆ ☆

What we know of the president's involvement comes primarily from tapes which he himself made of his White House conversations. No one investigating Watergate even knew about these tapes until July 1973, when Haldeman's aide, Alexander Butterfield, mentioned them in passing to the special Senate committee investigating the crime. From that point on, the legislative and legal investigations focused on getting hold of the crucial tapes.

Nixon considered the tapes his personal property and had no intention of turning them over to anyone. When he was ordered to do so by Judge John Sirica, who presided over the tapes litigation, the tapes started mysteriously disappearing. In October, Nixon's lawyer informed Sirica that two of the subpoenaed conversations had never been recorded. Less than two weeks later, the hapless lawyer told the judge that another of the subpoenaed tapes had an 18½-minute gap— this right in the midst of the very first White House discussion between Nixon and Haldeman on Watergate.

Who erased these crucial 18½ minutes?

Rose Mary Woods, the president's personal secretary, testified before the court that she might have caused a gap by reaching for the telephone while transcribing the tape and accidentally hitting the tape recorder's delete button. But when she was asked to demonstrate how this might have happened, she had to stretch herself into an extremely convoluted position. Stretching credibility even further was her testimony that her telephone conversation lasted only four or five minutes and therefore could not account for the remaining erasures. Nor did the testimony of Nixon's chief of staff, Alexander Haig, alleviate suspicion: it was just like a woman, he said, not to realize how long she'd been talking on the phone.

A court-appointed panel of experts concluded that the 18½-minute gap had been caused by hand operation of the controls, not the foot pedal, as Woods claimed. In addition, the panel stated that the gap had been caused by at least five and perhaps as many as nine separate erasures, and that the evidence was "consistent" with traces left by a deliberate erasure. At this point, even the conservative *National Review* threw in the towel, writing: "Believers in the accidental theory could gather for lunch in a phone booth."

The worst, for Nixon, was still to come. He eventually had to release some of the tapes Sirica requested, and on those tapes he can clearly be heard discussing payoffs and offering advice on how to commit perjury. A tape from June 23, 1972 came to be known as the "smoking gun" and it is indeed that: Nixon can be heard giving explicit instructions that the CIA should tell the FBI to lay off the Watergate investigation.

The June 23 tape proved beyond any doubt that Nixon had been guilty of obstructing justice, and once it was released his resignation was inevitable. But, it must be stressed, it was this involvement in the crime's cover-up that brought Nixon down. Nothing on the tapes he released indicated he'd had any direct involvement or knowledge of the crime itself.

Inevitably, some Nixon apologists continued to maintain that he was innocent. The 1991 book, *Silent Coup,* became a best-seller by portraying Nixon as a victim not just of Dean (whom it accused, you'll recall, of planning the break-in to find out about his girlfriend's call-girl ring) but of Alexander Haig, the president's chief of staff. In the Colodny/Gettlin scenario, Haig was "Deep Throat," the anonymous source to whom *Washington Post* reporter Bob Woodward regularly turned when he was stumped in his Watergate investigation. When that wasn't enough to bury Nixon, Haig took it upon himself to put the final nails in the president's coffin by erasing those 18½ minutes. The missing minutes, Colodny and Gettlin speculated, included nothing at all incriminating; Haig erased them solely to embarrass the president.

Responding to *Silent Coup,* Woodward denied Haig was Deep Throat; the *Washington Post,* where Woodward still worked, ran a savage review calling the book's documentation "pathetic." More objective historians and journalists were also critical of the book, though some did admit Colodny and Gettlin raised some intriguing questions. The debate will undoubtedly go on.

But even if a somewhat revised history of Watergate ultimately emerges, some basic facts won't change. Even if Nixon's participation in the details of the Watergate cover-up turns out not to have been as central as previously thought, there is no question that he did participate—the tape of June 23, 1972, is still as smoking as ever. Furthermore, no amount of revisionism can ever explain away all the spying, dirty tricks, and other forms of harassment of enemies that characterized the Nixon presidency—and of which Watergate was only a part.

For years Nixon's operatives spied on Democrats and reporters. They attempted to break into George McGovern's office. They asked the IRS to harass Nixon's enemies. When they couldn't come up with any dirt on his opponents, they didn't hesitate to invent some—as when E. Howard Hunt forged some cables indicating the Kennedy administration had been responsible for the 1963 assassination of South Vietnamese President Diem. Long before the Watergate break-in, some of the same burglars were working for the White House "Plumbers," a group whose quaint name came from its original task of plugging White House leaks but whose assignments included a variety of other spying jobs.

This, then, was the context of Watergate—a context in which Nixon's apparent bewilderment as to *why* anyone would want to break into the DNC can only be seen as an extraordinary performance. "In a lifetime of bold and brazen acts, this was the boldest and most brazen, as well as the most successful," wrote Nixon's premiere biographer, Stephen Ambrose. "That students, scholars, and the general public continue to ask these questions, as if they were legitimate, as if there were some unsolved mystery here, constitutes a triumph for Nixon." For whatever else he knew or didn't know about Watergate, Nixon understood full well why it happened.

☆ To investigate further:

The White House Tapes. These are the primary source for any Watergate investigation. The most readily available transcripts are still Nixon's own edited version, which he made public in April 1974 and which were subsequently published in paperback by the *New York Times* and the *Washington Post*. Unfortunately, these transcripts were soon shown to be very selective—and not just because of the infamous references to "expletive deleted." As for the tapes themselves, some (though not all) can be heard at the College Park, Maryland, location of the National Archives.

Bernstein, Carl and Bob Woodward, *All The President's Men*. New York: Simon and Schuster, 1974. How the two *Washington Post* reporters broke the story. Also worth reading is their second book, *The Final Days* (Simon and Schuster, 1976). The first book puts you inside the *Post* newsroom; the second inside the White House.

Higgins, George V. *The Friends of Richard Nixon*. Boston: Atlantic Monthly Press, 1975. For Higgins, himself a former prosecutor as well as a master of crime fiction, the heroes of the story are the prosecutors; everyone else—including not just Nixon's friends but quite a few of his enemies—is subject to Higgins's biting wit.

Dean, John. *Blind Ambition*. New York: Simon and Schuster, 1976. Almost all of the participants in the crime and cover-up penned memoirs; some more than one. Dean's two entries, this and *Lost Honor* (Stratford Press, 1982) are invaluable.

Lukas, J. Anthony. *Nightmare: The Underside of the Nixon Years.* New York: Viking, 1976. One of the first and best works of Watergate investigative journalism.

Nixon, Richard. *RN: The Memoirs of Richard Nixon.* New York: Grosset & Dunlap, 1978. Though obviously self-serving, this is nonetheless highly revealing—perhaps more so than Nixon intended.

Haldeman, H. R. *The Ends of Power.* New York: Times Books, 1978. Like Dean, Haldeman produced two invaluable works, this and and the remarkably frank, posthumously published, *The Haldeman Diaries* (G.P. Putnam's Sons, 1994).

Hougan, Jim. *Secret Agenda: Watergate, Deep Throat and the CIA.* New York: Random House, 1984. Much of what made such a splash in the Colodny/Gettlin book was first published here, along with evidence that the CIA's role in Watergate was pervasive.

Ambrose, Stephen E. *Nixon* (Vol. 1, *The Education of a Politician,* 1987; Vol. 2, *The Triumph of a Politician,* 1989; Vol. 3, *Ruin and Recovery,* 1991). New York: Simon and Schuster. The best biography of Nixon, including (in Volumes 2 and 3) a thorough presentation of the "orthodox" interpretation of Watergate.

Colodny, Len and Robert Gettlin. *Silent Coup: The Removal of a President.* New York: St. Martin's Press, 1991. Even its detractors admit it raises some questions that ought to be pursued further.

Kutler, Stanley I. *The Wars of Watergate.* New York: Knopf, 1990. There are numerous Watergate books by journalists but this was the first comprehensive treatment by a historian; perhaps as a result, Kutler argues that the role of investigative journalists has been much exaggerated and that most of the Watergate revelations were the result of judicial investigations.

Emery, Fred. *Watergate.* New York: Times Books, 1994. The latest history by a journalist, which restores the primacy of the journalistic and congressional investigations. *Very* thorough.

Chapter 30

What Did Reagan Know About Iran-Contra?

Throughout the early 1980s, Congress was engaged in a heated debate over whether to support the contra rebels in Nicaragua. Supporters of the contras, among them President Ronald Reagan, portrayed them as anticommunist freedom fighters; opponents decried them for being more interested in profiteering than in democracy or human rights. In the summer of 1984, the contras' congressional opponents prevailed. Capitalizing on public fears that support for the contras could enmesh the nation in another Vietnam, they passed the Boland amendment, which banned any further military aid to the contras. Then in October 1986, Nicaraguan soldiers shot down a cargo plane carrying arms to the contras. The captured pilot, Eugene Hasenfus, confessed that he was part of a covert U.S. government-supported operation—an operation in clear violation of the Boland amendment.

Not true, Reagan assured reporters. Although he adamantly supported the contra cause, his administration had had to abide by the will of Congress. Hasenfus was a private citizen working on behalf of other private citizens. "There was no government connection with that at all," Reagan stressed.

A month later, just as the furor over Hasenfus's statement was dying down, a Lebanese newspaper reported that the Reagan administration had shipped arms to Iran in an effort to win the freedom of

American hostages being held in Lebanon. Again the White House was plunged into crisis. In this case, the problem was not so much that such arms shipments were illegal (though they were a violation of the Arms Export Control Act), but that they directly contravened the administration's own oft-stated policy of not negotiating with terrorists. In fact the Reagan administration had been actively pressuring other countries to join an arms embargo against Iran. If the arms-for-hostages story were true, the administration looked like hypocrites, or worse, like fools—for once Iran had the weapons in hand, what was to prevent the terrorists from seizing more hostages?

The administration's response again was to deny the story. Yes, the president said in a televised talk on November 13, the United States had been in contact with some groups in Iran, but this had been purely an effort to bolster those moderates in their efforts to seize power from Ayatollah Khomeini. "We did not—repeat—did not trade weapons or anything else for hostages, nor will we," Reagan said.

Then, on November 25, the president opened a press conference by admitting he had not been "fully informed" of the nature of his administration's dealings with Iran. At that point Attorney General Edwin Meese took the podium and announced that some weapons had indeed been sold to Iran. Even more shocking, Meese continued, was that the profits from these arms sales—approximately $12 million—had been used to finance the contra war efforts. So the Iran and contra stories were not only true, they were linked.

The man responsible for the "diversion" of the $12 million, Meese said, was a mid-level staffer at the National Security Council, Lt. Col. Oliver North. North had now been "relieved of his duties" and his superior, National Security Adviser John Poindexter, had resigned. But if Meese thought that would put an end to the scandal, he was mistaken. Over the next seven years a series of investigations delved deeper and deeper into the Iran-contra affairs, attempting to find out who knew what—and when. Above all, what they wanted to know was this: Did Reagan himself know about—or authorize—the covert operations of his National Security Council?

Eager to make clear there was no cover-up, the president quickly appointed a commission to investigate the affair. The Tower Commission (named after its chairman, ex-Senator John Tower) interviewed key figures, including Reagan. On the subject of aid to the contras, Reagan was clear: he told the commission he had not known about the activities of the National Security Council staff. On Iran, he was more confused. In his first interview, he said he had approved a shipment of arms to Iran; in his second interview, he retracted this position. Then in a letter to the commission, Reagan wrote: "The simple truth is 'I don't remember.'"

The commission accepted the president's word. After all, Reagan's reputation had always been that of a hands-off manager, one who set broad policy but paid little attention to the details. It was easy to imagine his being oblivious to the actions of the NSC staff members. The Tower Commission report was highly unflattering to the president—the forgetful, confused figure who emerges in the report's pages was hardly the image Reagan wanted to project—but it exonerated him of any wrongdoing or knowledge of wrongdoing.

Next up were the House and Senate, each of which appointed a select committee to investigate the Iran-contra affair. The most dramatic testimony before the joint committee was that of North. Having been granted "use immunity" by Congress—which meant nothing he said could be used against him in any future criminal proceedings—North admitted he'd shredded documents, falsified evidence, and participated in other illicit activities intended to aid the contras and cover up the arms-for-hostages deals. But in spite of these admissions, North emerged from the hearings a star—and, to many, a hero. His patriotic fervor, his military bearing, his all-American looks made him seem far more likeable than his congressional inquisitors. Also working in North's favor was the fact that the committee had decided to avoid any substantive discussions on the merits of contra aid (and that seventeen of the twenty-six committee members had voted *for* aid). North could speechify about freedom fighters without fear of being contradicted.

In addition, North emphasized he was no lone ranger; he was a loyal soldier following orders. When the Boland amendment was passed, North's boss, National Security Adviser Robert McFarlane (who preceded Poindexter in the job), came to him with instructions directly from the president. These instructions, North told the committee, were to keep the contras together, "body and soul." McFarlane, in his testimony, confirmed that Reagan had said this to him, and that he had passed it on to North.

A man so good at following orders that a fellow marine once said: "Ollie North's commanding officer should never even think out loud." UPI/Corbis-Bettmann.

Did this mean Reagan had ordered the diversion of funds from the Iran arms sales to the contras? North didn't know. Neither did McFarlane, who had been replaced by Poindexter before the diversion. And Poindexter testified that he had *not* told the president about the diversion. "The buck stops here with me," he told the congressional committee.

After Poindexter's testimony, the committee eased up on Reagan. Its report was harsher than that of the Tower Commission—the president was blamed for creating or at least tolerating an environment where those who did know of the diversion could easily believe they were carrying out the president's policies. But on the key question of whether he ordered the diversion or even knew about it, he was off the hook.

In retrospect, many have speculated about why the committee backed away from investigating what else Reagan did or didn't know, what else he did or didn't order. After all, the diversion was merely the point at which the Iran and contra scandals intersected; it was hardly the entirety of either scandal. Why didn't the committee take a deeper look at Reagan's role in the Iran arms sales themselves, or in the overall National Security Council effort on behalf of the contras? Why did the diversion become the focus of the investigation?

In his autobiography, North suggested one reason why the administration chose to focus on the diversion:

> This particular detail was so dramatic, so sexy, that it might actually—well, *divert* public attention from other, even more important aspects of the story, such as what *else* the President and his top advisers had known about and approved. And if it could be insinuated that this supposedly terrible deed was the exclusive responsibility of one mid-level staff assistant at the National Security Council (and perhaps his immediate superior, the national security adviser), and that staffer had acted on his own (however unlikely *that* might be), and then, now that you mention it, his activities might even be *criminal*—if the public and the press focused on *that,* then maybe you didn't have another Watergate on your hands after all. Especially if you insisted that the President knew nothing about it.

In other words, the administration used the diversion as a diversion.

Still, the congressional committee went along with the focus on the diversion. This can be explained partly by the committee's makeup. Its members were, by and large, moderates; they had no desire to uncover information that might bring them uncomfortably close to a discussion of impeachment. And partly, the committee was following the lead of the public, which just wasn't that interested in the scandal. At one point, the *New Republic* tried to stir things up by holding a contest to come up with a jazzier name for the "Iran-contra affair". Entries included "Contraversions," "Ronnybrook," and the winner, "Iranamok." None caught on.

The underlying problem was that, in contrast to the dark and brooding Nixon, Reagan remained ever cheerful and popular. The committee's members had no desire to undercut that popularity. Moreover, the committee had early on set a ten-month timetable by which they wanted their hearings and report finished, and time was running out. So the hearings ended and the report came out—with many questions unanswered.

Lawrence Walsh, the independent counsel appointed by a three-judge panel to prosecute any illegal activities associated with Iran-contra, was not burdened by the political or time pressures felt by the congressional committee. His investigations continued until 1993 and resulted in criminal charges against fourteen individuals. Among these were McFarlane, who pleaded guilty to four counts of withholding information from Congress; North, who was convicted of altering and destroying documents, accepting an illegal gratuity, and aiding and abetting in the obstruction of Congress; and Poindexter, who was convicted of conspiracy, false statements, destruction and removal of records, and obstruction of Congress.

But though Walsh was not burdened by the political or time pressures on the congressional committee, he was bound by its grants of immunity. North and Poindexter appealed the convictions, arguing that witnesses at their trials had to have been influenced by the highly publicized congressional testimony. The appeals court admitted that was possible and reversed the convictions. North then declared himself "totally exonerated." But that was nonsense. The only reason North went free was that the crimes he'd been charged with were crimes he'd admitted to while under immunity.

The North and Poindexter reversals did not dissuade Walsh from pushing on—up into the highest levels of the Reagan administration. After a lengthy investigation, Walsh concluded that then Vice President George Bush was not nearly as "out of the loop" as he later claimed. Bush was regularly briefed on the Iran and contra operations, though he probably didn't know about the diversion. In the end though, Walsh decided not to prosecute Bush. Unlike the Tower Commission or the congressional committees, whose job had been to un-cover the truth, Walsh's mandate was more limited. His responsibility was merely to prosecute criminals, and Walsh did not have enough evidence to prove that the vice president had violated any criminal statute. Still, the investigation kept Bush on the defensive throughout the presidential elections of 1988 (when he defeated Michael Dukakis) and 1992 (when he was defeated by Bill Clinton).

Walsh also investigated the roles of Secretary of State George Shultz and Secretary of Defense Caspar Weinberger. Shultz and Weinberger, Walsh admitted, were peculiar targets. They were the only high-level members of the Reagan administration who had consistently *opposed* the arms deal with Iran. But Walsh argued they'd known what was going on and conspired to cover up the Iran arms sales in order to protect the president.

In the case of Shultz, Walsh eventually decided there was a reasonable doubt as to whether he'd willfully given any false testimony and Walsh decided not to prosecute. In the case of Weinberger, Walsh charged him with four counts of false statements and perjury. Then on the eve of the trial in December 1992, President Bush took his revenge on Walsh. In one of his final acts before turning over the Oval Office to Clinton, Bush pardoned Weinberger. In doing so, Bush argued that Walsh was prosecuting officials because he disagreed with their policies, not because of any actual criminal activities. Walsh, in turn, accused Bush of pardoning Weinberger to cover up his own role, and that of Reagan, in the Iran-contra affairs.

Objective observers, including Theodore Draper, the leading Iran-contra historian, have criticized both Walsh and Bush. Walsh was faulted for pursuing a Shultz and Weinberger conspiracy theory that was never entirely clear or convincing and that was, in any case, tangential to the main Iran-contra issues. And Bush's action was suspiciously self-serving: Had the Weinberger case gone to trial, Bush would certainly have been called as a witness and his claims to have been out of the loop would have been strenuously contested.

As for Reagan, he had slipped beyond Walsh's grasp well before the pardons. Reagan's testimony (via videotape) at the Poindexter trial and his subsequent interviews with Walsh revealed a man who seemed genuinely unable to recall even the main events of Iran-contra. Perhaps, in retrospect, Reagan was already suffering from the early stages of Alzheimer's disease (which was later diagnosed). In any case, Walsh concluded, Reagan's conduct, like Bush's, "fell well short of criminality which could be successfully prosecuted."

Nonetheless, of the three official reports on Iran-contra, Walsh's came down the hardest on Reagan. "The President's disregard for civil laws enacted to limit presidential action abroad," Walsh wrote, "created a climate in which some government officials assigned to implement his policies felt emboldened to circumvent such laws." By directing McFarlane to keep the contras alive "body and soul," by disregarding the warnings of Shultz and Weinberger against selling arms to Iran, by openly encouraging individuals and other countries to fund the contras during the ban on U.S. aid, Reagan set the stage on which Oliver North acted. In this sense, there is no question that the man responsible for Iran-contra was Ronald Reagan.

☆ To investigate further:

Tower, John, Edmund Muskie and Brent Scowcroft. *The Tower Commission Report.* New York: Times Books, 1987. The first official report.

U.S. House of Representatives Select Committee to Investigate Covert Arms Transactions with Iran and U.S. Senate Select Committee on Secret Military Assistance to Iran and the Nicaraguan Opposition. *Report of the Congressional Committees Investigating the Iran-Contra Affair.* 1987. The second official report.

Cockburn, Leslie. *Out of Control.* New York: Atlantic Monthly Press, 1987. Contends that well before the Boland amendment was passed, the administration was involved in a wide range of activities that circumvented Congressional restrictions on aid to the contras. Also presents evidence that the contras were involved in drug smuggling and that the CIA knew about it.

Cohen, William and George Mitchell. *Men of Zeal.* New York: Viking, 1988. Two senators on the Iran-contra committee tell, among other things, how the television cameras affected their inquiries and why they gave North immunity.

Segev, Samuel. *The Iranian Triangle.* New York: The Free Press, 1988. Focuses on Israel's role in the Iran-contra affair and on the Israeli side of the triangular U.S.-Iran-Israel relationship.

Reagan, Ronald. *An American Life.* New York: Simon and Schuster, 1990. The presidents own version, or at least that of one of his better ghostwriters.

North, Oliver. *Under Fire.* New York: HarperCollins, 1991. The number one best-seller from the man so good at following orders that a fellow marine once said: "Ollie North's commanding officer should never even think out loud."

Draper, Theodore. *A Very Thin Line*. New York: Hill and Wang, 1991. A thorough reconstruction of the Iran-contra affair and the numerous crossings of the thin line that separates the legitimate from the illegitimate exercise of government power.

Wroe, Ann. *Lives, Lies and the Iran-Contra Affair*. New York: I. B. Tauris & Co., 1991. A British journalist's provocative perspectives on the moral and political philosophies underlying the affair.

Kornbluh, Peter and Malcolm Byrne. *The Iran-Contra Scandal: The Declassified History*. New York: The New Press, 1993. A useful documentary history.

Walsh, Lawrence E. *Iran-Contra: The Final Report*. New York: Times Books, 1994. The results of the independent counsel's seven years of investigations.

McFarlane, Robert. *Special Trust*. New York: Cadell & Davies, 1994. Like the books of most of the principals (almost all of whom wrote one), McFarlane's is somewhat self-serving, but his has more pathos—and perhaps more credibility—since he was the only figure involved to show some remorse about his role in the affair. So much remorse, in fact, that in February 1987 he attempted suicide.

Timberg, Robert. *The Nightingale's Song*. New York: Simon & Schuster, 1995. An elegant multiperson biography, which traces Iran-contra back to its origins in the experiences of McFarlane, Poindexter, and North at the Naval Academy in Annapolis and later in Vietnam.

Index